Conflict, Power, and the
Landscape of Constitutionalism

Conflict, Power, and the Landscape of Constitutionalism

Editors

Gilles Tarabout

Ranabir Samaddar

Routledge
Taylor & Francis Group

LONDON AND NEW YORK

First published 2008
by Routledge

2 Park Square, Milton Park, Abingdon, Oxfordshire OX14 4RN
711 Third Avenue, New York, NY 10017

Routledge is an imprint of the Taylor & Francis Group, an informa business

First issued in paperback 2018

Transferred to Digital Printing 2008

Copyright © 2008 Tarabout and Samaddar

Typeset by
Bukprint India
B-180A, Guru Nanak Pura, Laxmi Nagar,
Delhi 110 092.

British Library Cataloguing-in-Publication Data
A catalogue record of this book is available from the British Library

ISBN 978-0-415-44542-9 (hbk)
ISBN 978-1-138-38417-0 (pbk)

For

Maurice Aymard

*Historian, and an inspiring figure for intellectual
endeavours across the boundaries.*

Contents

Introduction   **1**
Ranabir Samaddar

1. Constitution-Making in the Process of Decolonisation   **14**
   Dietmar Rothermund

2. The Exception and the Rule: On French Colonial Law   **27**
   Olivier Le Cour Grandmaison

3. Law and Terror in the Age of Constitution-Making   **50**
   Ranabir Samaddar

4. The Citizen and the Subject: A Post-Colonial
   Constitution for the European Union?   **80**
   Sandro Mezzadra

5. The Silent Erosion:
   Anti-Terror Laws and Shifting Contours of
   Jurisprudence in India   **93**
   Ujjwal Kumar Singh

6. The Post-Communist Revolution in Russia   **129**
   and the Genesis of Representative Democracy
   Artemy Magun

7. The Acts and Facts of Women's Autonomy in India   **144**
   Paula Banerjee

8. The Limits of Constitutional Law:
   Public Policies and the Constitution   **167**
   Virgilio Afonso da Silva

9. Regulation of the Particular and Its
   Socio-Political Effects   **182**
   Rastko Močnik

10. Constitutionalism in Pakistan:
The Lingering Crisis of Dyarchy   208
Mohammad Waseem

Bibliography   227

Notes on Contributors   241

Index   246

Introduction

Ranabir Samaddar

This is an unusual but significant collection of commentaries on the double nature of law and legal texts—the power-limiting and power-enhancing functions of law. These commentaries on conflicts, law and constitutionalism deal not only with various political and social conflicts and the constitution's capacity to deal with them, they also bring out, in the process, law's paradox in claiming universal efficacy. At the same time, they assert the specific, rigorous, non-partisan, and particular nature of law. Drawing from various experiences around the globe—Pakistan, India, France, Eastern Europe, Russia, Brazil, and the general experience of decolonisation—the texts of this collection argue that in order to study constitutionalism, it is necessary to closely follow the juridical–political history of the different tools of rule in the light of the dynamics of power and the contending spheres of legality and illegality. Cast in a comparative mould, yet retaining a critical attention to the specifics of the constitutional cultures of different countries, this collection raises a number of significant questions with which our political minds are greatly agitated today. For instance, how does law deal with illegality? Can law produce dialogic culture? How shall we understand the fact that a constitution, that applauded the instruments of democracy, produces and tolerates differential citizenship? What happens to the outlaws and half-legal entities such as illegal migrants, refugees, women, and oppositionists who are, in the eyes of rulers, 'terrorists' under constitutional regimes? In other words, what is the nature of legality and how are we to understand it in the light of the conflicts of our time?

These articles throw fresh light on the genealogy of rule of law as a plank of governing, and re-examine the relation of rule of law with democracy, popular politics, and ways of representation.

Finally, they engage with the fundamental question, namely, how does law constitute relations, and why must therefore any legal document including the basic legal text, be seen as a relational text, or as a contentious document? If the paradoxes of law thus constitute one major strand of inquiry in this collection, the other strand is the engagement with 'exceptional powers' which constitutions through the ages have tried to end but have always come to accept as part of the constitution or the basic legal system. This too, of course, is a paradox, but with a more direct relevance to how we contemplate politics, and how we always try to become autonomous political subjects, freeing ourselves from our subjection to the exceptional powers of the sovereign. Universality, particularity, power matrix and power relations, and political subjectivity—these are the themes of this collection. The readers, therefore, will find in these texts hard juridical concepts, constitutional provisions and legal notions flirting with philosophy and politics, as all these essays engage themselves with an examination of law's relation with the big outside world. Essential political concepts such as sovereignty, responsibility, union and division of powers, popular politics and revolts, rule of law, democracy and representation appear in this volume through a legal mirror. Law, in this sense, is congealed politics—politics in fiercely material forms.

I

Who is not familiar with the theory according to which every good constitution rigorously separates the legislature, executive and the judiciary from each other, and thereby guarantees the independence of each of these powers thus ensuring life, liberty and security? If a constitution symbolises power and produces power, the implication is that it has taken care to separate one site of power from another, and to distinguish one form of power from another. Ironically, the other implication of this formulation is that power, when it is undifferentiated (undivided) or because it is undifferentiated, becomes its own limit because it cannot be exercised in an effective way. This is because any division of power limits power, and thereby limits absolutism. Therefore, the idea that total power is undivided power in that judgment is a paradox. However, precisely because it is undivided, power collapses early. The political problem in creating governmental institutions is not therefore how they can exercise power but how they can limit unbridled power, ensuring at the same time that this separation produces more power at the end. This is how law has been always entangled with philosophy, even though its original mandate was to explain the mystery of power in heaven and on earth.

This book presents a collection of essays that seek to explain this mystery by way of investigating how power acts on power; how limits placed on power produce excess; how separation of powers produces the union of powers, represented by and sanctified by the constitution. Ironically, the constitution guarantees the division of powers, but this division is, at the same time, a myth and a reality: a myth because power that is produced is, in the end, indivisible; a reality because each form of power corresponds precisely to its own sphere only, therefore non-corresponding with other spheres and forms. These essays address this dual nature of basic legal texts.

In order to undertake this agenda, the essays have to simultaneously address (*a*) constitutions; (*b*) the vast sphere lying outside the constitutions, that is, the societies. The essays address both the spirit (to use Montesquieu's term) and the physical reality of laws. As these essays tell us, we must treat the story of constitutionalism as a political culture of laws as well as one of the dynamics of power. Constitutionalism says, for instance, that ministers must give an account of their administrations; judiciary must show that rule of law exists and political nobility must subject itself, when required, to this judiciary in a free state. Also, legislature must demonstrate that rule of law is intrinsically better than rule of men and rule of orders, and administration must show that government can govern relations judiciously by assuming custodianship of life, liberty, and security.

This volume is therefore not so much concerned about the separation, but the combination, fusion and liaison of various forms of powers achieved through distinction, division and classification. These forms, achieved through the act of division or partition, enhance the political effect, which a legal text creates through the process of setting institutions almost from nought. Many of the essays in this collection show how the institutional practices originating from a legal text create a matrix of power that is neither division nor unison, and that owes its life not to a contract between men, or one between state and men, or even one between society and men, but to *relations* established, organised and formalised by laws in the form of a matrix. The philosophical implications of the problematic are therefore concerned with method—in this case, the method of studying societies. As the essays suggest, therefore, the problematic of legal knowledge is not related to genesis and end of human societies, but to the nature of things knowable only through studying the relations. We are thus studying laws and constitutions here in the context of facts— facts of relations, which are often facts of conflicts—and therefore, there is a decisive attempt here to break with the tradition of natural law, or even vague political laws, and return to facts of relations that settled governments and settled ways of rule produce.

II

This is a concrete task, yet it is associated with what can be called a paradox, the 'concrete universality of law'. Is this task of coming to terms with the double nature of the legal texts a minor or self-evident task? It may seem so now given the flourishing of legal studies everywhere since the emergence of the modern state. But we have to remember that law initially meant simply a command, and this meaning remains, till this day, fundamental to many of the constitutional expositions. This is precisely what some of the essays in this volume say in great detail while speaking of the extra-ordinary nature of the state, and the paradox of the legal approval of the 'permanent exceptions' to law. Law gradually attained its special domain by achieving a new status that was capable or had the function of explaining the nature of relations between material objects—men, property, institutions, and material situations—the physics of social life. As Montesquieu said, law had the form of 'a fixed and invariable relation' between variable terms. Here is a contradiction. Law was to be invariable in settling variable relations that produce conflicts. It was to be universal. It was this universality that bound constitution and laws together in a journey that has continued till today. Constitutional study is thus always a *universal* study, by which we mean (and this volume demonstrates too) a *comparative* study, since universality emerges from the game of comparing. In the old sense, law was an order and an end pronounced by a master, or a god, or by morals; people therefore appreciated that law could be differential because masters, gods and morals could be different. Yet, because the source was important, even though these sources could be different, law could only be the command of a superior agency. This is what philosophers call *concrete universality*. Therefore, from now on, law would mean a matrix of relations—a combination of the invariable and the variables—applying *the method* everywhere, to every situation, to every human being, to every place. What happens then to the facts of difference on which rule rests? What happens to that fixed method which at times dissolves in the face of the immense facts of difference? The jurist would term this problem as the 'paradox of concrete universality'. This collection addresses the paradox through a series of case studies on the interplay of the universality of law, and the specifics of the situations requiring legal intervention.

We must face up to the implications of this theoretical, in fact, legal revolution, based on the concept of concrete universality, when dealing with a comparative story of constitutions. Such a theory assumes that it is possible to draw from human institutions and human conditions themselves—irrespective of differences in these institutions and conditions—the instrument and the ability to think that the diverse conflicts have a constancy of resolution in form of law. But the more significant implication of this theoretical revolution is that, as soon a constitution appears, law does not become in a place of command an expression of an ideal, say a democratic ideal, rather it becomes the symbol of a relation immanent to the material things. In fact from the time constitution starts working, law starts *constituting* the relations. The theory then is, if there are material things, there is law. To press the point further, it is law—rather basic law—that constitutes the 'material' things, or the 'materiality' of things. Constitution of law is thus what we call the *Constitution*, and these essays try to face up to the implications of this theoretical revolution and critically examine its implications for a political society. Laws constituting the materiality of the political life in different contexts are the objects of investigation in this collection of studies.

Let me illustrate an implication of the stance taken by this collection of texts. Mohammad Waseem's essay on constitutionalism in Pakistan, for example, shows how the juridical problem

of power is finally a political problem of relations of forces, and
not simply a juridical problem concerning the definition of legality
and its spheres. In fact, as he shows in course of his analysis, the
enterprise of juridical definition of power invites political com-
plications. This essay, provocative in many ways, along with some
other similar texts of this volume (see Rothermund's insightful piece
on the general relation between constitutionalism and decolonisation; also, Artemy Magun's essay on the form of Soviet legality),
casts light on the difficult question—what is a constitutional regime
or a constitutional government? Along with that, what is a moderate
government, or, is a moderate government a constitutional government? Once again we are back to the question of law, constitutionalism and power, and the double nature of law, that is, *law controlling
power, law producing power*.

The issue of moderation is, of course, a famous problem in
politics. What is moderation? A juridical concern and respect for
legality? Is it a separation of powers or separation of organs or
agencies? Or, the line beyond which any arrangement of power is
enough to bring a collapse of government? Does it guarantee liberty
or guarantee against passion—either of the ruler or of the people—
the guarantee every legal philosophy and philosopher dreams of?
Moderate government is thus a government of moderation against
both absolutism and popular revolutions. Once again, the essays
by Ujjwal Singh, Sandro Mezzadra, and Rastko Močnik examine
how constitutionalism—the gospel of moderation—can become
the foundation of rule where moderation is the key word. The
fundamental issue is therefore: the problem of conflict, law and
constitution is defined by the absolute limits of the theoretical or
the conceptual field in which the problem is posed. In simpler
terms it means posing the problem of conflict and law as a function
of legality; similarly, moderation as a function of legality, indeed,
as the argument will go, legality as moderation.

But, what proves that power is being exercised in a moderate
way? Or, that this is moderate power? The answer will be 'any
power being exercised constitutionally'. The problem apparent in
this formulation lies in the way by which we define the interiority
and exteriority of a problematic. In this case the problematic is of
law emanating from its dual nature, indicated by the term 'concrete
universality'. Its exterior is the concrete engagement with a conflict;
its interior is a universal method, because of which law never

admits that there can be areas beyond legislation. The answer, methodologically speaking, then would lie in finding out those acts, processes, or elements that reflect on that interface of the internalities and the externalities (of law). Thus one can ask as a beginning: who breaks the law? By what means do people combine legality, semi-legality, and illegality? How is a semi-legal situation created? The question suggests the line of solution, because it immediately connects law to non-legal spheres and makes possible a study of law amidst a setting constituted by the externalities. This is a solution which legal philosophers never considered. Apparently we are returning by this to the traditional solution of the school of natural law, which thought that civil society and the state as juridical concepts began from some foundations (the genesis), and we would have to return to genesis in order to solve the problem of illegalities or semi-legal existence. This collection of texts however takes a different line. It suggests that the answer may lie in the dialectic of the exteriority and the interiority of the problematic, particularly the exteriority. Thus the essays ask: what does a law consist of? What are its constitutive elements? Why do people not obey it always? Why do they perceive the relations differently from the way law does? Why does legal equality produce political and social inequality? Reduced to a schematic expression, people's attitude and inclination to semi-legality and illegalities is a problem outside the domain of law, yet it becomes a problem for law. What emerges from this identification of the problematic is the continuum of legalities and illegalities and their distinction, also the ceaseless desire of law to absorb within its situation the phenomenon of illegality. The concrete universality of laws indicates all these facets.

III

The question remains: what to do with conflicts that themselves generate illegalities, particularly in view of the fact that law does not solve conflicts but only negotiates them? That is, the main question will be: how does law cope with illegalities that mark conflicts? In some ways, this is the most profound question of popular politics, which carries illegalities and subversive sites within it. Olivier Le Cour Grandmaison, Ranabir Samaddar and

Ujjwal Singh—have all produced significant texts for this collection in order to engage with the phenomenon of exceptional or extraordinary powers of the state in dealing with the illegalities. Does the state thereby become exceptional, even though it may be constitutional; is exceptional within the bounds of normalcy, or does a democracy indeed require and encourage these monstrosities? Grandmaison raises this question in the context of colonial French rule over Algeria, Samaddar discusses the issue of law and terror in colonial Bengal, and Singh produces a dateline history almost of what can be called a 'deficit of democracy'.

It is ironic for any legal discussion, since one of the responses to the political turmoil in which the world had been thrown after the *annus mirabilis* of 1989 was the renewed interest in laws and constitutionalism, and the promise of law that it would solve conflicts. Rarely do people today expect a constitution to solve an acute political or social conflict, or hope that a particular constitutional culture can be the answer to today's fundamental questions of political existence. Indeed, to the deviant minded, the ability of constitutions to address those questions was so obviously insufficient. The question is how had we ever believed in the capacity of constitutions to deliver peace? In fact some realist historians even attribute the 'long peace' that we had during the almost 40 years of post-war era to a strategic balance of power between two great adversaries, that gave the world not only world peace, but social, regional and local peace as well.

This was for instance the argument of John Lewis Gaddis, and it had its antecedents in the history of thinking on conflicts.[1] After all, the realist thought that political and military power and its symmetry brings peace in the last analysis, and nothing else can, had always paralleled the hope of Kant, Burke, and others, that constitutionalism promoted peace by solving conflicts. Why is there, then, the renewed interest in law and constitutionalism in this conflict-ridden age?

We can hazard three answers:

- First, in this age of restoration (of liberalism, peace after the savagery of the Balkan war and third world civil wars in countries such as Rwanda, Cambodia and Afghanistan), lawmakers and constitutionalists are seen to be the primary engineers and technicians in putting the state to order. From this follows the entire recent history of the proliferation and domination of jurists and lawmakers in the international political field. They can help effect the 'democratic transition', they know how to fix the nuts and bolts of the new restorative legal machines, and they can restore social peace.

- Second, the renewed interest in law is partly because the received lesson is that *rule by men* was bad and capricious, *rule by order* was also arbitrary, while *rule of law* is better because it is rule of rules. Courts, statutes, constitution, a basic law, jurists' heritage, verdicts, arbitration, and commentaries—all those great characteristics by which a modern legal–constitutional system is marked—represent law and help a political society to escape, forget, and transcend the violence with which it was founded.

- Third, all conflicts call for neutrality (if there is no conflict, there is no need to be neutral), and law appears as the most congealed form of neutrality.

These foundational beliefs of the modern age are not only characteristic of the Euro-American world; the processes of decolonisation world over also contributed to those beliefs. Indeed, more than Kant or Burke, or the *Federalist* fathers, colonial politics and decolonisation had contributed to the universal ascendancy of *rule of law*. The problems of rule and governing deepened the belief in the capacity of law, and at the same time aroused interest in the actual record of this universal social instrument. Law showed that if conflicts could not be solved, they could be negotiated in the interest of rule and government. The *defence of the realm* could be built only with the help of a structure of orders that necessitated law and constitution. This is one important issue discussed at length in these texts we present here. Thus the fundamental problem of representative democracy is marked by one great query: namely, in what specific ways can rule of law be held to be the foundation of democracy, and in what way does it disconnect from popular politics and popular representation? Readers will find echoes of this problematic and animated discussion in the essays of Sandro Mezzadra, Artemy Magun, and Afonso da Silva respectively on the questions of constitution-making for a federal Europe, instituting representative legislative system for post-1991 Russia, and the role of public policies as limits to constitution-making in recent Brazilian juridical–political history.

IV

'Concrete universality' of law, yes, but as four texts in this collection show, what can be more concrete than the colonial experience, and the universality of that experience? The book begins therefore with a generalised presentation of constitutionalism and decolonisation, and then proceeds with three accounts of colonial and post-colonial experience (Algeria, India, and a post-colonial Europe on the way to integration). Readers should find these texts significant in studies of law, because of at least two reasons. First, it gives the colonial and post-colonial experiences a justified place of significance in studies of law and constitutionalism. It shows that while Montesquieu, Kant, and Burke each in their own way were promoting the spirit of laws, on the other side of the world a more significant history of law-making was being enacted in order to defend a particular rule—colonial rule—and a particular type of government—the colonial government. As many researches, including the papers of this collection, have shown, the colonial history of law-making was essential to the development of the entire legal culture and tradition of the Euro-American world. The colonial history left its impact on constitutionalism everywhere. It taught the rulers that governing by law-making was not a pure process. Rule of law had to be mixed appropriately with rule by men and rule by orders. Second, this collection draws attention to another legacy that again neither Kant nor Burke wrote of, namely that constitutionalism was to be built on the principle of difference. As some of the essays in this collection demonstrate vividly, race, gender, caste, communal identity, and locality—all, and most fundamentally, race, built this principle of difference. Constitutionalism and law-making did not invent difference; they only gave them formal shape in the light of the principle of governing on the basis of the principle of difference. At times, constitutionalism took away the right to be different also, in the sense that everyone had to subscribe to the homogeneity that the legal order was creating. Thus exclusions and inclusions evolved as the two strategies of rule, playing on the fundamental reality of difference. Constitutionalism promised citizenship, but this was a promise to grant differential citizenship.

Yet, the fact of difference as the mark of constitution-making is overshadowed often by the claimed universality of law, a feature we have already noted. This all-season or all-weather machine called constitution naturally wants to avoid the antinomy of violence and dialogue—the two fundamental processes by which politics runs. Both play on forms of power. Both require no pre-explanation; both act as the site of political strategies. Constitution therefore wants to play on both. We may recall, in this context, Burke who wanted to avoid this antinomy by thinking of a machine called the constitution in which every small detail would have a specific function, and this constitution would act as the fountainhead of laws fixing every such small detail of society. He said:

> I must see with my own eyes, touch with my own hands, not only the fixed, but the momentary circumstances, before I would venture to suggest any political project whatsoever, I must know the power and disposition to accept, to execute, to persevere…I must see the means of correcting the plan, where correctives would be wanted. I must see the things; I must see the men… The eastern politicians never do anything without the opinion of the astrologers on *the fortunate moment…* Statesmen of a judicious prescience look for the fortunate moment too; but they seek it, not in the conjunctions and oppositions of the planets, but in the conjunctions and oppositions of men and things. These form their almanac.[2]

This collection shows the interplay of violence, the dialogic functions and powers in the process of rule by law, known as *rule of law*. Law allows this interplay as it occupies the middle space. But how does it ascribe to itself this space? The brief answer is that, and one has to read Afonso da Silva particularly, it can occupy the middle ground by claiming to reach all spheres of life, by claiming universal applicability. This is what happens when governmentality overwhelms law and constitutional operations. Law occupies manners and morals, education, and civil religion. It has the goal of setting up the practical arrangements for a permanent moral reform intended to cancel out the effects of the social interest groups, which are constantly arising and active in society. It ceaselessly defends and restores the purity of the individual conscience. Political laws, civil laws, and criminal laws have the essential supplement in the form of custom and common law (the basis on which manners and morals stand)—a power that great legislators too have to bear in mind. Laws therefore impact constitution by bearing on the latter the stamp of common sense—both together make the great machine of rule, governance, and continuity.[3]

Finally then, how would rule of law account for exceptions? I have already indicated in this brief introduction that the great strength of the book is the insight it offers on the dynamics of exceptional powers even under a constitutional government. In that sense we can see that even the colonial story of constitution-making, assumed hitherto as a story of exception in the development of 'rule of law', was an inbuilt element in the universal story of law. Giorgio Agamben has shown that the long history of exceptional powers was uninterrupted in the democratic time. The sovereign always required exceptional powers to dispose of bodies. What Ujjwal Singh or Le Cour Grandmaison or Ranabir Samaddar describe in this collection are not exceptions or aberrations, they show the limits of law, law in non-relation to life, when law thinks that it can now kill or dispose off lives that laws were supposed to preserve. Agamben comments, in conclusion of his fascinating account of *State of Exception*, 'Politics has suffered a lasting eclipse because it has been contaminated by law, seeing itself at best as constituent power (that is, violence that makes law), when it is not reduced to merely the power to negotiate with law'.[4] Precisely when under the shadow of 9/11 George W. Bush was demanding exceptional powers from the Congress in the name of defending the constitution, Agamben had to write this history of exceptional state; the English translation of which came out in 2005. Precisely at that time, some jurists, philosophers, historians and critical thinkers assembled in Paris to take stock of the exceptional state, which combines law, governmental functions, constitutionalism and summary powers, to become the permanent exception.

What happens to popular revolutions then? Constitution cannot allow daily plebiscite or daily dialogues to determine political relations in as much as it cannot allow unregulated violence. No rule can leave the people to their passions alone—the passions of blood and friendship. Popular passions need the bridle of deliberation of the wise, and thus the science of governing has to be combined with the art of keeping popular passions in check by innovating ways of selecting the wise men who can control the fury below. Constitutionalism raises the issue of political representation and citizenship. This collection discusses therefore, quite appropriately, the politics of representation and the dynamics of the political subject called the citizen, who is at once the symbol of both subjection and subject-formation. Readers will recall in this particular context the essay by Paula Banerjee, which not only brings into light Indian legislations on women, but also discusses the nature of the particular legality aimed at negotiating the gender problematic. The collection in this way illuminates the mysterious process of a people becoming subjected to ruling politics, and simultaneously becoming political subjects in their own rights.

That of course is another topic of another conference and a volume. For the present I must thank, at the outset, my co-editor Gilles Tarabout. Working with him has been a great pleasure and a lesson. His short and precise comments and his patience made the conference and the collection possible. He and the great French institution for collaborative research—the Maison des Sciences de L'homme in Paris, which organised the conference (Paris, 16–18 February 2005), and Maurice Aymard in particular, made all resources available for the conference. Similarly my thanks go to the collaborating institution in Kolkata, the Calcutta Research Group. We also thank the contributors who readily agreed to join and delve into discussions on the difficult questions mentioned above, and to colleagues who offered secretarial assistance, Rosette de Montfalcon and Ayan Mukherjee, in order to make the conference and the volume successful. Some of the papers have been published in their earlier form in *Diogenes* (© ICPHS: International Council for Philosophy and Humanistic Studies, with the Support of UNESCO, 2006, by permission of Sage Publications Ltd., UK) and in the Algerian journal, *Naqd*—our thanks go to Luca Scarantino and Daho Djerbal for these efforts. Finally, we thank all other participants in the deliberations that made this volume possible. After all, this is only a rough selection from the enormously rich and variegated discussion, which went on for three days in that particularly bitter winter of Paris.

Notes

1. Gaddis (1987).
2. Edmund Burke, cited in Bickel (1975: 15–16).
3. The principal jurist among the fathers of the Indian Constitution, B. R. Ambedkar repeatedly emphasised on what can be called the juridical common sense in defending draft articles and opposing certain major amendments moved against those draft articles; see for example, his speech to the Constituent Assembly on Article 61.
4. Agamben (2005: 88).

1

Constitution-Making in the Process of Decolonisation

Dietmar Rothermund

In addition to the two world wars, the rapid decolonisation since 1947 has been the most important phenomenon of the 20th century. The two wars in fact led to the decline of the European colonial empires and speeded up decolonisation. This process spawned more than one hundred new nations which did not exist in this way before. It also fixed territorial boundaries most of which have remained unaltered ever since. In the course of decolonisation, constitutions have been made which have also survived unless they have been suspended by military coups. Many of these constitutions bear the stamp of the process of decolonisation because they were framed with a view to facilitate the transfer of power. Usually the grant of independence was preceded by various steps in the devolution of power which left their traces in the constitutional documents. Since this devolution implied the prescription of administrative procedures, these constitutional documents often contain a great deal of contingent detail, whereas 'normal' constitutions are restricted to statements of fundamental rights and basic principles. This led to such ironies of fate that the Independence of India Act, which subsequently formed the basis of the Indian constitution, is the longest Act ever passed by the British Parliament which itself is based on an unwritten constitution.

The formidable Independence of India Act and its impact on the Indian constitution is a typical example of the problem which will be discussed in this chapter. Except for the insertion of fundamental rights, the constituent assembly which produced the Indian constitution added nothing of importance to the existing constitutional arrangement. Whenever the departments of government were asked for comments on the paragraphs debated in the constituent assemby, they invariably endorsed the *status quo* because they were working within the framework predetermined by the British. In the course of the Indian freedom movement, Jawaharlal Nehru had frequently asserted that the constitution of independent India would be framed by a constituent assembly based on universal suffrage and unfettered by the constitutional arrangements made by the colonial rulers. This remained a dream; the actual constituent assembly was based on the limited franchise introduced by the British in the 1930s, and it proved to be completely fettered by the colonial precedent.

The formative influence of the process of decolonisation on the respective constitutions was more or less the same in all ex-colonies. With the exception of the Japanese who lost their colonies—Korea and Taiwan—at the end of the Second World War, all colonial rulers bequeathed constitutions to their departing colonies. Even the Belgians who left the Congo very hastily convened a constitutional conference in Brussels before doing so. This chapter does not aim at a comparative study of all those constitutions; that would fill many volumes. The aim here is rather to illustrate, with a few examples, how constitution-making played a role in the process of decolonisation, and to what extent crucial decisions of that time have influenced the further course of political development. In the first part of this chapter we shall discuss the basic functions of constitution-making, the setting of an agenda of how politics should be transacted, and the setting of the arena in which political contests should take place. Frequently, the constitution-makers resorted to federalism in the process of decolonisation. This will be discussed in the second part of the chapter. The final part is devoted to a blind spot in this process which concerned the control of the armed forces. This proved to be a fatal oversight as many of the carefully contrived constitutional arrangements were soon swept aside by military coups.

Agenda Setting and Arena Setting

In functional terms, a constitution is an agenda which regulates the transactions which are considered to be relevant in the political life of a nation. It can do this by formulating a few principles, leaving everything else to the 'due process of law', but it can also prescribe detailed rules of procedure. It must contain references to the structure of government which may sometimes be of cryptic brevity. Thus the Indian constitution contains the sentence: 'There shall be a Prime Minister'. This is meant to imply that the type of government will be a parliamentary one and that the conventions governing the powers of the Indian Prime Minister are the same as those of the British Prime Minister. But none of this is stated explicitly in the Indian constitution. There is nothing in the Indian constitution that would preclude the appointment of a prime minister of the present French type. Actually, Jinnah who inherited the same constitutional framework for Pakistan as Nehru did for India, opted for what may be called a Gaullist interpretation of this constitution whereas Nehru followed the British precedent.

In the British sphere, much of this informal constitutional agenda-setting preceded the final act of decolonisation. Introducing legislative assemblies and appointing the head of the largest party as, 'Leader of Government Business', was a step towards parliamentary government. African politicians like Kwame Nkrumah held this position before they became prime ministers in the next round of constitutional reform. Parliamentary democracy, which was the only form of government with which the British were familiar, had to be transferred gradually, because in its full-fledged form it would have left no room for the powers of a colonial governor. The introduction of an incomplete parliamentary democracy, however, made those, from whom its complete form was withheld, even more eager to get the genuine article. Accordingly, most nationalists in British colonies never even thought of other forms of government. As we shall see, when the British experimented with federalism in the process of decolonisation, this was usually resented by nationalists who saw in it a devious ploy of the colonial rulers. Parliamentary democracy basically implies a unitary state and, therefore, federalism was seen as counterproductive in this context.

While the British style of agenda-setting was more or less uniform, it was nevertheless adapted to local conditions. The British produced tailormade constitutions for each colony. Some of them fitted better than others. In some places they made interesting experiments of doubtful value. Ceylon provides a striking example of this procedure. The so-called Donoughmore Constitution of 1931 was in many ways 'progressive', but it also contained negative features as far as further political development was concerned. Universal suffrage was combined with communal representation; the model selected for the structure of the government was not the usual parliamentary one but that of the London County Council with a committee system and seven 'ministers' in charge of their respective portfolios. This did not contribute to the aggregate national interest but encouraged a kind of bargaining within the political elite. In the end, this ensured a rather smooth transfer of power with no dramatic, 'freedom struggle'. The real conflicts emerged when Ceylon graduated to a parliamentary system and 'interest disaggregation rather than aggregation' became a persistent problem.

The French type of agenda-setting was very different from the British one. The Cartesian mind of the French politicians and administrators projected a uniform pattern of imperial governance. Even when the machine had to be put into reverse gear, i.e., a process of decolonisation, it was operated with the same mindset that had prevailed so far. This was clearly expressed in the 'Loi Cadre' (Framework Law) which was applied to all French colonies in Africa in 1956. Under this law they were all blessed with universal suffrage, they all had elected territorial councils and they could send a limited number of representatives to the French national assembly. They were all considered to be part of a French Union, a concept which will be discussed later on in the context of the uses and abuses of federalism. The number of representatives sent to Paris had to be severely limited, because otherwise the French 'natives' would soon have been governed by a black majority. The 'Loi Cadre' was a grand scheme, but it was bound to be a halfway house. It stimulated the demand for independence, but in Paris there was no plan for further agenda-setting. This was also due to the lack of stability of the Fourth Republic which was much more directly affected by the problems of decolonisation (including the Algerian problem), than the British government ever was. It was left to General de Gaulle to cut the Gordian knot. His idea of agenda-setting was not at all clear to begin with, but he soon took surprising initiatives. Initially, he just built on the foundation of the 'Loi Cadre' and held a referendum on the new constitution of the French Union of 1958 which he expected would be universally endorsed. When he was defied by Guinea he first reacted in a very vindictive manner. He also hoped that Guinea would collapse, thus demonstrating what happened to those who did not accept his agenda-setting. When Guinea did not collapse and the Algerian problem became worse, he finally cut the Gordian knot completely and announced the grant of complete independence to all African colonies in 1959, finally achieved by most of them in 1960. This made an immediate impact on British agenda-setting. Macmillan rushed to Africa in January 1960 and made his famous 'wind of change' speech. But, for the British it was not that easy to decolonise with the French speed. They had no 'Loi Cadre' supplemented by the constitution of 1958 and had to follow a piecemeal approach. Nevertheless they managed to release most of their African colonies in the course of the 1960s, for the most part, in terms of a full-fledged parliamentary democracy.

In addition to the setting of the political agenda, the setting of the arena of political contests is of major importance. This means the delimiting of constituencies, the granting of the franchise, the election system, etc. Most constitutions contain no reference to this field at all. It is left to specific legislation by the respective parliaments. However, even the best constitution may not work if the pitch is queered by restrictive or even deliberately contorted arena-setting. Early American political practice has produced a term which graphically describes one aspect of arena-setting: 'gerrymandering'. It refers originally to the clever redrawing of the boundaries of a constituency in the district of Essex, Massachussetts, under the auspices of Governor Elbridge Gerry in 1812. Since the constituency had the irregular shape of the spots of a salamander, it was portrayed like that animal in the caricatures which were circulated throughout America. The term was soon applied in a more general way to all kinds of political cheating to serve party interests. In trying to secure a social base for their rule the colonial powers often resorted to such schemes. They limited the franchise in terms of property qualifications favouring those on whose support they thought they could rely. They vetted the lists of voters and controlled the registration of trade unions and political parties. They introduced communal representation by specific electorates. Finally, they channelled political activities into arenas which would not directly affect their central control of the respective colony. The scheme of 'provincial autonomy' introduced in India in the 1930s is of special relevance in this context. It will be discussed later as it was part of the federal scheme of the Government of India Act of 1935.

All these attempts at 'gerrymandering', in the most general sense of the term, originally played a role in the usual game of 'divide and rule' which characterised all colonial empires. The results of this type of arena-setting were, of course, still very much in evidence when decolonisation became the order of the day. They could not be suddenly eradicated, and sometimes they were even continued and improved upon to assure a smooth transfer of power uninterrupted by oppositional forces. Special problems usually arose where the population of the respective colony did not have a homogenous population, but had been significantly affected by foreign immigration. This was the case in the sugar colonies which depended on Indian labour such as Mauritius, Guyana and Fiji or in African colonies which had attracted white settlers such as Algeria, Kenya, Rhodesia and Namibia. In the three sugar colonies, Indian labourers and their descendants more or less outnumbered the indigenous population or other immigrants. The colonial powers then tried to contain these Indian majorities by means of communal representation, etc. This caused an ethnic conflict which poisoned the political atmosphere even after independence had been achieved. The white settlers in Africa were small minorities. Here, measures were adopted to artificially enhance their political weight. This often led to violent conflicts such as the war in Algeria or the Mau Mau rebellion in Kenya or the guerrilla warfare of black nationalists against settler-dominated governments in Rhodesia.

Instead of going into the details of individual constitutions we shall now turn to the application of federal designs in the process of decolonisation, which have in some cases turned out to be of permanent importance but in other instances have been of a transitory nature.

The Uses and Abuses of Federalism

Federal designs have been applied to different levels of political organisation in the process of decolonisation. At the highest level they concerned the linkages of the metropolitan power with its colonies which were supposed to survive decolonisation by transforming imperialism into some kind of partnership. The model for this was the British Commonwealth of Nations which in a rather attenuated form did survive until the present day. Initially it was based on the Dominion status of ex-colonies like Canada and Australia. This status was also conferred on India and Pakistan at the time of their being granted independence. The same applied to Ceylon a year later. India insisted on becoming a republic which would no longer recognise the British monarch as the head of state represented by a Governor-General. A new formula was then found which enabled India and Pakistan to remain members of the Commonwealth as republics, while acknowledging the monarch as the head of the Commonwealth. Ceylon later on followed the same path when becoming a republic and adopted the name Sri Lanka.

The French Union was originally conceived in a similar way, but it did not provide for such an elegant form of attenuation as the Commonwealth did. In fact, it contained a great deal of uniformity and centralisation which was exemplified by the Loi Cadre that has been mentioned earlier. As a consequence of this tendency, the older quasi-federal structures of French West Africa with its Governor-General at Dakar and French Equatorial Africa with its Governor-General at Fort Lamy (N'Djamena) withered away to be replaced by more direct ties between Paris and the individual colonies. General de Gaulle's superimposition of the Constitution of the Fifth Republic on the Loi Cadre in 1958 at first seemed to produce a very strong tie which firmly attached the colonies to the French Union. Within a short time, however, de Gaulle had to abandon this construction, and what was left of the French Union in 1960 after most French colonies had attained individual independence was a mere fraction of the original. Actually this process contributed to the Balkanisation of Africa which many African leaders such as Félix Houphouet-Boigny and Barthélemy Boganda had wished to avoid.

The Union which the Dutch had created in order to contain the rebellious Republic of Indonesia was doomed to an even earlier demise. The Republic of Indonesia owed its origin to the unilateral declaration of independence proclaimed by Sukarno in 1945 at the end of the Japanese interregnum. For the Dutch who returned to Indonesia as colonial rulers, this Republic was a natural enemy which they tried to contain by forging links with leaders of the outer islands which the Republic did not yet control. Being dependent on American aid themselves, the Dutch could not exterminate the Republic. The conservative elements in Dutch politics would have liked to do that to be able to impose their political will. Finally the design of the Union only served as a transitory figleaf at the time of granting independence to the Republic which soon scrapped the Union, and asserted its control over the entire archipelago.

While the colonial rulers introduced many federal schemes, the ambitious plans of colonial nationalists were doomed. Most African nationalists had been inspired by Pan-Africanism and Kwame Nkrumah had advocated the creation of a United States of Africa. But all that the African leaders could finally produce was the Organisation of African Unity (OAU). Julius Nyerere later on said that the OAU had become a trade union of African heads of government who jealously guarded their sovereign rights. The leaders of ex-colonies were caught in the cage of inherited constitutions and did not dare to transcend the limits imposed by those arrangements.

At an intermediate level, the British tried to use federal designs in regional contexts in the process of decolonisation. The most successful one was the Union of India which has retained the federalism imposed by the colonial rulers until the present day. The Government of India Act of 1935 which contained this federal design was a clever piece of constitutional engineering for the purposes of a centrally controlled 'devolution of power'. It consisted of two parts, one concerned the newly introduced feature of 'provincial autonomy', the other a federal centre in which the Indian princely states were supposed to act as a conservative counterweight to the British Indian provinces which were for the most part dominated by the Indian National Congress. 'Provincial autonomy' actually worked, and to some extent did serve the purpose of diverting the attention of Indian politicians to this arena which had been set for them by the colonial rulers. The major leaders such as Gandhi, Nehru, Patel, et al. did not descend to this arena and formed a 'High Command' which aimed at taking over power at the center in due course. They were, quite naturally, anti-federalists as they saw in this construction a device to thwart their national ambitions. It so happened that the federal part of this constitution did not come into operation, because the required assent of at least 50 per cent of the Indian princes was not forthcoming. As a consequence of this refusal, all powers of the federal centre were left in the hands of the Viceroy who was now more powerful than ever before. This constellation led to a strange amalgamation of centralism and federalism in independent India. A powerful centre was transferred to the 'High Command' which nevertheless did not abolish federalism, but weakened it by specific legislation which embodied the heritage of the interventionist British colonial state that had emerged during the Second World War. In independent India, federalism, in setting a variety of political arenas, has contributed to the stability of the Indian Union.

Similarly, the Federation of Malaya, designed by the British, produced a rather stable political structure. The first plan of a Malayan Union was scrapped very soon because it was rejected by the Malays. It would have provided equal citizenship to the Chinese settled in Malaya and it would have curtailed the powers of the Malay sultans. In 1948, the British introduced a new constitution for a federation of Malaya which favoured the Malays and retained the powers of the sultans, one of whom would be the head of state, now called the 'King of Malaya'. This high office was to be filled by rotation. This rather unique construction has stood the test of time and is still working.

Another federation which was designed by the British for the purposes of decolonisation was the West Indies Federation. The Commonwealth Caribbean consists of a string of small islands of which Jamaica and Trinidad are the biggest ones. The political leaders of these two big islands—Norman Manley in Jamaica and Eric Williams in Trinidad—were ardent supporters of the idea of a West Indies Federation. It was inaugurated in 1956 and if it had worked it would have led to the simultaneous grant of independence to all islands of the British Caribbean by 1960. Unfortunately, neither Manley nor Williams were ready to become the prime minister of this federation and left this honour to Grantley Adams of Barbados. The federation was a weak construction, it was not even a customs union. W. Arthur Lewis from St. Lucia, who later received the Nobel,was the economic advisor to Adams and had high hopes for the future of the West Indies Federation. But the whole scheme collapsed before it could take off. Manley, who was sure of the great value of the federation, submitted the plan to a referendum for which the Jamaican opposition had clamoured. He lost both the referendum and the subsequent elections. Jamaican nationalism had defeated the federation. Jamaica and Trinidad became independent seperately in 1961. The smaller islands had to wait, some of them for a long time, before they could reach this goal.

A more enduring federation established by the British was the state of Nigeria which has retained its federal character until the present day. This federation, however, has been preserved with great difficulties and enormous sacrifices. These difficulties had their origin in the peculiarities of the constitutional development of colonial Nigeria. The British thought very highly of the system of indirect rule which they had established in Northern Nigeria. This was a region dominated by Muslim Amirs who were converted into 'native authorities' by the British. They tried to construct such native authorities in Southern and Eastern Nigeria as well. The Ibo of Eastern Nigeria are Bantu people who have no chieftains but have an elaborate system of age grades which regulate local governance. In such areas chieftains had to be invented by the British. In the process of decolonisation the British tried to rely on the native authorities in the three regions, and instead of taking steps towards creating a parliament for the whole of Nigeria, they diverted political activities to the three regional arenas. When they finally did create a federal parliament they queered the pitch by favouring the North to which more seats were allocated than the other two regions. This practically predetermined that the federal prime minister had to be from Northern Nigeria. Having set the arena in such a way that national interest aggregation could not be achieved and that the North would predominate, the British contributed to a violent power struggle which soon engulfed Nigeria. Finally there was even an attempt of the Eastern region to secede that was eventually suppressed in a bloody civil war. Instead of an aggregation of democratic interest, military dictatorship preserved the federal state. It is only recently that Nigeria has tried to retrace its steps by introducing democracy once more.

A rather infamous British federal scheme was the Federation of Rhodesia and Nyasaland. It owed its origin to the white North Rhodesian labour leader Roy Welensky, an engine driver who had earned fame as a boxer and then became a politician. The white settlers of North Rhodesia were a small minority and looked to the more powerful settlers of South Rhodesia as their main support in an uncertain future in which the black majority would play an important role. Welensky would have favoured a merger of both Rhodesias, but his Labour Party friends in London told him that this would be impossible, whereas a federation which would also include neighbouring Nyasaland could find favour in London. Welensky returned home as an ardent federalist and managed to get the federation going in 1953. A senior South Rhodesian politician became its first prime minister, Welensky was his successor in 1956 and remained in charge of the federation until its bitter end in 1963. It was a complex construction; each of the three states had its own prime minister and its own British governor. The not so hidden agenda of this construction, the preservation of the political power of the white settlers, was soon affected by the 'wind of change' which Harold Macmillan conjured up in Africa in 1960. In North Rhodesia, Kenneth Kaunda and in Nyasaland, Dr. Hastings Banda led their respective African nationalist parties to democratic victories which could not be ignored by Macmillan. He knew that the Federation was doomed but tried to humour Welensky to prevent him from appealing to the British public. In 1963 Macmillan finally scrapped the Federation and soon thereafter Zambia (North Rhodesia) and Malawi (Nyasaland) achieved their independence. South Rhodesia was left to its own devices, and under the radical leadership of Ian Smith it then proclaimed a Unilateral Declaration of Independence in 1965. The Federation had been a halfway house. Its construction had not led to a smooth transfer of power. It had delayed the independence of two of its components and had prepared the ground for the radical reaction of the third component which gave the British a great deal of trouble.

A Blind Spot: The Civilian Control of the Armed Forces

One item which was missing in the constitutional debates preceding the transfer of power was the control of the colonial armed forces. Their existence was taken for granted both by the colonial rulers and by the politicians who would inherit their power. Some constitutions made in the process of decolonisation contained references to the conditions of service of the bureaucrats and judges. But the armed forces which soon proved to be of crucial importance in the life of the newly independent nations were of no concern at the time of decolonisation. A cynical expression of this neglect was the formula 'After Independence=Before Independence' which the Belgian commander of the Force Publique of the Congo wrote on a blackboard for the instruction of his black soldiers. He caused a mutiny in this way which determined the future course of the history of the Congo. A civilian reaction to the stark facts of military power after independence is best exemplified by that of Mahatma Gandhi in India. He had reluctantly agreed to the partition of India but was surprised when he was told that this would also mean the partition of the British Indian army. He had not given any thought to this at all and when he was compelled to do so, he clearly predicted that the two armies which would come into existence in this way would soon fight each other. This prediction came true within a short time when Indian and Pakistani troops faced each other in Kashmir.

India under Prime Minister Jawaharlal Nehru then managed to keep its large army under strict civilian control whereas Pakistan was ever again subjected to military rule. Both countries had inherited the British tradition of politically neutral professional armed forces. The difference in the further development was only due to the strength and stability of the civilian government or the lack of it. Most newly independent nations had inexperienced and unstable governments and could thus easily fall prey to military dictatorship. Clear lessons were in the form of the mutiny of the Force Publique (mentioned earlier) and the East African mutinies of 1964. The latter could only be repressed because the ex-colonial power sent in troops for disarming the mutineers. Also, the mutineers did not yet have trained leadership and could be easily overcome. Wherever an indigenous command structure had been fully developed, military coups succeeded and usually led to the permanent replacement of civilian government. There were only a few instances where the civilian government was resourceful enough to build up an army tied to it by means of patronage. The government of Forbes Burnham in Guyana is a case in point. Burnham was also defence minister and recruited his army almost exclusively from his own Afro-Guyanese community. He saw to it that everybody in these armed forces owed him a debt of gratitude. Other political leaders were not so circumspect. Sylvanus Olympio of Togo, for instance, was murdered by disgruntled soldiers of the small colonial army whom he had to demobilise in the interest of balancing his budget. If he had acted like Burnham he would have remained alive and powerful—at the expense of his nation. There were also cases of highly irresponsible and unconstitutional actions of civilian politicians which paved the way for their own overthrow by a military dictator. Milton Obote of Uganda, for instance, who was prime minister in 1966 ordered his military commander, Idi Amin, to storm the palace of the Kabaka of Buganda who was the President of Uganda. The Kabaka fled and Obote himself became President and Prime Minister, but he enjoyed his power only for a short time. Idi Amin overthrew him and subjected Uganda to a regime of brutal terror.

A very special case is that of the politicised armies of Southeast Asia which owed their existence to the Japanese interregnum of 1942–45. The Japanese trained about 6000 Indonesian officers in this short period of time, leaving a legacy to this nation which proved to be of great importance for its subsequent political development. The Indonesian army then had to fight the returning colonial rulers and could claim credit for freeing the nation. It therefore felt entitled to play a political role.

In most other decolonised countries the armed forces had not been involved in fighting for national freedom. One important exception is Algeria, but there the military which captured power had actually been prevented from fighting the French colonial rulers. Colonel Boumedienne's well organised troops were bottled up in Tunisia during the Algerian war; they entered Algeria only after the war and then enabled Boumedienne to seize power and to retain it for a long time.

The lesson to be derived from all these examples is that the internal command structure of an army provides a 'constitution' which is simple and stable. It also has clear operational rules within the limited sphere of its action. But this 'constitution' does not refer to the more complex tasks of civilian government. This means that once the army takes over these tasks will be neglected or performed in an arbitrary manner, but nobody can complain about this because the military 'constitution' does not permit insubordination.

2

The Exception and the Rule: On French Colonial Law

Olivier Le Cour Grandmaison

'The indigenous are nor comparable with the French [...] They have neither their moral quality, nor their level of education nor their religion [...] nor their civilisation. The mistake is generous and pretty French; it was made by those who drafted the 'Declaration of the Rights of Man and the Citizen' instead of simply drafting the 'Declaration of the Rights of the French Citizen.'

—P. Azan (1925)[1]

'The indigenous have demeanour, laws and a fatherland which are not ours. We do not make their happiness, neither according to the principles of the French Revolution, which is our Revolution, nor according to the Code Napoleon, which is our Code.'

—F. Eboué (1941)[2]

Extracts of works written at different times by authors coming from distinct disciplines and professions, the quotations above indicate the remarkable continuity of particular representations of others and of the world; they also show the spirit of an age whose contemporaries–exceptions are rare–profess a radical political and juridical relativism. Based on racial, cultural, and religious considerations, this radicalism is based on an anti-universalism which has long since been theorised and vindicated by many who affirm that neither the principles of the Declaration of the Rights of Man and the Citizen, nor those of the Republic that followed are capable of being extended to the colonies. In these distant parts of the empire, where 'primitive' people live, the laws and the fundamental liberties cannot be established because of the differences arising out of the specificities of the civilisations.

The climate, the manners, the religion, the ancestral customs and mentalities prevent it. So believe the authors, jurists and politicians of the time, who find in the recent developments in the science called 'coloniale'[3] the essential and proper scientific justification for the orientations/policies and measures which they defend.

On Some Fundamentals of Colonial Law

Numerous ethnologists, sociologists and anthropologists agreed to put their expertise and, sometimes, their respective disciplines to the service of the empire. The leaders of the Third Republic, who frequently confronted new problems, difficult to be resolved (due to the rapid expansion of territories overseas, and because of the importance and diversity of the people who had since then been placed under the bondage of the metropolitan country) often sought to solicit the views of well-known authorities of these disciplines. The ambitions and the desire to know on the one hand, and the pressing need, on the other, to subjugate almost everything to the grand imperial design of the metropolitan country, thus favoured an unwritten agreement between the sciences and the state.[4] The overwhelming majority of the actors of France's colonial politics (whether councillors or legal professionals, legislators or ministers) therefore felt that specific policies elaborated and applied to these parts of the colonies should take account of the inferiority and peculiarity of the 'indigenous' people and the countries in which they live, without forgetting the superior interests of the metropolitan country and the imperative of preserving colonial public order. The establishment of this public order, along with its pitiless defence in the face of the people described as savage or barbaric, is a major task before which the 'juridical scruples and sentimental considerations should efface themselves'.[5] Indeed, they did effectively efface themselves.

Rights of Man and the Colonies

At the heart of these dominant conceptions (since they structure the analysis, the discourse and the practice of the majority of the contemporaries interested in the affairs of the empire) triumphantly resides a hierarchical and racial principle. This destroys the concept of humanity as an ensemble of individuals, certainly different but equal and, in this sense, capable of having subjective and inalienable rights which they recognise as possible. Beyond the people, historically situated and observed, exists the alter ego. For this alter ego, the differences are indifferent, and it ought to benefit, at all times and everywhere, from an equal dignity, sanctioned by prerogatives which cannot be denied without committing a grave crime. This challenge interests us. When the contemporaries thought of 'the Arab', the majority among them could see only a barbarian, so menacing that he could never be assimilated. The 'black', living in a savage land or thought of as a 'big child', should be controlled by a firm authority lest he escapes during his minority. As for the 'Annamite', mysterious and impenetrable, he comes from an important civilisation surely, but one which is inferior in many points. If the unity of the human space is thus difficult to construct—unequal races and people do exist—then it would be vain, even hurtful, to apply a common law to everyone. J. Harmand, for example, believes the recent 'progress' of knowledge bears testimony to the essential and irreconcilable diversity of men, which would, on that count, make it impossible to put everyone under the principles of universal law. Considered more as antiquated heritage, such principles and laws are henceforth rejected in the name of the development of 'ethnological science'. The latter, happily influenced by 'positivism' and under the guidance of Broca and Le Bon, has allowed the break with the French 'practice' of 'universalism and uniform centralisation', whose assimilation, when applied to the colonies, would be disastrous. This classic denial of assimilation opens, more fundamentally, a radical critique of 'the revolutionary ideas' and their 'utopias' as presumably dangerous, because they are the cause of the decline of imperial power. As for the Rights of Man, they sound like the 'artificial ideas dear to the evangelists of the French Revolution',[6] but in fact have been rendered obsolete by the progress of the science mentioned earlier.

Beyond the authors discussed by J. Harmand (the scientific nature of their work had not been fundamentally established though their works were being discussed) and his own particular position, the principal arguments were pretty current at that age. In effect, questions arise about the feasibility of the laws being implemented in the colonies. Indeed, the 'indigenous' characteristics are put forward in advance to justify the impossibility of extending these laws, which were made basically for the 'civilised races'. Reflecting on the virtues of rigorously imposing work ethic in W. Africa or Congo, R. Cuivillier-Fleury wrote, in a treatise on law, that he would not hesitate to suppress 'the freedom to work' or to considerably restrain it, should the circumstances and the mentality of the Blacks so demand. According to him, in these countries such dispositions had 'excellent effects…from the point of view of moral and material amelioration' of the 'indigenous', who should be taken away from 'idleness', 'war' and 'plunder', and among them one ought to develop the healthy 'habit of work'.[7] As for the immediate abolition of slavery in the colonies recently conquered by France, he would consider that to be premature on account of the unfortunate consequences it would have on the agriculture of the concerned areas. Also, freeing them would mean that given their contempt for 'work on the field', they would abandon themselves to their innate and principal vice—'idleness'. He was thus in favour of a 'transitory state of semi-control' which would permit the old slaves to 'prepare themselves for the new status of free men'.[8] These examples—which can be multiplied—prove that institutions and practices long condemned in France continued to be advocated at times in the colonies, even though they were contrary to basic principles. More generally a line of thinking emerges, and this is close to the verities established by the 'colonial sciences': the inferior races and the superior races should be subject to juridical and political regimes which are exact opposites.

It is convenient to extend the benefits of democracy, the rule of law and the procedures meant to guarantee civil and civic privileges to the citizens in the advanced countries of Europe and North America. In the 'backward' and 'un'civilised countries of Africa, Asia and Oceania, it is necessary to impose other institutions and a system of justice which, freed from the subtleties of the notion of 'the separation of administrative and judicial authorities', will make the indigenous people accept that 'the Europeans are the masters'.[9] The author of the statement is none other than Girault who was greatly applauded by the participants at the International Congress of Colonial Sociology. Fiercely opposed to the idea of assimilation of the colonies and the colonists, the politics of assimilation was officially rejected in 1900 by the powers that be as a chimera, dangerous to the stability and integrity of the empire. It also asserted that 'supreme' authority should be vested in a 'person who in some ways incarnates...the metropolitan and who has the power to break all resistance which might be produced'. Three years later, he affirmed at the inauguration of the London session of the International Colonial Institute that all the 'civil, judicial and even military authority should equally be vested in him'. In conclusion, he felt that the new imperial orientation in France, on its positive side, suggested only one line of thinking for the future: 'the good tyrant is the ideal form of government for the colonies.'[10]

Such then are the major elements of the quasi-official creed of colonial politics and juridical science in the Third Republic. As for those who laid down the fundamentals of colonial law and deduced the practical consequences of the birth of such law earlier, the fact that is often ignored today or considered of secondary importance, is that they were perfectly aware that these laws were extraordinary in nature, and contrary to the basic tenets of democracy. Better still, they did not even seek to conceal or find a euphemism for the situation these laws created. Such views are, however, quite well known on account of the works and treatises dedicated to colonial legislation. Such material was notably used at l'Ecole libre des sciences politique of the Law faculty and at L'Institut d'ethnologie of the University of Paris. It was presided over by Levy-Bruhl and was established in 1925 with the active support of public authority.[11] Convinced of the legitimacy and imperious necessity of this particular type of legislation for governing the Empire, and supported by the 'colonial sciences' which provided its psychological, ethnological, anthropological and sociological justification, the jurists and responsible politicians put forward, precisely and without qualification, what should be the good law for the colonies.[12] Yet, many men of that époque proved to have a clairvoyance which eludes many of our contemporaries, who forget or ignore that France of the Third Republic was neither 'a unitary state, nor a federal state', but 'like England, an *imperial state*'. This is what J. Barthelemy and P. Duez did so effectively.[13]

Of the Metropolitan Law in the Colonies: The Exception and the Rule

The consequences of this division, between a republican metropolitan and the territories of the empire subject to a permanently exceptional rule, are immense from a political and juridical point of view. In effect, 'it is not a branch of law which, transplanted to the colonies, could undergo more or less profound transformation', wrote P. Matter, the *procureur-general* of the *Cour de Cassation*. After many others, he ascertained that the 'regime of decrees' to which the colonies had been subjected, further accentuated the differences and favoured the emergence of a 'special law whose peculiarities are always more numerous and more striking'.[14] The origin of this situation is found in Article 109 of the Constitution of the Second Republic which, while declaring 'the territory of Algeria and the colonies' as 'French', also added that they would be rewarded by 'particular laws which will be made in accordance with the special law under the present constitution'. One knows what followed: the transitory regime, so conceived, became definitive. This was interpreted in terms of a principle, which generations of jurists and responsible politicians believed for nearly a century.[15] Important for the constitutional principle that it involves and for the consequences for the 'indigenous' people, this principle has been described by P. Dareste thus: *'the metropolitan laws do not [stretch] as far as the colonies which [are] ruled by a proper legislation'*.[16]

It is then clear and precise: two radically different political–juridical orders could henceforth develop along legal lines under the auspices of the Fundamental Law of 4 November 1848, which was both republican and reputedly generous. Let us add, in order to dispel all ambiguity and to get nearer to the essential procedure which establishes the laws, that the rule was simple: metropolitan laws and regulations were not applicable to the colonies save in exceptional cases which would be decided by the regulatory authority or competent legislative authority.[17] The inapplicability of metropolitan legislation to the territories of the empire would lead us to the fundamental judicial principles of colonial law and help to discover its essential elements: the colonial law was not derogatory to the republican principles or national dispositions in a marginal or superficial way or by virtue of an exceptional conjuncture whose effects were limited in time and space for the concerned individuals. In fact, the colonial law was, in essence, derogatory and discriminatory because it systematically detracted from all the principles declared in the metropolitan country, and from all the texts adopted there.

These principles ran up against two limitations—one is territorial and the other relates to the quality of individuals; the conjunction of their effects had been the origin of the singular situations in which the colonies and their people find themselves. Considered French (it allowed France to affirm sovereign power over the countries conquered by her) these colonies would, however, not be privy to the horizontal extension of the laws and decrees of the metropolitan country. This particular territoriality was not absolute since the colonists who resided in the empire could enjoy the rights and liberties guaranteed in their motherland. This evidently was not the case with the 'indigenous'. In this case the jurists point out, finding their evidence was almost a triviality; these men were only *'subjects*, protected and administered by the French, and not *French citizens'*.[18] Thus conceived and applied, law continued to sustain the exclusive benefit of the people coming from the metropolitan country, to ensure the restrictive effects of territoriality, and to establish two opposite status: that of the indigenous who were merely *subjects*, and the French who enjoyed full civil and political rights.

More generally, the interpretation of Article 109 of the Constitution of the Second Republic, an examination of its major consequences on the juridical conditions of the colonies and of the colonised, permits the observation that at that inaugural moment the *exception became the rule* in the territories of the empire. This was enabled by the proclamation of its permanence on the one hand, and the inscription of a particular juridical order on the other. The juridical order which authorised this exception thus became legal, and for many legitimate, simultaneously favouring the emergence of a colonial law which contemporaries found to have proliferated extraordinarily, while remaining both complex and variable. 'No branch of French law is as obscure, confused and open to contradictions as colonial legislation',[19] remarked R. Doucet. The origins of this situation can be found in the mechanism, which will be studied, and in the dispositions of such laws in different parts of the empire. These dispositions were not subject to any general principle, stranger to Fundamental Law and, adopted in the metropolitan countries or in the colonies. Born of diverse juridical and geographical situations, these dispositions kept on adding one to the other and never ceased to vary in time and space. The governor in the colonies, who dispensed these, possessed the powers to render them valid in the territories under his control and thus established a regime of decrees. These decrees escaped even the control of the parliamentarians who often took cognizance only when these were published in the *Journal Officiel*.[20]

These diverse elements tell us that a major characteristic of colonial law was that it was 'frankly particularist',[21] and as Vernier de Byans saw, it was not a vice but an indispensable quality necessary for the preservation of peace and security in the conquered territories. The essential point then is that these laws were not universal and could therefore hardly extend to individuals the privileges which were guaranteed everywhere and on every occasion. These principles, the permanence of laws and the relative stability of the laws, had a reverse side: colonial legislation recognised only the actual 'indigenous', particular situations of the people and singular conjunctures. The law was subject to these elements. At the same time such laws were 'supple' and had constant variability. Many contemporaries praised the ability on the part of the metropolitan authority, or of the governors, to quickly adapt or modify, by passing the legislative procedure or normal control, the rules to respond to new or particular situations without delay. Such were the principal advantages of ruling by decrees through which proper dispensation could be extended to each colony. If such regimes had occasionally been critiqued, it could not be wished away on account of its remarkable longevity. They were abolished only after the Second World War. In fact, one thing can be said about colonial law: it was a law without principles; it was, however, possible to add that it did have an underlying but constant principle: to be of service to the politics of subjugating the 'indigenous'.

'Indigenous' Subjects and French Citizens

From this discussion arises a singular situation whose juridical effects, traditionally confined within the limits of a geographical frontier where all the nationals enjoy identical rights, disappear in the colonies on account of the establishment of a second frontier founded on the basis of racial and cultural considerations. Within the limits of the second frontier the residents of the empire were discriminated on the basis of their origin, race and religion. This has the effect of actually creating 'two classes', separated by a 'proper divide': one of subjects, that is to say, subordinates who are bound by a specific legislation and the other of 'citizens'.[22] The difference which separated the condition of the former from that of the latter is not marginal; on the contrary, these were differences of nature. In fact, two different worlds were organised which were ruled by dispensations meant to enslave the 'indigenous' and to guarantee plenty of rights to the colonists. In a final analysis, this ensured the domination of the latter over the former. This was always seen to be a *sine qua non* for the preservation of public security as well as the stability and prosperity of the empire. Regarding the 'generic' and modern 'concept of persons',[23] it was obviously ruined by the colonial law which established an order where there was, not a 'single personality' conforming to the principles declared in 1789 abolishing privileges, but 'several', gifted personalities with completely different attributes.

This is nothing new as Tocqueville had earlier pleaded for a similar organisation. *'Nothing absolutely prevents, when the Europeans are concerned, to treat them as if they were alone; the rules that we are making for them necessarily being applied only to them'*,[24] wrote Tocqueville in 1841 in his famous work on Algeria. Rule of law was, for the colonists, coming from the old continent; for the 'Arabs' or the *Kabyles* there was no equality, no civil society, no universality of law, neither today nor tomorrow. In effect, Tocqueville did not fix the terms of the situation which could perpetuate the juridical dispensation subject to the principles, affirmed earlier by the Declaration of the Rights of Man and the Citizen, that without universality of law there could be no equality. In France, law, reputedly an expression of the General Will, 'should be the same for those it protects and those it punishes',[25] according to the formula long established. The Constituents, having been anxious to inscribe in the Constitution several articles a few weeks earlier abolishing the privileges and sanctioning a natural equality to the members of the society, could not be privy to this. This is why in the new society, which knew only free and equal individuals, any positive law ought to have been submitted to that major principle. Let us add that in order to effectively establish equality before law, it was necessary to equally apply that major principle. To recall briefly, what was destroyed in Algeria were the essential conceptions and dispositions. These disappeared to create a situation whereby in one country existed not two different sets of legislations, but also two different regimes for two distinct peoples. The rule defended by Tocqueville may be summed up by this formula: 'law should not be the same for everyone'. All the same, the consequence of such attitude was that law would not be uniformly applied to the colonial space. It is not surprising that in place of equality and equal liberty, proclaimed and established in the metropolitan country, inequality with its multi-layered discriminations triumphed in the colonies. This is characteristic of the juridical order which is dedicated to the cause of enslaving the 'indigenous' people.

In his report presented to the National Assembly in June 1842, Beaumont said the same thing. 'For long', he affirmed in making a convenient argument, 'an exceptional legislation would be necessary (for Algeria); it would not be on account of public safety alone: the differences of climate, the varieties of people, different manners and different needs would call for different laws'. Indeed, such precision is interesting. At the risk of being original, they tell us this: Just as the military situation was transformed to the benefit of the army in Africa, other factors like climate, habits and customs of the 'indigenous' people oblige the authorities to maintain, for an indeterminate period, the exceptional dispensation of the common law. Taking almost word for word the formulation of his friend Tocqueville, who like him, was a member of the sub-commission in whose name he was expressing his views, Beaumont adds, 'Thus, there is in Africa two societies, one distinct from the other and each day moving further apart from each other; for each there is a regime and a set of laws'.[26] The extreme limits of the juridical conditions vis-à-vis equality, hierarchy or liberty, clearly establish the submission of the 'indigenous' population to the superiority of the metropolitan. Decades later the jurists and the politicians of the Third Republic, in their discourses and accounts of events, conformed to the positions already defined by Beaumont and Tocqueville. The author of *Democracy in America* was now being recognised as a great specialist of colonisation and those who strongly argued in favour of increasing the powers of the governor-general read, cited and commented on his writings with enthusiasm. It is not being suggested that Tocqueville directly inspired this imperial politics prevailing around 1900, but that contemporaries used some of his texts where they found tools of analysis or elements of legitimacy, in a different situation, to defend their own attitudes.[27] He was certainly not an inspirer; but his writings and discourses on Algeria served as a point of reference to those who cited them to claim a long and prestigious history for their policies.

In 1938, R. Maunier stated that 'there is not, in the colonies, equality of the citizens and subjects, but hierarchies... distinctions...subordination of subjects ...there were the French, but also the French who are not citizens'. Fierce supporter of this situation, he always defended it as perfectly suited to the 'primitive' or 'backward' peoples of the empire. It was also necessary to establish the supremacy of the colonists and the authority of the metropolitan country. He added, by way of conclusion: the 'indigenous' people have 'less right', 'they are inferior and not equal.' This is why the word 'subject' which was in vogue in the colonies... 'defines all the conditions of the inhabitants'.[28] In Algeria, in terms of the decree of 24 October 1870, all the territories were unified, and assimilated in the metropolitan country with the establishment of the departmental system. At the same time the 'indigenous mussalmans' became 'French subjects'. This 'fundamental rule' is 'characteristic of their juridical condition',[29] wrote E. Larcher and G. Rectenwald, who considered this to be the price for maintaining French rule in North Africa. Thus, in all the colonies, as a result of particular situations and their specific statutes arose 'double legislation', a 'double government', a 'double administration', and a system of double justice where 'each' has 'his judge' and 'each' has 'his laws'.[30]

Proof, if there is any need of it, that the republican character of the institutions in the metropolitan country was hardly considered by the men of the Third Republic when they thought of the colonial state or imperial legislation, is found in the description of the necessity to administer far away territories and 'primitive races' or simply 'backward' people. The reality of principles applied in the empire and the juridical situation in the colonies, where the special dispensations are applied, are for all to see. As for assimilation, often described as a distinct mark of colonisations '*à la* French' and reputed to be a generous policy calculated to elevate the people in their charge (thus employing a vocabulary convenient at that age), it was vigorously condemned and abandoned at the turn of the century by a majority. Finally, the uniqueness of a number of measures vigorously applied in the empire is only a myth when compared to certain measures adopted by other European colonial powers. In the Dutch East Indies, for example, by virtue of an organic law of 2 September 1854, relating to the government and justice of those territories the 'indigenous' were assimilated. Trying to know the descendants of the Muslims of Hindustan and the Chinese in particular, they put them to a particular type of justice which the Europeans evidently escaped. In the German colonies likewise, a principle strongly stated by the jurist Otto Kobner asserted that *'ensemble of rules comprising private laws, penal laws and the procedure and organization of the judiciary are to apply only to the white population* '. In the case of the 'indigenous and other coloured men, the application of imperial law and the ordinances…is unlimited',[31] because they came under special measures. In what sense do these differ from the essential dispensation of colonial law of Republican France? In no way, as we can now see. As for Belgian Congo, the rules and codes of the neighbouring indigenous French were applied there, for the autochthons submitted to the control which obliged them, for example, to take a passport and authorisation of the territorial administrator to leave their original home. Add to this the fact that forced labour and capitation, vigorously in force in a number of French colonies, also existed here.[32] Thus all forms of state, whether a republic or a constitutional monarchy or a Reich, put into operation an extraordinary, discriminatory and racist law which established an exceptional state, permanently imposed on the colonies.

The strange situation in the French empire, including Algeria, did not escape the notice of many contemporaries who felt that the colonial regime and the condition of the 'indigenous' people were analogous to the feudal regime. Initially developed by Fr. Charveriat, Professor at the Law School of Algeria, this analysis was further popularised by E. Larcher in the work referred to here. This had virtually become the Bible for all studies and courses on colonial legislation. 'The French citizens could be compared to the nobles and the seigneurs; they were to be judged only by their counterpart; only they, in principle, could carry arms. The indigenous people, simply subjects, had a situation that was comparable to that of the plebeian or the serf', wrote Larcher. Anxious to illustrate this general proposition by concrete examples, he maintained that the *mussulmans* could not travel without passport, and also certain kind of 'forced obligations' to the French authorities, like the *diffa* (reception obligatorily given by the chiefs in their tents) and 'the service of *postes-vigies* which resembled the old feudal services'. To this may be added, says Charveriat, the requirement of various labour—like digging or the fight against the invasion of the locusts which may be likened to corvée or forced labour adapted to the conditions of different societies. Should one be surprised at this? Not if one follows Larcher, who wrote, 'We are in Algeria in conditions similar to those in which the Franks found themselves in Gaul—a victorious race imposing its yoke and domination on a vanquished race'.[33] In his course on colonial law taught at the Faculty of Law at Paris in 1938, R. Maunier followed the old and well-known texts to pedagogically establish the general condition of the 'indigenous'. 'In more senses than one, the relationship between the metropolitan and the colony, *stricto sensu*, was one of vassalage', said this illustrious professor and academician, who called the natives 'subjects', who had no other rights than what 'one recognises as belonging to the subjects everywhere'.[34] This is what the thesis generally established, but it lacked demonstrative precision. More important, these eminent contemporaries, face to face with the particular legislations of the empire, had to fall back on the feudal age in France, in order to discover the elements of comparison to satisfy their need for analysis and understanding.

They did not, however, cite old examples to oppose what they saw; they approved of it. There were, at the same time, some critics of the colonial politics, who used some of these points and conclusions of these theses to denounce the 'aristocracy of race', which was established in Algeria with great deal of severity. They also critiqued the conditions to which the 'indigenous' were reduced; they were made 'an eternal plebeian in the name of the raison d'Etat'. This was expressed by Ch. Dumas, a socialist parliamentarian in charge of an enquiry into the conditions of the *mussulmans* in North Africa. He was also one of the rare individuals who fought for a rigorous application of human rights in the colonies to combat the oppression and exploitation of the autochthons.[35] Benito Sylvain, Doctor of Law, officer of Marine in France and aide de camp of the Emperor of Ethiopia, compared the condition of the indigenous to that of a serf, 'manipulated at the mercy of the ancient regime', on account of forced labour and numerous juridical discriminations imposed on them. To end this situation, he pleaded for the application of the principles of civil equality in the colonies. He felt that the Third Republic was faithful to that principle only in the old continent. Moreover, the Republic had shamelessly and absolutely betrayed 'those of a pure heart, who represent the ideals of civilization.'[36]

Be that as it may, the numerous apologists and rarer critics of colonisation, though they came to opposite conclusions, knew the extraordinary character of the fundamentals of the colonial legislation and the concrete measures adopted to administer the empire, entrusted to the Republicans. Two of them will now receive our attention: administrative internment and collective responsibility. These were the essential dispensations imposed on the colonial order by France. These are exemplary evidences of the situation to which the 'indigenous' had been subjected. They also allow us to observe the radical negation of the major democratic principles.[37]

On Some Exceptional Measures

Of Administrative Internment

Occasioned by the 'imperative' of the war of conquest in Algeria, the administrative internment was defined by a ministerial order of September 1834, and this was added to repeatedly during the 1840s. It progressively became a permanent arrangement, quite detached from the context of the war which provided the original justification, and survived the changes of regime until it was confirmed by a ministerial decision of 27 December 1897. In the colonies the exception thus became the rule, and internment became a permanent practice. Because of its frequent use and the modalities of its execution, it did appear to the local population to be an extraordinary regulation and produced a permanent apprehension. The motives for which it was possible to have recourse to this measure were: the defence of the public order and then, in 1902 and 1910, the pilgrimage to Mecca without authorisation.[38]

It was not possible to make an appeal against the decision of the governor-general. He could pronounce that internment in the colonies would take the place in an 'indigenous penitentiary' or in tribal village or a nomadic tent from which he could not leave without detention, or it could be deportation to Calvi. Moreover, (a major peculiarity of the measure), its duration was, more often than not *indeterminate*; neither the place nor the form of detention could be predetermined, and the governor-general had the monopoly to decide these matters. Finally (a second extraordinary element of detention), it could be a major punishment or could be served with another verdict given by a tribunal. In the latter case it was a major violation of common law. There was no remedy in the judicial system, neither for the condemned nor for the judge. Contrary to all the principles of separation of powers and liberty conforming to the Declaration of the Rights of Man and the Citizen, an administrative agent—in effect, the juridical status of the Governor-General—could intern individuals on his own terms.

Expression of sovereignty, the internment had the character of absolute control over the 'indigenous', because it took away, as a consequence, all privileges. More precisely, this jurisdictional disposition sanctioned a *'sans-droit absolu'*, whereby the defender could not invoke any legal text in his defence. The interned was considered neither as an individual nor as a human being, in the judicial sense of the term because he had no right in such a situation. The modalities of internment and the juridical conditions of the internment are not comparable to the conditions in any other age; we then find a major innovation which is without precedent since the Revolution and the emergence of constitutional regimes in France.[39] In effect, the delinquent, the criminal, and the prisoner of war having committed a mistake were judged by these precise dispositions which determined the procedure, the nature, the conditions and the execution of the servitude, its duration and the conditions of appeal, if and when they existed at all. The interned 'indigenous' was not considered a prisoner, who was serving a term pronounced by a tribunal, nor as an accused who, at the same time as he was incarcerated, had the right to defend himself or seek his release. The internee does not belong to any of these categories because his situation was created by an administrative fiat necessary to preserve public order and therefore recourse to all laws were denied to him till such time as the governor-general pleased. *This is how the procedures of internment unfolded themselves: depriving a man of his liberty and destroying his rights even as a subject.* This measure need not be confounded with other deprivations of liberty, which never had the consequence of completely destroying the juridical personality of the condemned. Internment then is that exceptional disposition which had the extraordinary power of reducing law to nothing.

Of Collective Responsibility

Apart from internment, the Governor-General also had the power, as per the Circular of 2 January 1844, of putting an entire tribe to collective punishment. In this case too he had discretionary powers and his freedom of action was complete. He could then use this collective punishment. In consideration of mainly political factors, he was the sole judge of the necessity and the opportunity to execute it. Initially it was used for issuing sanctions against tribes, some of whose members had committed acts of hostility against the colonial regime, its representatives or against the Europeans. Later, its use was extended to crimes or acts of delinquency committed collectively and also applied in cases where the alleged culprit was not handed over to the French authority by his tribe.

It was by virtue of the exercise of this extraordinary power, whose equivalent legislation was unknown in the colonies or in the metropolitan, that the Kabyles tribe, who rebelled in 1871, were subjected to a punitive payment which gradually rose to 63 million francs. Incapable of meeting this huge demand, many of them were forced to sell their cattle or land. This was a direct cause of the permanent impoverishment of the region. 'Contrary to the less debatable principles of our penal laws', commented E. Larcher, notably the essential principle of the 'individuality of the accused',[40] guaranteed and sanctioned by the French legislative texts, collective punishment was integrated to the law of 17 July 1874. It was extended to incidents of fire and its prevention in Algeria. In the matter of their application, the Governor-General reserved all his powers and the freedom of action which nothing could restrain. It was enough to follow a summary procedure: to take an order from the Council of Government.

The Third Republic maintained the particular form of this dispensation. If a tribe was suspected to be responsible for a fire, even the innocents were affected simply because they were members of that tribe. They could be total strangers to the incident. In the eyes of the coloniser, by complete reversal of principles applied to the Europeans, the 'indigenous', almost by definition, was presumed guilty; he had to pay for the alleged fault of his group, even if he could bring proof of his personal innocence. Again, these dispositions saw the disappearance, in the corpus of colonial law, of the concepts of the individual and the man. Thus these people were reduced to a mass of de-individualised people, on whom the measures of exception could be permanently imposed. These measures were applied on them for alleged violation not as individuals but as members of a 'racial' community. They were constantly clubbed together and were found to be, in the eyes of the French legislators, always guilty. This whole thing was subjected to a novel juridical concept, unknown to us: that of guilt without any action or responsibility. In 1935, J. Melia summarised the situation in these terms, 'never did any regime, particularly the forest department of Algeria, listen to the complaints of the 'indigenous' […]. A forest is on fire. The indigenous Muslims of Algeria, who lived there or nearby, were suspected of causing the fire. They thus became guilty and their responsibility was extended to the entire tribe. An exaggerated punishment, in the form of collective responsibility, is imposed on the innocents, who are thereby reduced to utter misery'.[41]

Administrative internment, collective responsibility and sequestration—the last was considered as a legal spoliation—were the measures which proved that the body and the property of the 'indigenous' could be seized in accordance with the summary proceeding which was opposed to all the principles proclaimed since 1789. These measures thus confirmed the extraordinary legal situation whereby their person and well-being could never be protected by any sacred and inalienable right, because these were submitted to the sovereign and unlimited powers of the colonial state and its actual principal representative: the Governor-General. In the name of public order, he could dispose of the colonised or their land, thereby creating a veritable *hors-la-loi* (outlaw) for the first time in the case of internment and then by sequestration for a second time. Therefore, the liberty, property and security, guaranteed 'for all men at all times', according to the beautiful slogan of the French Revolution of 1789, were, for the colonised, destroyed for the benefit of the state. The personal and juridical insecurity of the colonised were abandoned because of general fault or for crimes they did not commit. This insecurity is one of the major and structural effects of ruling by decrees. And the particular consequence of the different measures studied was to institutionalize them making them an essential element of the condition of the 'indigenous'. These not only made them subjects, as the jurists and politicians of the Third Republic never ceased to declare: because of it they were also the condemned men, who lived in a world where, because of 'a legislative anarchy',[42] the laws of the empire were neither assured to them nor guaranteed. This particular condition confirmed what Girault and Maunier said on the nature of the regimes imposed on colonised France.[43] Personal and juridical insecurity, one knows since the time of Aristotle, is one of the characteristics of tyranny, and in the contemporary world, of totalitarian domination and dictatorship, as H. Arendt has so well analysed.[44]

> 'Let us not deceive ourselves. Let us not cheat. For what should we disguise truth? Colonisation, from the beginning, was not an act of civilisation, or a will of civilisation. It is an act of force, a force that was interested. It was an episode in the struggle for life, of a grand conjuncture, which from men to groups, from groups to nations, propagated itself across the vast world. Colonisation is from the beginning a project of interested persons; it is unilateral and egoistical, accomplished by the strong over the weak. This is the reality of history.[45]

Who is the author of these lines? A fierce critic of colonisation, whose political position discredited it? No. It is Albert Sarraut, the minister of colonies, in the course of his official discourse on 5 November 1923 at the inauguration of the course at the *L'Ecole Coloniale*. It is worth noting that on 23 February 2005, a majority of French parliamentarians voted, with the endorsement of the government and the prime minister, a law in which the 'positive' character of the 'French presence overseas, particularly in North Africa' [46] was officially proclaimed. Curious times!

Notes

* Translated from the French original by Subhas Ranjan Chakraborty.
  1. Azan (1925: 39). General Azan (1874–1951) was the director of the historical division of the army. Author of a number of works on Algeria and colonisation, he received the Grand prize of the French empire for his works.

2. Eboué (1941: 3). An old student of the l'Ecole coloniale, Eboué´ (1884–1944) was the Secretary General of Martinique (1932–1934), then governor of Guadeloupe in 1936. He joined General De Gaulle and became the governor of AEF in 1940. His ashes were transferred to Pantheon.

3. Appearing at the turn of the century, these sciences were officially consecrated by the Third Republic in 1922 with the creation of the Academie des sciences coloniales which aimed at, among other things, 'complete colonial knowledge', as P. Mille declared during the 10th anniversary of the 'Compagnie'. Academie des sciences coloniales (1933: 20). As for G. Hanotaux, member of the Academie francaise and a specialist on colonial questions, he exclaimed enthusiastically: 'Colonial science has become a living and active reality. Colonial science! But that is entirely a science'. *Idem*: 23.

4. 'That (ethnology) should and would guide governments', wrote J. Chailley (1854–1928) in his Preface to the celebrated work of J.C. Eerde (1927). Chailley was, among others, founder member of L'Institut colonial international, founded in 1894 and Professor at L'Ecole libre des sciences politiques where he taught 'Colonisation Compared'. Eerde was Professor at the University of Pays–Bas and Director of the ethnological section of L'Institut colonial d'Amsterdam. An eminent representative of colonial sociology was R. Maunier (1887–1951), author of a voluminous and ambitious treatise—*Sociology coloniale*—in three volumes published between 1932 and 1942. Equally famous as a jurist, Maunier was Professor at the Law faculty at Paris and a member of l'Academie des sciences coloniales.

5. A. Girault (1865–1931), 'Condition of the indigenous populations from the point of view of civil and criminal law and distribution of justice', in *Congres international de sociologie coloniale*, Paris, Rousseau, 1921, t.1, p 66. Celebrated professor at the Law Faculty of Poitiers, Girault played a major role in that Congress at Paris in 1900, held with the support of the French authorities. Girault is the author of *Principes de legislation coloniale*, chez Larose, 1895. Becoming 'the obligatory manual for the students of law', and 'academic men', 'this new colonial Gospel' ran into six editions by 1943. See Masson (1906: 23).

6. Harmand (1910: 55, 18, 248). A friend of G. Le Bon, Harmand (1845–1921) was Ambassador of France. His book is a classic which is often cited by the specialists on colonial questions. 'Humanitarianism', wrote Ch. Regismanset, 'is a general superstition, a strange malady springing from the defective idealism of 1789, entertained by romantic literature, nursed by the pseudo-liberalism of Lafitte and Royer-Collard, aggravated recently by a resurgence of the Huguenot spirit'.

This man from the regime of Louis Philippe concluded, 'Let us renounce the destructive theories. More abstractions without sense. No politics of assimilation' (Regismanset 1912: 52). Regismanset is also the author, along with G. Francois and F. Rouget, of a successful book, which had four successive editions, entitled: *Ce que tout Francais devrait savoir sur nos colonies*, Chez Larose, 1924.

7. Cuvillier-Fleury (1907: 33). France initially refused to sign the Geneva Convention (that was promoted by the International Labour Organisation in 1930) to prohibit forced labour in the colonies. It was finally ratified in 1937, but suspended two years later. The abolition of forced labour in the empire was finally sanctioned by the law of 11 April 1946.

8. *Ibid.*: 27. See also Bonet-Maury (1900: 162), where this position is defended. 'Except in rare circumstances', he wrote, 'the immediate abolition [of slavery] would be more harmful than useful to the blacks themselves. It is necessary to prepare them, educate them and to defend them against their own instincts'.

9. Girault (1906: 71, 253). Almost in the same vein A. Billiard declared, 'in the barbaric countries, the formalities of justice should be simplified and delays eliminated, in order to ensure an *energetic repression, always quick, and summary*' (italics mine; Billiard (1901: 47). Billiard was administrator of mixed communes in Algeria and inspector of the department of indigenous affairs in Constantine.

10. Girault (1903: 36). 'Never', he added, 'did the colonies make so rapid a progress as from the time the Republic gave them the good tyrant about whom I am going to speak now' (37–38). Familiar with the politics of the great European powers in their respective colonies, he was particularly impressed by Holland, because the governor-general of Batavia enjoyed 'absolutely extensive powers'.

11. That is R. Maunier who was entrusted with the teaching of 'colonial economy and legislation'.

12. Penant (1905: 86). 'Under the present constitution in the French colonies, legislation is in discordance with our republican principles', stated D. Penant, Director of Recueil general de jurisprudence et de legislation coloniale, who, however, did not condemn the situation. On the contrary, he found the arrangement to be perfectly suited to the peculiarities of the empire and to its diverse population. Penant felt that one of the essential functions of the jurists was to 'facilitate the task of the legislators in colonial matters'. In 1906, Clementel, the minister of colonies, declared that 'the principle of separation of powers was unintelligible [to the primitive people]'. That is why we 'are not keen to apply' to Congo 'our complicated laws and rules of procedure made only for a perfect civilisation', *Les lois organiques*

des colonies: Documents officiel's procedés de notices historiques (1906: 446–47). Twenty seven years later, in their celebrated *Traité de Droit constitutionnel* (1933), J. Barthélemy and P. Duez wrote with lucidity, 'The metropolitan is organized in the liberal mode; the colonies on the authoritarian mode. Our law poses the principle of native equality of men[...] our imperial system presupposes inequality of races' (rpt. 1985: 289; italics mine).

13. Barthélemy and Duez (1933) rpt. 1985: 283.

14. P. Matter in his Preface to Dareste (1931: v).

15. Likewise in Algeria this situation and rule by decrees were abolished by the ordinance of 7 March 1944 and confirmed by the law of 20 September 1947.

16. Dareste (1931: 233). P. Dareste was an honorary advocate with the Council of State and the cour de cassation; Director, *Recueil de legislation, de doctrine et de jurisprudence colonialés*; and President, Comite des Jurisconsultes de l'union coloniale.

17. Sol and Haranger (1930: v). The authors are both inspectors of colonies.

18. Solus (1927: 15). Solus was a reputed professor of law at the University of Poitiers.

19. Doucet (1926: 57). Author of many works on colonisation, Doucet was the chief editor of *Monde economique*. A great specialist of colonial law, P. Dislère (1840–1928) had already noted in 1886 that there are only 'a few' legislations which 'present to a degree the diverse character and variability; moreover they do not extend to subjects equally complex'. Later, he added, 'it is easy to recognize that these legislations [...] do not follow a general idea or a principle' (1914: x). Dislère, a polytechnician, was the master of requests of the Council of State in 1881; Secretary of State of the colonies in 1882; and President of the council of administration of the l'Ecole coloniale (established in 1889).

20. 'The rules, the decrees are adopted unknown to us, almost hidden from us, and we know about them only when they are put in the Journal officiel'—Gascony, a deputy, declared bitterly at the National Assembly on 9 February 1888 (*Debats parlementaire* 1888: 344).

21. Vernier de Byans (1912: 8). 'The inherent stability of the acts of the National Assembly does not harmonise well with the evolving character of colonial legislation [...] it would still be required for a long time to keep the suppleness and the easy applicability of such legislation' (10).

22. Larcher and Rectenwald (1923: 364). In the case of Algeria, he added, 'It would be a chimera to believe that the fusion of two classes [...] is approaching [...] All the Algerian politicians, on the contrary, are keen to maintain their separation' (*ibid.*). Larcher was Professor at

the faculty of Algerian law and an advocate at the Cour d'appel. Rectenwald is a doctor in law, counselor at the Cour d'appel and Vice President of the mixed tribunal in Tunisia. This work became a classic and was an obligatory reference for both the teachers and the students of the time. It simply came to be known as 'le Larcher'.

23. Supiot (2005: 60).
24. Tocqueville (1991: 752).
25. Article 6 of the Declaration of the Rights of Man and the Citizen, 26 August 1789.
26. Beaumont (1843: 2, 9).
27. 'In 1847', declared O. Dupont, 'that is, long before the likes of Jules Ferry, Burdeau, Jonnart and Jules Cambon [...] who have now given an impetus to the study of the Algerian question, M. de Tocqueville told the Chamber of deputies, "it is necessary to create for Africa a machinery of government more simple in its mechanism and quick in its application than the one which works in France"' (Dupont 1901: 64). Dupont was the administrator of mixed commune and sous-chef of indigenous affairs of the Government of Alger.
28. Maunier (1938: 320–21).
29. Larcher and Rectenwald (1923: 408–9)
30. Maunier (1938: 14, 206). To illustrate this general point, Maunier quotes governor Pasquier of Indo–China. 'To each his judge, to each his law'. Perfectly aware of the importance of this characteristic of colonial law, Maunier adds, 'such is [his] principle'.
31. Les lois organiques des colonies, t.3 (1906: 227, 341–42).
32. Strouvens and Piron (1945: 497, 537).
33. Larcher (1902: 200). Diffa consists of the obligation, against fixed reimbursement by the French authorities, of furnishing to the officers or duly authorized agents, transport, supplies and water. See also Charve'riat (1889).
34. Maunier (1938: 253). A. Hampaté Bâ wrote: [the blacks] 'are the absolute masters of the countries. It is not for nothing that they are called the "the gods of the bush". *They have all the rights under us and we have only duties'. Yes, my commandant!* (1994: 193; italics mine).
35. Dumas (1914: 5).
36. Sylvain (1901: 398, 523).
37. It has not been possible to treat here the Code of the Indigene, qualified by Girault, who thought it to be 'monstrous' (1927: 305). Larcher and Rectenwald wrote a few years later, 'The indigenous regime taken together is a juridical monstrosity' (1923: 477). On this very important point I would like to refer the readers to Grandmaison (2005) for the history of deportation, administrative internment and collective responsibility. On the code of the indigene, cf. Merle (2002).

38. Cf. Sautayra (1883: 328). Administrative internment was extended to other colonies. The practice reveals that it could be decided to omit the salute to the commandant or to the French flag. Cf. Hampaté Bâ (1992: 504). Introduced in A.O.F in 1887 and New Caledonia in 1897, the decree of 21 November 1904 limited its operation to ten years. Equally in A. E. F. after 31 May 1910. As for Algeria, the law of 15 July 1914 replaced internment by 'surveillance', sort of residence for two years. This new dispensation was to be applied only in the civil areas. Everywhere, though, internment continued. Cf. Larcher and Rectenwald (1923: 233).

39. 'We do not have, in our French law, any punishment comparable to internment [...] It is contradictory to all principles', wrote Larcher. He added: internment is 'exorbitant, contrary to our public law' and 'prejudicial to the separation of powers...' (Larcher 1902: 87, 90).

40. Larcher and Rectenwald (1923: 537).

41. Melia (1936: 71). Collective punishment for suspected support to 'rebellion' or damage to forests was used in Indo–China towards the end of the 19th century by the decree of 9 January 1895. Similar dispositions apply themselves also to AOF by virtue of the decree of 4 July 1935, relative to the regime of New Caledonia. Identical measures were also adopted in British India. Cf. Nielly (1898).

42. Doucet (1926: 64).

43. Maunier affirmed that the governors in the colonies 'had functions, but they were all sort of dictators' (1938: 281).

44. Cf. Arendt (2002).

45. Sarrault (1923: 8)

46. Article 4 of law no. 2005-158 of 23 February 2005: 'On recognition of the nation and national contribution in favour of the French repatriates'.

3

Law and Terror in the Age of Constitution-Making

Ranabir Samaddar

In this exploration into the intimate relation between terror and law, I attempt, first to show that the relation between terror and law is not a simple question that merely relates violence to law, but is connected to the very process of constitution-making.

Second, I want to show this by arguing that the laws, which relate to terror, may or may not find a formal place in the constitution. However, this relation is essential to the working of the basic law, of the *rule of law*, and the working of the constitution.

Third, I want to show the key place that intelligence-gathering occupies in this relation, and this activity, which has almost no mention in any constitution the world over, is the fulcrum on which reasons of State stand.

Fourth, intelligence-gathering is principally based on the close monitoring of human movement—of the body and of various physical activities (such as when one is meeting somebody, writing, talking, seeing, reading, sleeping somewhere, etc). In this peculiarly physical form of politics, we witness the convergence of 'body' and 'reasoning', terror and constitution, violence and law.

Finally, what appears in the following description is specifically an account of the Indian experience, yet it may have larger significance in terms of retrieving the history of constitution-making. I have tried to capture this significance by means of the term—'colonial constitutionalism'.

These themes may not be very clearly delineated in this exploration. In view of the current reality, these themes may even require a separate book that sheds light on their inter-relatedness. This essay is thus to be viewed as an exploratory attempt only.

Uncertain deaths are terrifying matters for the State, because above all they bring unsanctioned and unwarranted deaths. In this sense, while the form of the State has undergone change since the time it made its appearance in the world, the State in all its forms has experienced terror at the prospect of uncertain deaths; that is to say, deaths that bring or symbolise uncertainty. Extra-ordinary measures are taken, juridical serenity breaks down, and schizophrenia takes possession on such occasions. Most of the time we know this prospect as 'terror'.

Terror implies uncertainty that has the capacity to scare, 'terrorise' (since it is an exception to law). It is evocative of violence, symbolic violence, extraordinary methods, unaccountability, uncertain prospects, different rules (if you understand them) of engagement and murder, and different methods. The act and the response, both are locked in death acts. Since terror denotes uncertainty, the State wants to make sure that the world of terror becomes law-bound, its grammar is subjected to cognition, so that terror is stripped of uncertainty; it is made certain in terms of definition, knowledge, action and retribution. This is how 'the uncertain' is legally defined, becomes subject to State's reasons, to the world of knowledge, therefore to calculated decisions. Yet (surprisingly), the process of attempting to subject the essential uncertainty to the most extreme certainty—*law*—is coupled with a recognition of the limits of this enterprise; and therefore this process is accompanied with a frenzied invocation of the great arbitrary method of governing since time immemorial, namely, *intelligence-gathering*, that forms the bedrock of the trinity—State, terror, and law. Governing must be preceded by collection and analysis of information; law must protect not only ways of govern-ing, it must also be backed by information. Indeed, the effectiveness of collecting information will determine how law can help the State to face, employ, and counter terror.

In speaking of the trinity of law, terror and the State, I am aware of the momentarily embarrassing irony of the question that this exploration should inevitably raise—how can law be so close to terror that one can never think of terror without its legal definition, without the legal mechanisms to cope with it—indeed, without terror becoming one of the most significant moments, or at least the next moment, in the development of law? The entwined and entangled story of law and terror presents to us the appearance and disappearance at will of what we can call the 'the will to legislate'. In a situation where the State at one moment goes beyond law to combat or inflict terror, and then shrinks back at the next moment to the confines of law to take stock and legislate in order to forge an appropriate tool of terror and counter-terror, the *will to legislate* becomes contingent on elaborate phantom-building exercises. Defining terror, so that at some level terror becomes acceptable or normal in politics, becomes a juridical task of high priority—where normalisation refers both to bringing the phenomenon back to a 'normal' level, and the 'normalising' of the level achieved. The story of constitution-making in colonial times in India in the background of the twin development of terror and law is significant. It demonstrates the material conduct of the state in an age when terror appears as one of the most essential ingredients of politics, and physical control therefore becomes, once again, one of the chief instruments of ruling.

I

The colonial state in India was an extraordinarily war-like state. In some way, it had continued the record of the pre-colonial state in making war, conquest and large-scale murders the basis of state foundation, expansion and consolidation. But the colonial state raised the level of violence to an unprecedented level. Throughout the 19th century, the truly colonial century in India's history—wars, plunders, conquests, battles of attrition, destruction, mutinies, revolts, massacres, famines, pestilence, a high death toll, and widespread depopulation marked the country's state of affairs.

In this war-torn century, empire-making meant terror at every level and every step. It meant employing warriors and guns, the raising of mercenary armies, creating of anarchic modes and consequences of taxation, seizing land, forcibly colonising tracts with huge loss of lives, and imposing trade rules with devastating effect. A war-struck century meant a terror-struck century. It also meant that a huge land mass dotted with points of intense violence needed to be aggressively ruled by guns and regulation-making at a ferocious pace. The pacification that started with Regulation III of 1818 did not quite achieve the success that it claimed. With the onset of the new century, violence struck the political horizon of the country again. The early terrorists had learnt the lesson that a violent colonial state understands only the language of terror, or at least mass movements must be laced with appropriate measures of terror and violence. The size and the spread of violence and terror in all forms throughout the century—assassination, internment, deportation, exile, physical torture, random death penalty, increasing monopolisation of the means of violence by the colonial state, and murder (by which, murder by an individual became an occasion for the state to decide who was guilty and confer the death sentence), incarceration, artillery development, punitive taxation, collective punishment (as in the suppression of the Mutiny), race violence, forced labour employed by the army, and starving unto death of massive groups of people—meant that violence had a deep impact on the political forms of action in the society. In this uniquely ubiquitous violent society, terror was the birthmark of politics.

The sheer physical dimension of the only possible form of anti-colonial political activity ensured that with the accumulation of martial strength and various means of terrorising, modern politics and terror would make simultaneous appearance in the colonial land. It also ensured the centrality of the body in such politics; in other words, the central significance of the sheer physicality of terrorist opposition to colonial rule. The early terrorists (the militant nationalists) were nurtured and brought up through innumerable organisations devoted to the inculcation of physical discipline—indeed, the two most well known militant anti-colonial organisations, 'Anushilan' and 'Jugantar', grew out of such efforts. The famous garden of Maniktola, one of the early terrorist organisers Upendranath Bandopadhyay tells us in his memoir, housed one such centre, where study of anti-colonial politics, culture of the body, meditation, physical discipline, abstinence from all temptations, cooking and cleaning oneself, all formed a sort of curriculum for militant nationalist pedagogy.[1] The name *Maniktola bagan* associated with the fame of the Maniktola Conspiracy Case became soon a household name in nationalist Bengal and a model for several such efforts though the centre was disbanded after a police raid in 1908. Such organisations called *samities* and *akhras* were founded in many districts; and ironically the more the leaders of the terrorist organisations claimed that 'the people must be trained up spiritually to face dangers'[2] the more they stressed on the perfection of the body as the tool for anti-colonial resistance. To live a physical life of a soldier—to train the body to attack, to destroy the bodies of the occupiers, and then to die to accomplish the mission—was the journey of a rebel. Another terrorist leader, Bina Das, confessed years later that on hearing the massacre of the prisoners in Hijli prison she was seized with frenzy; she became insane; she knew that only death could relieve her from madness and give her peace. 'I felt I would go mad if I could not find relief in death... My object was to die nobly fighting against the despotic system of government'.[3] In the colonial wars, violence, and terror were a physical reality—bodies were being tormented, killed, forcefully put to labour, starved to death, dumped, or confined and controlled in torturous ways, and the physicality of the milieu marked the articulation of politics. Indeed, as we shall see, terror had no other purpose, than to make a political declaration; and politics had no other purpose, at least at the outset, than to strike terror in the enemy camp.

The literature on the Great Game has made us familiar with the colonial wars of conquest, annexation and suppression on the western side of India. What we immediately did not see was the connection between the Wahabi threat to colonial rule and the imperial policy of guarding the frontier. It became clear much later when Lord Mayo, the Viceroy, was assassinated in the Andaman Islands by the Wahabi prisoner Shere Ali in 1872. Indeed, the British punitive and pacification policy created something new in Indian reality: the modern jail system. As one historian describes, the colonial society became a penal society, where the social, political, and physical order was sought to conform to the norma-tive order of colonialism.[4] Jails became the breeding grounds of the early terrorists. State surveillance only increased hatred. The colonised was not just a subject, but a convict-subject bound by rules of segregation, punishment, impressive spectacles of power and benevolence, and obedience to personalised authority. Colonial penal policy grew directly out of the needs of conquest and pacification, and thus from the beginning, penalising had little to do with reform but with control. The procedural forms of punishment were elaborately laid out with formalisation with the Penal Code, Criminal Code, Evidence Act, and the jail system. All these were reinforced with a bizarre paradox, and which generated only hatred, namely that while justice theoretically might be individuated, punishment was to be, whenever required, collective. Where guilt was collective, the punishment to the individual was to be severe and 'equal', thus denoting the collective reality behind the crime and the punishment. This was as if the colonial rule, law, justice, order and magistracy, by the acts of hanging, lynching, caning, exiling, interning, torching, confiscating, impounding, were addressing not the subject of law, but the collective society behind that individual subject. Thus, no wonder, shame and hatred spread rapidly. Law was born out of conquest, and war ensured that only hatred could be the site of politics. Revenge, punishment and pacification were uppermost in the colonial conduct in the wake of the South Indian wars of conquest as well. After the defeats elsewhere in the later period of the 18th century, British governing and military establishments went on the offensive, not just in terms of warfare, but also in terms of rule and suppression on a massive and successful scale. The fall of Tipu Sultan and Seringapatnam was in that sense more significant than or at least equal to the exile of Bahadur Shah II, killing of the latter's sons by Hudson, and the fall of Delhi 58 years later in the suppression of the Mutiny. Hereafter, colonial rule was to be a race-rule, law was to provide how this rule was to demonstrate terror when necessary, anti-colonial terror became the dominant form of the other side of the war; and as identities solidified and multiplied, terror, which is always linked to a politics of identity, became the universal form of politics.

If on the Western side, the Wahabis symbolised the role that terror played in the development of colonial legal system, in the East the conquest of Assam played the same role. By Article 2 of the Treaty of Yandabo the King of Burma had renounced all claims on Assam. Now if Assam was annexed to the empire, how was this to be done? The upper portion of the Brahmaputra Valley went under British administration; the frontier tract, inhabited by the Moamarias, Khamtis and the Singpos were excluded from direct administrative control; the Assam Light Infantry was posted to protect the frontier to prevent both Assamese and the hill tribes from killing each other and to control both; the sons of chiefs of the tribes were taken and kept as hostages, and yet by 1830 rebellions broke out in the frontier tracts. In 1842 new areas— Sadiya and Matak were annexed; civil rebellion in North Cachar had to be suppressed. There is no doubt, however, that with the Treaty of Yandabo a huge new tract had been prised open. Access to Burma meant all adjoining territories were also to be annexed. In the following 75 years, the Cachar Plains, Khasi Plains, Jaintia Plains, Assam Hills, North Cachar Hills, Garo Hills, NEFA, Lushai Hills, and the Naga Hills were subjugated in 1830, 1833, 1835, 1838, 1858, 1873, 1875, 1890, and 1904 respectively. Conquest was followed by rational rules of administration that necessitated measures one after another such as the Scheduled District Act of 1874, Backward Tracts Act of 1919, and finally the Excluded and Partially Excluded Areas Act of 1935. By the enactment of special powers such as the Armed Forces Special Powers Act that conferred immunity from terror to the conquerors and administrators, the rulers eventually sealed their conquest. By conferring immunity on the security forces they covered their foot soldiers; by rules of exclusion they had already divided the subjects, and pacified them; and with all these they were able to guard the frontier. But the necessity of defending the frontier meant that first, colonial law had indeed created 'permanent exceptions', and second, that law came only in the wake of conquest, wars of physical annexation, physical violence, physical resistance and disorder.

No one was more aware of the two-fold developing reality of permanent exceptions and the physicality of politics within a constitutional rule than the two adversaries—the colonial state and the early terrorists.[5] Upendranath Bandopadhyay in his reminiscences of his stay at the Andaman Islands Cellular Prison tells us of an exchange of words with Reginald Craddock, the well-known colonial administrator and the Home Member at that time, when he had gone to inspect the Island Prison in 1913. Bandopadhyay and other prisoners had asked Reginald Craddock the reason as to why they were being denied the facilities under the jail manual. Craddock's reply was that they were terrorists, they had 'done conspiracy' against the State. Again on being asked why their trial had not been public, Craddock had answered that, 'these things did not call for or require evidence', and that the State should have killed them in the first instance. To this, the prisoners asked, 'If so, why were then the entire ceremony of law and court, and the unnecessary spending of public money carried out? The work could have been finished briefly.' Reginald remained silent, only cryptically adding that discipline had to be maintained whatever might be the merits of the demands.[6] After he left, the torture of the prisoners resumed with frenzy. Ullaskar became insane; the Ghadar prisoner Prithwi Singh died after spending six continuous months in a cell; two others died after merciless beating and then dysentery; three died in hunger-strike; Chatta Singh was caged and alternatively exposed to the sun and darkness for days—he died in the cage. Amar Singh was caged similarly. Jyotish Chandra Pal, the accused in the Balasore Conspiracy Case went mad in his cell, and died in Baharampur Asylum in Bengal after he was sent back to mainland.[7]

With these and countless other incidents of extremely brutal punishment, we must therefore come to the issue of law—law that follows conquest. It is here where we shall find the true story of constitution-building. With conquest and engagement with terror everywhere in the colonial history, began the modern story of constitutional and legal administration and rule. This administration, from day one, had granted 'permanent exceptions', or built itself upon them. This was the administrative—legal strategy to tackle resistance invented by the colonial rule, which had to be a mix of terror and the principle of responsible government. Indeed, the two discourses of exceptions and responsibility emerged in colonial rule in India roughly at the same time. The invention of the wheels of responsible government did not come much later than 1818. We have already noted that terror, necessitated by conquest, was a physical fact. Yet, this was not enough. The task was to combine terror with law, suppression with responsibility, conquest with constitutionalism—a juxtaposition that I have referred to elsewhere as 'colonial constitutionalism'.[8] Built on the physicality of the fact of rule was a discursive strategy of the colonial power to name the opposition to its rule, particularly subaltern opposition, as terror-driven and to counter-pose its norms of 'responsible governance' to the 'terrorist' methods of the opponents. These two techniques combined effectively in devising permanent exceptions, thereby making colonial rule a success. With colonialism began the paradox; we can in fact say that almost from the beginning of liberal jurisprudence, the world of juridical–political knowledge had taken a somersault. The distinctions between terror and terrorism, colonial rule and constitutionalism, control and freedom, security and democracy, individual guilt and collective punishment, and information and intelligence, vanished as a result of this acrobatic feat. In this upturned world of juridical knowledge, the operation of law-making had one important aim among several, namely legally defining 'terror'. The task at hand was how to include some acts as acts of terror, and omit others from that definition. This was the founding moment of law. Yet the moment was never completely legal, because defining terror was dependent on gathering of intelligence about militant opposition. This founding moment of law, as the 19th century history of India showed, was as much a mythological moment as a legal moment, because each enactment depending on 'external sources' was marked with fearful anticipation that this definition could soon prove inadequate calling for new necessities and new enactments in the wake of new attacks on the State. The Regulation III of 1818 was to be thus succeeded with many measures in the first part of the 20th century, including the Defence of India Rules. Law-making and terror-acts thus went hand in hand in colonial times.

II

In terms of constitutionalism, the significance of the development of the legal discourse on terrorism was evident in India. India's colonial history proved two tasks of statecraft as important—making terror a subject of law and making intelligence operational, an exercise fundamentally beyond law—a crucial instrument in this exercise of legality. The second, I submit, was more significant of the two. Intelligence-gathering became critical because: (a) intelligence was a grey area in State operation, little controlled by law and norms of accountability; and (b) terror had become 'democratic', with means of violence within reach of many, hate becoming widespread and opposition to rule deep—all these therefore required the State to gather greater and greater information about 'irresponsible opposition'. With every development of military technology of the superior powers, the terrorists were also learning new modes or using old modes in new ways—an equally potent revolution in military affairs, half-noticed and half-understood. New techniques of gun-making, bomb-making, clandestine voyage, radio transmission, new organisational techniques, financial laundering, printing fake currency notes, robbery, cryptography, train-wrecking, improved graphics printing for forging papers and travel permits, combined with old forms like stabbing, beating, or tying with rope to death—intelligence files abound with all this information.[9] Terror became cost-effective and democratic. Therefore intelligence-gathering became crucial. As a result, spies and intelligence officers of the government became the most hated objects of the militant nationalists or the early terrorists. (For instance, in 1910, the Deputy Superintendent of Police (DSP) of the Criminal Investigation Department (CID), Shamsul Huda was shot dead on the corridors of the Calcutta High Court; the same year, CID Inspector Sarat Chandra Ghosh was attacked in Dhaka—the former was associated with the investigation of the Maniktola Bomb Conspiracy case, the latter with Dhaka Conspiracy Case. In 1911, the Head Constable attached to the intelligence department Sirish Chandra Chakraborty was killed. Then, the CID Chief Denham was attacked. In 1914, it was Inspector Nripendranath Ghosh's turn to die. In 1916 died DSP Basanta Kumar Chatterjee who had escaped the earlier attempts on his life.) Consequently, before law could pronounce certain truths, it was important for the colonial rule to find out who killed whom, when, where, and by what means—even now, a key issue in military affairs relating to terrorism. Thus, as soon as the Chittagong Armoury Raid took place, followed by the deadly attack in Dhaka on the Inspector General of Police (IGP) Lohman and the Superintendent of Police (SP) of Dhaka Hodson, the Bengal Criminal Law Amendment Act of 1925, which was to expire on 21 March 1930, was given a new lease of life in form of the Bengal Act VI of 1930. Empowered by this new legislation that conferred enormous powers to investigate and dispense with the necessity of evidence and corroboration, the government formed special tribunals, arrested and sentenced scores of political activists. Long-term prison sentences were handed out on a massive scale to the entire ranks of the Jugantar Group. The verdict of the Mechuabazar Bomb case resulted in scores being sent to jail for periods sufficient to break the backbone of the terrorist organisation; these included, among many others, Satish Pakrashi, Niranjan Sen Gupta, Sudhir Aich, Mukul Ranjan Sen Gupta, Sudhangshu Das Gupta, Nishikanta Ray Chaudhury, Ramendra Biswas, and Panna lal Das Gupta.[10]

To understand the critical role that the task of developing consti-tutional rule in the colonial time accorded to intelligence, we have to note the most important fact that the role of intelligence-gather-ing had become strategic. Earlier, intelligence was meant for the king, for the benefit of his counsel, for selected things and targets, and its role was tactical. Now intelligence became strategic, it called for analysis and recommendations on political goals.[11] For instance, in report after report, intelligence agencies and officers inquired the impulse behind forming secret societies, their nature, organisation, membership, sustainability, and the reasons behind their periodic rise. The techniques of forming secret societies by the early terrorists became the object of study—techniques such as oath-taking, raising money by robberies, rules of introducing new comrades, rules of secrecy, contacting, networking, reading sacred texts in groups, group study, or, 'infiltrating legal societies and association'.[12] What was noticeable was the way the intelli-gence officials analysed the declarations that the early terrorists like Barindranath Ghosh made to the police on being arrested or before the court during trial, and turned these into confessions to be subsequently used as material for building up a conspiracy case. The Maniktola Bomb Conspiracy Case was one of the early instances of this technique. It also helped to bring in charges against a group and pave the way for group punishment. 'Confession' or 'declaration' was therefore one of the murkiest issues in the ranks of the revolutionaries, and if one of the early nationalist bomb-makers Hem Chandra Das Kanungo is to be believed, it sowed and encouraged suspicion. According to Kanungo, Barin Ghosh was also guilty of making such a declaration/confession.[13] Indeed, the *Sedition Committee Report* of 1918 mentioned explicitly the tech-nique, and Hem Kanungo too drew attention to the *Report*. The Intelligence Bureau published in colonial India two books that went beyond the simple goal of collecting piecemeal information on some individuals and activities, and presented strategic analysis on colonial security threatened by terrorist activities—the first, *Political Troubles in India: 1907–1917* by J. C. Kerr, Special Assistant to the Director of Criminal Intelligence from 1907 to 1913, and published in 1917 (to which we have made reference already), and the second compiled by H. W. Hale specially deputed to the Intelligence Bureau for this purpose, in 1937 to cover the period between 1917 and 1937. Taking great pride in introducing the book,

Ewart, the then Director of the Intelligence Bureau indicated the strategic role that intelligence was playing as a technology to buttress the colonial rule, 'The book in final form represents an immense amount of research among the scattered and defused contemporary records'.[14]

The wisdom of the colonial administration enriched by the Irish, Indian and similar experiences of intelligence-gathering elsewhere was a significant source of juridical development of rule of law. Indeed Act XIV was enacted in India in 1908 at the advice of the intelligence officials. Likewise, in the promulgation of the Ordinance of 1924 and the Defence of India Rules intelligence advice was crucial. Again it was the intelligence community, something that took shape in India in the first quarter of the 20th century, which began analysing the interface of mass 'non-violent' movements and militant violence—a problem that exercises the CIA and the Israeli intelligence minds today. While colonial political leadership was baffled at times at the strong mixing of the two currents, the intelligence report was busy *analysing* the import of the intermingling of the two.[15] In 1932, R. E. A. Ray, Special Superintendent, Intelligence Branch, CID, prepared a 'Brief Note on the Alliance of Congress with Terrorism in Bengal', where he noted the progress made by the early terrorists in influencing mass non-violent movement with their ideas of militant nationalism. In 1921, he noted that terrorists had taken part in the Non-Cooperation Movement, after coming out of prisons following the Royal Proclamation of December 1919. They then managed representation in the Bengal Provincial Congress Committee in 1922. In 1923, they supported C. R. Das in 'return for his connivance with the secret conspiracy'. The key part of Ray's report dealt with his analysis of 'terrorists' views on their connection with the Congress'. It noted the popular nature of the issues related to civil liberty, ignored in the Gandhi–Irwin Pact of 1931. Prisoners were still in jail, hundreds were awaiting trial for years, many were not even chargesheeted, there was large scale detention without trial, several persons were being deported or interned, many were being executed—the situation was inflammable, and then the report tellingly cited a letter from an undertrial accused in the Chittagong Armoury Raid to Gandhi in 1931, 'You cannot certainly deny the fact that in almost all the provinces the Congress programme has been worked out by the men most of whom have got violence as their policy in heart and especially in Bengal where the disobedience campaign has achieved the highest amount of success, 90 per cent of the Congress workers are open revolutionaries to whom no doubt all the credit of the success goes'.[16] This letter could have been the result of some intelligence ploy; but there is no doubt that the hawk's eyes were on strategic questions of politics.

All social forms that supported militant nationalism were, therefore, put under the scanner. More significant is the way in which the analytic community was pointing out one of the chief indices of the popularity of a cause—the decentralised organisational set up, the flexibility in the organisation of war, and the myriad ways in which the party of war and contest permeated existing organisations and institutions. Both Anushilan and Jugantar, the two major terrorist groups in British Bengal gradually developed their specific ideas, tactics and views of building up and/or aligning with political and social organisations such as the Ramakrishna Mission, the Indian National Congress, the Swarajya Party, Indian National Educational Board, or the Shankar Math. Relations between these and the terrorists ranged from being purely instrumental and tactical to integral.[17] Historians of civil society should take note of these in sketching out their ideas on the problematic of the civil/political in anti-colonial political milieu where, contrary to their ideas of a neat division, everything was civil and at the same time, political. Seen in this light, it should not appear strange that in colonial India intelligence officials were also investigating the town structure of Benaras (Varanasi today) in order to understand how that town could patronise large-scale terrorist activities.

The Denham report spoke of the visit of Tilak to Benaras in 1900, and noted the congenial atmosphere that Benaras offered to the 'Poona Party' 'so closely connected with the murders of 1897', and suggested that it was the 'Marhatta' connection that had led to the beginning of Bengali terrorist activities in the town. It mentioned various names and castes, and cited the instance of the founding of Anushilan Samiti in Benaras by Sachaindra Nath Sanyal and Deo Narain Mukherji. The report spent quite some lines on Basanta Kumar Biswas who had come to Benaras in 1910. Basanta is, of course, one of the illustrious names among the early terrorists of Bengal and in fact in the entire country. Basanta was a member of Jugantar; he was conspicuous for his organisational skills, and was an important intermediary between the Calcutta office of the Jugantar and the 'co-conspirators' in Chandannagar. He was very young, started to work on his own in 1910, was sent to Puri and eventually to Benaras where he was said to have taken shelter in Ramakrishna Mission. In 1911, he came into contact with Rashbehari Bose who was in Dehra Dun and who himself had been in close contact with Benaras. Basanta along with others had organised money supply for the activities—something that came to light later in the Benaras Insurance Fraud case. Sachaindra Nath Sanyal[18] and Rashbehari Bose, the two veterans, linked up the Bengali diaspora in almost all major towns outside Bengal, principally Puri, Patna, Benaras, Dehra Dun and Delhi as the sustaining network for militant activities, and Basanta was one of the principal activists. Many other names occur in this strange story. Basanta's story comes to an end when he was finally apprehended and was subsequently hanged on conviction in the Delhi Conspiracy case in 1915.

Denham's report on Benaras is a part of the systematic gaze that the colonial rulers cast on the landscape of violence in the country, and read in details tells us of the way in which the colonial state buttressed its law, order and justice machinery by raising intelligence activity to the status of strategic necessity.[19] Again, we know for instance that Basanta was not given death penalty in the lower court on the ground of lack of sufficient evidence, but was hanged on appeal, where the ground lay on the strength of the presenting a 'conspiracy'. What is conspiracy? That, of course, law does not define. Also, we have no select indices of that. In what precise way does it connect to sedition? Again we have no answer. Was the last emperor of a free country, Mughal India, guilty of conspiracy and sedition, and could he be deported under Regulation III of 1818?[20] Was he a subject of the British sovereign? To build up the factual–legal–mythological world of sovereignty (which could then form the basis of the entire law and justice machinery), the intelligence machinery provided the relevant framework. In that sense intelligence has been to rule of law what epistemology has been to philosophy: the problems have to do with ways of knowing, making meaning out of knowing, the meaning of knowledge. A rule must be backed with knowledge about its ways, means, consequences and impediments. Intelligence must be built around a core of solid body of knowledge about organisational style of the terrorists, the *modus operandi* of the activities such as political robbery, the decentralised functioning of the main groups, etc. Therefore, a published government report titled, *Terrorist Conspiracy of Bengal, 1 April–31 December* described in detail several organisational networks of the terrorists.[21] The *Report* had significant implications for legislations to control and suppress terrorism, and develop constitutional rule.

To legislate, however, the State had to know the identity of the subject who was going to be legislated upon. In fact, modern law never freed itself from its early days—from the trap of the question of identity, and always had to solve the question in its framing, operation and verdict—who are the law-breakers, who are the culprits, what are his/her intentions, who are the subjects, and given all these what is the gravity of any violation of law? No amount of objectivity has freed law from these questions, and so we find the colonial officials repeatedly asking, interrogating and examining the biographical background of the terrorist. H. L. Salkeld, a magistrate on special duty and F. C. Daly, the Deputy Inspector General (DIG), Special Branch, wrote on investigating and reporting procedure in exhaustive detail, enabling the Government to break through the veil of secrecy and identify the deep dissenters. Therefore, each year the colonial administration produced history sheets of persons and organisations, detailed their caste identities or caste bases, behavioural proclivity, and the dress, the look, the handwriting style, the manner of speaking. So we have in the government files, the photograph of a *baboo*, a coolie, a terrorist-baboo, a raider,[22] and then in a move, as if the Government wanted to resolve once for all its own sense of enigma as to who the terrorist could be, we find the Government spending pages on a terrorist's love for death. Thus for instance, the Government wanted to know why Charu Chandra Bose, who was hanged in 1909 and had a crippled hand, had joined the movement? Why had Charu, just a few days before he enacted the fateful act of killing the public prosecutor in the Alipur Conspiracy Case, gone to a studio to photograph himself? Why did he want to meet his relatives before his death? Why, had he, a meek, silent and disabled person, done 'this'? And the intelligence officials took therefore another photograph of Charu before he was being sent to the gallows. Could a photograph then give any clue—that photograph taken by Charu and this one taken by the intelligence officers?

Thus the search would go on: who are these terrorists? As I have mentioned earlier, the Bengal Ordinance was important. The publication *Terrorist Conspiracy in Bengal* (mentioned earlier) refers to the need for continuing Regulation III as a special measure, and the need for other special measures.[23] The Bengal Criminal Law Amendment Act came in 1925 close on the heels of the 1924 Ordinance. The Government noted the appearance of what it termed 'New Violence Party'. It prepared yet another Memorandum on the History of Terrorism in Bengal. It spoke of 'want of evidence' that justified the Revolutionary and Anarchist Crimes Act of 1919 preceded by the Indian Criminal Law Amendment Act XIV of 1908, because what was needed was speedy and one-sided trial, 'where the accused shall not be present during an enquiry, unless the magistrate directs, nor shall be represented by a pleader during any such enquiry'. Section 15 of the Amendment Act said, 'If the Governor General-in-Council is of the opinion that any association interferes, or has for its objects interference with the administration of the law or with the maintenance of the law and order, or that it constitutes a danger to the public peace, the Governor General-in-Council may, by notification in the official gazette, declare such association to be unlawful.' Thus, several associations, the *samities* in Bengal, were banned in January 1909 under this Section 15 (2b). And as the gloss of the Royal Proclamation of Amnesty in 1919 wore thin, Section 121 A of the IPC started to be invoked again to defeat the 'waging war against the King' (Barisal Conspiracy Case); and two successive Bengal Criminal Law Amendment Acts came in 1925 and 1930.

In understanding who the terrorists were, and on the basis of that understanding, recommending strong punitive measures, the most unambiguous was the decision of the Court of Commissioners constituted under the Defence of India Act, 1915 in the Lahore Conspiracy (that included the bomb attack on the Viceroy on 23 December 1912) case, 1916. The Commissioners spoke of terror as of, '... dacoits, seduction of troops, villagers and students, manufacture and collection of arms and bombs, projected and accomplished attacks on railways, bridges, arsenals, and general communications, and finally projected as general uprising, which was to be the culminating act of war'; and then the Commissioners declared, 'We regard acts done up to July–August as acts of conspiracy to wage war; acts thereafter, when once the war had started as acts in furtherance of that war, and in abetment of such war'.[24] The Commissioners were severe—in the first case of the 82 accused, 78 faced trial, and of them 24 were sentenced to death and 26 were sentenced to transportation. Only five were acquitted. One was sentenced to death and promptly hanged in a separate case and had no opportunity to face the trial. In the second trial, 17 were tried, of them one approver was pardoned, six were hanged, and five were transported for life.

The issue of the identity of the terrorist had another import too, from the rulers' point of view. The issue was regarding access to arms. Clearly, terrorists were those who challenged the colonial state's monopoly over the means of violence. Everything else could be ignored by the colonial state, tolerated, or postponed, but the fact that they were armed, they wanted access to arms, and were taking any step necessary to acquire them, was singularly grave. Therefore, the colonial discourse stressed the fact that the terrorist was an armed man, and all legal and penal provisions were directed at disarming him. From finding out and blocking supply routes of arms to tracing the factors behind the increase of the skill in manufacture of arms and drying it out, stopping the mixing of armed men with unarmed population, to finally killing the armed man. It was nothing short of war. The attrition between the terrorists and the colonial state reflected this war at the most basic level.

The legal task of defining a terrorist was thus a product of contentious politics. Also linked with this realisation was another lesson, namely that, beneath identification and definition lay a process of law, the act of legislating, and the dynamics of 'preparing the brief' which included calculations of war, punishment, analysis, intelligence operation, knowledge of the enemy, capacity and the means to terrorise those who wanted to oppose the rule, and ways and means to disarm an entire population. It was as a part of the preparation of this brief that the CID came into existence in 1906. The provincial special branch was expanded and upgraded as the Special Branch in 1910. Armed constabulary was organised along Irish lines. Laws and other measures were enacted. This was thus a roulette game: you have to define the attributes in order to define a person; you can define the attributes only when you have defined the situation; you can define the situation only when you have summed it up in an exact way, that is in a juridical way; you can sum up the juridical essence of a situation only when you have analysed the situation properly by observing the person of the terrorist. Thus, rules of organisation-building, behaviour, *'modus operandi'*, 'enticement of minors and young boys', spreading 'ideas' and increasing the capacity of their 'reception'—all were under the scanner of J. E. Armstrong when he sat down to report on who the likely terrorists and terrorist organisations were. Everything was to be found out, if necessary by torture, so that everything could be closely examined.[25] Torture was, in this way, the deep voice of law. At times, even law could not recognise its own voice, so deep it was. Torturing the terrorist, then, was essential for the law to operate. It was the signature of the sheer physicality of the colonial world.

Even though it may surprise us as to how little of this physical world was reflected in the legal history of the colonial rule, yet these laws were like the hardened crust of earth and foam that enormous convulsions leave from time to time. It began with Regulation III of 1818 for detention of suspects. The Act I of 1900, known as the Press Act, was passed to regulate publication of newspapers and other printed material and to contain sedition and seditious literature. The Defence of India (Consolidation) Rules of 1915 conferred wide powers on the Government to detain people on the ground of anti-government activities. The infamous Rowlatt Act found its new form in the Indian Penal Code (Amendment) Act No XVI of 1921; it amended Sections 121 and 122 of the Code. The Criminal Law Amendment Act of 1925 strengthened the ordinary criminal laws; close on the heels came the Bengal Suppression of Terrorist Outrage Act of 1932. Police circulars became more detailed. For instance, one such circular suggested that police evidence alone was enough at times for a *'prima facie'* case; reports were to be exact, meaning it was enough if they were streamlined in terms of the format. Explosives Substances Act and Arms Act were pointed out as provisions under which culprits could be booked.

The intelligence files, the will to legislate, torture, and the litany of enactments—collectively then, this was the colonial state's unconscious. There we find evidences of deep fissures and fault lines left by the exasperating situations through the decades, threatening the entire machinery of law and order and thus the project of colonial constitutionalism itself. This was also a 'protracted war', marked by moments of tremendous violence. And though in the forties of the last century it seemed all a matter of mass movements only, with isolated terrorist acts appearing as marks of long past days, the violence of 1942, 1945–46, and 1947–48 showed that virtually the whole nation had become 'terrorist'.

III

Law reminds us of the principle of responsibility, and responsibility, as we know, is at the heart of constitutionalism. The colonial legal strategy in order to exclude some individuals and institutions from the rule of law depended on making 'responsibility' the cornerstone of legislating exercise. To talk of law is thus to talk of responsible government. Responsibility, then, was the principle that was being defined at different levels and purposes in course of the colonial state's battle with the early terrorists.

What makes the Indian colonial experience particular is that the principle of responsibility was laced with three elements of constitutional design that worked as both inclusive and exclusive strategies of rule: (a) *parliamentary system,* (b) *federal structure,* and (c) *the basic civil and criminal laws providing the backbone of the administrative system.* All three elements proved durable, and were left practically untouched by the new Constitution of independent India.

It all began with the exercise of *regulating acts* by the Home Government on the basis of which local governments and subordinate governments were set up. The essential design remained such that while the basic structure was provided from above, local participation at the bottom was gradually allowed. Rule of law also demanded a delinking from commercial interests as well as direct imperial interest—a form of government that would look like one that of Indians, albeit with the help of some Englishmen ruling India, or those being trained to rule India. The passage from Company's rule to the rule by the British Emperor, that is the rule of the constitutional government at 'Home', was the first step towards establishing rule of law. It came only with the suppression of the Mutiny, which had been, to the colonial rule, the most terrorising and horrific act by the Indians in that century. Already, the Governor General-in-Council by the Act of 1833 (Section 85) was to take steps to mitigate the state of slavery, and to provide by laws and regulations for the protection of the 'natives' from insult and outrage in their persons, religions and opinions. We can see how the multi-layered politics of responsibility was building up: the Crown was responsible for good governance; the Company was responsible to the Home Government; the Government was responsible for initiating Indians into self-governance and good governance, and the Indians were responsible for their self-education. Terrorism and mutiny were the evils that aimed to destroy this scheme; hence they had to be suppressed without mercy. Rule of law demanded this suppression and the destruction of the evils of violence. It also demanded that the regulations be transformed into law. The Bengal Regulations had been extended with some variations to North-Western Provinces. These Regulations were clumsy and intricate where administration was not detailed and was rickety. In the non-Regulation provinces and districts too a mass of executive orders were turned into law. Executive legislation, the usual way in which extraordinary measures begin, has thus an ancient beginning.

The thrust was towards codification, which in fact meant the consolidation of rule. The Regulation of 1781 (Impey's Civil Code) satisfied (in anticipation) the principle of 'cognoscibility of law', i.e., law should be capable of being known by persons whose rights and duties it determined—a principle that Bentham was to stress later. A Code of Regulations needed the Courts of Justice who could provide redress against infringement of the Regulations. By the Act of 1797 the Parliament sanctioned legislation and codification by the Governor General-in-Council. The Code of Gentoo Laws and Ordinations of the Pundits (1775) was the beginning; Judicial Regulations (1772–1806) followed it. Then came John Herbert Harington's three volumes of *An Elementary Analysis of the Laws and Regulations* (1805–17). Princep's *Abstract of the Civil Judicial Regulations* was published in 1829. And thinkers like Bentham and Mill who were powerless or unwilling to change the lot of their own country concentrated their energy instead on constitutional experiments in the colony. Indeed, Bentham wrote an essay, 'On the Influence of Time and Place in Matters of Legislation'[26] with the object of considering what modifications were required in transplanting his system of law codes to a colony. No wonder, all these thinkers honed their skill in liberal reforms during their stint at the India House.

Section 53 of the Act of 1833 upheld, '[...] such laws as may be applicable in common to all classes of inhabitants [...] of the regard being had to the rights, feelings, and particular usages of the people, should be enacted; and [...] all laws and customs having the force of law [...] should be ascertained and consolidated, and, as occasion may require, amended'.[27] The power of making laws and amending was vested in the Governor General-in-Council, and the task of ascertaining 'all laws and customs which have the force of law' was entrusted to a Law Commission. Thus, the First Law Commission came into existence. It was required by Section 53 of the Act of 1833 to streamline laws and provisions regarding administration of justice and police establishments, all forms of judicial procedure, nature of operation of all laws—civil and criminal, and suggest necessary alterations in the interest of rule of law. As can be expected, Macaulay compared the work of the Indian Law Commission with that of the Code Napoleon. Law was to be concise and lucid—we can see the reason for the frenzied search in the next hundred years for precise definition of terror, different crimes, and precise punishment. Even acts were divested of their names. The work on the Penal Code started around the same time, 1837. The Second Law Commission formed in 1853 assigned priority to a 'simple system of pleading and practice uniform as far as possible throughout the whole jurisdiction [...] which is also capable of being applied to the administration of justice in the inferior courts of India'. The work of the Commission was transferred from Calcutta to London. On the basis of its recommendations forwarded by the 'Home Government', the Legislative Council passed in 1859 the Code of Civil Procedure, in 1860 the Penal Code, and in 1861 the Code of Criminal Procedure. The High Courts Act came in 1861. The same year, the Third Law Commission was appointed 'to prepare for India a body of substantive law, in preparing which the law of England should be used as a basis'; and as if this was not enough, the Fourth Law Commission recommended in 1879 the following: 'English law should be made the basis in a great measure of our future Codes', but, as a concession to the colonised it said, 'its material should be recast rather than adopted without modifications [...] in recasting those materials due regard should be had to Native habits and modes of thoughts'.[28] And what was that English law? It meant, in the least developing legal response to factors and situations that were a consequence of the wars of annexation that had required repeated raising of money and men in the colonies; recurrent famines in the Isles, internal religious quarrels and conflicts; conflict in Ireland; the challenge of the Chartists; the past encounters with republicans and present encounters with poverty, vagabondage, and destitution. There was also industrial unrest, so much that 'the number of offences in Britain commanding death penalty by the end of the 18th century amounted to more than 200 (with) little wonder that the criminal statutes were known collectively as *The Bloody Code*.'[29]

When large-scale mutiny after 1857 became impossible for close to another three quarters of a century and the population had been completely disarmed, also with the relentless institution of an armed-to-the teeth colonial administration, through legal means, described in brief as above, terror in the incipient nationalist politics became the signature of the milieu; indeed, terror was the only way to become truly national in politics as opposed to the responsible politics of graded constitutionalism that colonialism was ushering in. The structure of administration initiated by Lord Ellenborough was in place by 1843 with separate 'Home' and Military departments besides Foreign and Finance. District administration was strengthened. Regulations were issued to set up a body of commissioners to take up municipal and police functions, as in Calcutta. The judicial administration was bolstered at the bottom by the union of the magistrate and the collector. The colonial administration was embarrassed by this, but it served them well. As we know, the union of judicial and police functions continued for long even after India became free. Equally important was the creation of the Civil Service whose members, Rivers Thompson, the Lieutenant Governor of Bengal, observed in 1883, 'have abandoned caste, (they) have surrendered religious feelings, (they) have broken family ties and set themselves against the devout sentiments and doctrines of their ancient creeds',[30] and selected on the basis of competition, and produced through special training; they became along with the judge, the police officers, intelligence officials, and the army generals, the main elements of the framework of rule that stabilised the empire shaken repeatedly by thousand mutinies, revolts and terrorist outbursts. Again, we must note that the strength of the framework was that it was 'legal'; the hundred years of law-making in this enterprise were as

essential as other critical aspects of colonial rule. We have no reason
to be surprised at this, because in classic liberal thinking, reform
had been one of the essential virtues. Reforming the society and
punishing the culprits were together one of the great tasks of the
liberal enterprise in India—therefore, setting up the police force,
courts and jails was more important than setting up schools and
colleges.[31]

The impregnable administrative massif that the nationalist
warrior would face was partly a result of the transfer of power
from the Company to the Crown—in many ways, as significant
as the much better known transfer of power nearly a century later.
It meant direct control of the colonial power, a ruthless transplantation of modes of politics prevalent in the 'Home' country—
for example with a cabinet mode of governing which had little to
do with parliament, but more to do with a centralised executive
mode led by the Governor General-in-Council. Thus, Lytton kept
secret his Afghan War and annexation of Upper Burma; similarly
under Kitchener, the most prodigious centralisation of all armed
forces in 1909 took place; and Canning candidly admitted,
centralisation should mean 'paramount authority of the head of
the government'.[32] Princes practically became feudatories. The
transfer of power further meant that the Anglo-Saxon legal system
was founded here, resulting in (as mentioned earlier) Law Commissions, plus the Penal, Criminal, and other Codes and Acts. By the
same token, with the Indian Councils Act of 1870 all regulations
for 'peace and good government' became parts of basic laws. The
transfer of power brought centralisation into the administrative
and social sphere. The result could be seen when the first signs of
organised terrorism against colonial rule were evident. Lord Minto,
the co-author of the 'liberal' Morley-Minto Proposals initiated
repressive laws and quartered the military and the punitive police
in an unprecedented manner in the service of what he termed 'Law
and Order'. The legislative councils, particularly the Imperial
Legislative Council, in their composition were to be rid of the
'influence of the professional classes'—the breeding ground of
protest politics and terrorism. It was only in this way that in 1915
the Defence of India Act with its provision of Special Tribunals
was rushed through the Council in a single sitting. This was in
the footsteps of the Defence of the Realm Act passed in England.
The Special Tribunals became notorious. Immediately, 24 persons

were sentenced to death at Lahore, although only six had been found guilty of murder.

The other significant transfer of power came in the form of the shifting of the capital from Calcutta to Delhi. With the institution of lieutenant governorships and chief commissionerships, provinces were strengthened, and though Bengal Partition was annulled, the country had been reorganised in one stroke. With the reorganised administrative structure of British India, honing of an electoral policy, a game along communal lines, centralisation of laws and codification, and the successful organisation of a stable military force, the colonial rule now was ready to face the militant nationalist threat. It could now take its time and say (as Curzon, a member of Lloyd George's coalition cabinet had indeed said) that its goal was 'to ensure progressive realisation of responsible government in India as part of the British Empire' and the British Dominion.[33] The *Rowlatt Committee's Report* was only one evidence, though the best known, of this strategy. By 1935, and subsequently the Defence of India Rules, the entire system of permanent exception, and permanent exclusion had been put in place so that the regulations could now work, acts could be the bedrock of the rule of law, and the state's reason could become amply clear so as to become the soul of the constitution.

A sense of history is therefore important because it helps us to understand better the juridical project that any regime has. All historical forms of rules have inequality, but what is different and particular to the modern form of rule is that it proclaims equality as its objective and claims that it can achieve it. Equality of law, equality before law, equality in the market place, equal rights, etc. are, therefore, the great principles on which constitutionalism stands. The freedom's laws that the constitutions include now as a matter of habit are the high symbolic gesture of acknowledgement of the principle of equality. Yet, for the first time, the legal definition of terrorism and its juridical invocation introduce the possibility of a constitutional sanction of inequality—on the basis of a person's or group's association with violence (other inequalities were matters of deficit). This makes some individuals, citizens, some half-citizens, and some outlaws on whom freedom's laws are not conferred. It thereby becomes a new way to define citizenship—earlier, gender, property, education, status, identity were the criteria, which constitutionalism long discarded. Now, two

tests become crucial—territorial location in the form of national
identity and an identification with violence. The refugee or the
non-state person (association with location) and the terrorist
(association with violence) become the two great outsiders to the
promised world of citizenship, i.e., of equality. While the relation
between the immigrant and equal citizenship is of a more recent
origin,[34] the political fact of the association with violence as one
of the disqualifications for citizenship is of older origin. The
strategy of 'extraordinary exceptions' that colonial constitutionalism initiated has produced the legal sanction of turning
people into half-citizens and non-citizens for whom the world of
citizenship holds no promise. We can see how the organic quality
of nation has depended from the beginning on inheriting one of
the essential features of pre-national political formations—armed
rulers and unarmed peasantry. In terms of liberal polity, it has
meant that those associated with violence will be disqualified from
citizenship. The disqualification began with the colonial strategy
of creating permanent exceptions.

We can thus suggest here a re-reading of the history of citizenship. In the received history, citizenship is associated with the
achievement of rights. In the re-reading that I suggest, a complicated scenario emerges. Some are not granted citizenship or would
soon be denied of it because of their association with violence. The
curve of militancy that went up via popular mobilisation comes
down with the grant of citizenship. Armed people cannot have the
right to vote. A permanent disqualification in the form of exceptions
to freedom's laws appears. Constitution-making in the independent country therefore has depended, to a great extent, on colonial
laws and enactments that foresaw who were to be disqualified. This
is admittedly a reading based on the reality of passive revolution
that independence through the specific route of decolonisation has
been to the once colonial countries. The terrorist is, therefore, the
first outlaw of a polity based on liberal legal principles.[35]

What then of the constitution-making exercise itself whose pre-
history we have recounted briefly? As we know, the Constituent
Assembly was a child of the Cabinet Mission. The Cabinet Mission
Plan that sanctioned the Constituent Assembly was, in reality, an
award. Although it granted that Indians had the right to frame
their own constitution, it laid down certain principles. Conditions
were now tied to the transfer of power, and the transfer of power

was, therefore, really an award. This transfer of power was to be complete with the accomplishment of two missions—formation of an interim government and the convening of a constituent assembly that, through its deliberations, would form a constitution to give birth to a sovereign country. In this hidden story of passive revolution, few things merit our attention more than the fact that in the operation of both these conditions, the existing regime of law and order developed through past 150 years remained intact.

Sovereignty came in this way. The Constituent Assembly, we are told, is the great instrument to ensure two most vital elements of democratic sovereignty—representation and consent. As the constitution-making exercise came to a close with the birth of a sovereign country, the past 150 years seemed like a state of nature and anarchy from which the country had recovered, with a representative assembly that represented the people and had their consent. The way in which sovereignty appeared is significant on several counts, some of which we may mention here in conclusion: (a) while the dreams of the colonised for freedom, independence and democracy, constantly acted on anti-colonial politics, and forced the nationalist leadership to reckon with them, the constitution-making exercise never touched on the regime of laws that was in place; (b) constitution-making exercise had to now keep out the politics of the street as the constitutional chamber had become, by this time, the locus of power; (c) the constitutional story significantly signalled stability, and the sustainability of the framework of institutions put in place amidst and as consequence of the disorder of the past time; and (d) it constituted for the first time in the life of the country 'a superior law', which legitimised all ordinary laws which had earlier lacked such sanction.

IV

To sum up, colonial legality never came to terms with what can be called actions in the public space symbolising opposition to law.[36] The deployment of coercive means in wars and domestic control in the colony presented two problems to the colonial rule: First, the requirement that to the extent the colonial ruler was successful in annexing territory and subduing population, the ruler had to now provide *rule* in terms of administration of land, goods, services and people. Therefore, now, conquest had to be normalised into a form of rule, i.e., energy had to be diverted from war to law-making and administration. Second, there was no way, however, in which the colonial ruler could ensure that a normal administration would be looked as such by the ruled, and coercion would become thereby an exception and not a matter of daily necessity to the ruler. The colonial strategy of rule, in the process, built a state that wanted to be both coercive and paternalist, where the precedence and the ongoing reality of violence and terror in politics posed a problematic to which the colonial rule had no answer. The strategy of conquest, coercion, domestication and normalisation faced one inveterate challenge—posed by the early nationalists who were also the early terrorists, and who were singularly insistent in their aim that this strategy of normalisation must not succeed. That challenge we know invited more coercion and more methods of administration, which in turn developed the modern state in South Asia.[37]

In a sense then the problem that terror and violence pose for law is elemental. Briefly, it can be formulated as this: how can law forget or come to terms with its own founding moment—the founding moment of violence? How can the countless murders that were originally perpetrated be normalised by law so that vengeance (that has now enveloped society) can be quarantined, its instruments brought back to the fold of state monopoly, and the order be satisfied with one or two sacrifices? Law's path of course, as shown by the colonial experience of vengeance, is to develop a well-policed society where public vengeance is the property of the judicial system. Law cannot afford that acts of terror appear as individual acts. Even though it may begin responding to emergency legislation, it recognises that such legislation can give it only a bad name. So, as colonial history showed, the will to legislate arises from the fact that law has to discount individual particularities and the uniqueness of a given situation. 'To act under its aegis is to apply a norm, to subsume a particular case under a general rule.'[38] Yet law's own founding violence cannot but generate a mimetic desire, at times not just desire, but monstrous repetition. It is in this sense that the entire colonised society immersed itself in terror in 1947 when it realised that the colonial judiciary's monopoly of committing murder was not to last any more.

* I am indebted to Amiya Kumar Samanta, Subhas Chakraborty and late Amitava Chanda for discussing with me some of my arguments and allowing me access to some of the material used in this chapter.

Notes

1. Bandopadhyay (1999: 8–35). First published in 1921 the book created a sensation; read and openly appreciated by Tagore, it has since then run into several imprints; see also Das (1987: 132–44). Pulin Behari Das was the founder of the Dhaka Anushilan Samity.
2. Barindra Kumar Ghosh, *Amar Atmakatha,* cited in Bandopadhyay (1993); see also *Sedition Committee Report* (1918: 20).
3. Cited in Bandopadhyay (1993: 152–53).
4. Sen (2000).
5. I am grateful to Benedict Anderson for drawing my attention to the close relation between early terrorism and early nationalism almost everywhere.
6. Bandopadhyay (1999: 102–103).
7. *Ibid.*: 104–109. See also, Bhaumik (1985: 55–80).
8. Samaddar (2002).
9. *Terrorism in Bengal* (1995, vol. 1: 32–33, 45; hereafter *TIB*) speaks of bomb-making, train wrecking, and the proliferation of small arms at places the intelligence people make the administrators aware of the organisational structures of the secret societies (*ibid.*: 221) – Home, GOI, 1937, Simla. The tragi-comic story of the early Bengal revolutionaries' attempts at bomb-making is documented in graphic details in Datta (1983: 151–53). For details of the various techniques employed by the early terrorists, the best account is Chakraborty (1981).
10. On this period, see also Ker (1973); also in this connection, see *Terrorism in India* (1974).
11. Michael Shapiro refers to the politics of surveillance as the 'bio-politics' of our age, when following Michel Foucault he argues that surveillance and control of bodies have become crucial for the State to manage security. I am grateful to Shapiro for providing me access to his essay, 'Every Move You Make: Bodies, Surveillance, and Media' (2005).
12. Some of these are drawn and discussed in detail by Kanungo in a chapter titled 'Gupto Samitir Adorsho Byartho Holo Keno?' (1984: 27–49); Chakraborty (1981: 23–92).
13. Kanungo (1984: 183–89).
14. *TIB* (1995, vol. 5: ii).
15. *TIB* (1995, vol. 1: 20–21, 34).

16. All citations are from R. E. A. Ray, 'Alliance of Congress with Terrorism in Bengal', *TIB* (1995, vol. 3: 957–93).

17. The jail lives of the terrorists were marked by intense discussions and debates on the merits and demerits of particular linkages. See, on this, Datta (1973: 159–70).

18. Indeed, Sachaindra Nath Sanyal's life is a great instance of a terrorist as an organised warrior. He along with Rashbehari Bose became legends in their lifetime for organising and leading a 'terrorist' army. On Sachaindra Nath Sanyal, his association with Rashbehari, and their joint work, see Datta (1390 B.S.: 120–32).

19. To understand the role of Benaras along with towns like Kanpur, Allahabad, and Meerut in the development of early terrorism, one needs to read Sachaindra Nath Sanyal's memoir which he wrote in several phases and only haphazardly completed before his death in 1943 (Sanyal 2001); also Chattopadhyay (1977: 147–91).

20. We can see, in this connection, the *Report of the Government of Eastern Bengal and Assam on Deportation* (1909). The *Report* dealt with deportations (under Regulation III of 1818) of Aswini Kumar Datta, Satish Chandra Chatterji, Pulin Behari Das, and Bhupesh Chandra Nag. The *Report* spoke of their activities, political profiles, and place in 'terrorist activities'. It must be noted that the *Report* nowhere spoke of their direct involvement, but always pointed towards their leadership roles in the districts of Bengal. In this regard, one can also see Pulin Behari Das' own revealing account: he wrote of the strength of the Dhaka Anushilan Samity, the near autonomous functioning of similar Anushilan Samities in eastern Bengal, and the fragile nature of the unity of the terrorist groups that depended on the state of the collective movement and the spread of the feeling among the ranks of the militant nationalists at a particular time about the need to strike terror in the ranks of the rulers to rejuvenate the masses. See Das (1987: 102–24).

21. Government of Bengal (1926).

22. *TIB* (1995, vol. 1: 353).

23. Government of Bengal (1926).

24. *TIB* (1995, vol. 5: v).

25. On the systematic use of torture by intelligence officials in the interrogation centres at the intelligence headquarters and elsewhere by the police in police custody, and in jails by jail officials, see the detailed accounts by Chattopadhyay (1977: 48–53). Chattopadhyay lists various methods used, the likely occasions when the prisoners would be tortured, and the attitude of the intelligence officials towards torture.

26. See on this, Stokes (1982: 51).

27. Cited in Chopra (2003: 303).

28. *Ibid.*: 302–16.

29. Farringdon (1996: 6).
30. Chopra (2003: 439).
31. On the influence of liberal thinking on the drafting of the Penal Code, see Stokes (1982: 140–233).
32. Cited in Sastri (1987: 62).
33. Simon Commission later admitted the fact of limitless centralisation that the one century of legal reforms had brought about. See *Report of the Simon Commission* (1929): Paragraphs 138, 139.
34. Here too colonial history has much to offer as lesson relating to teach the business of modern state running the world over—first, of course, it made the concept of race integral to the notion of citizenship; second, it showed how the global communities of colonial labour (mostly in indentured form) were de-linked from the democratic universe of citizenship of the decolonised countries. Thus, Indian labour abroad could not return to India after 1947. Various Acts were passed in the last decade of the colonial rule in India, such as the Registration of Foreigners Act (1939), The Reciprocity Act (1943), The Trading with the Enemy (Continuance of Emergency Provisions) Act (1947), The Foreigners Act (1946). One can also see in this context the deliberations on the Immigration into India Bill. For an insightful analysis of the relation between citizenship and decolonisation, see Banerjee (2002).
35. I am extending here some of the arguments of Wallerstein's essay (2003: 650–79).
36. Pierre Bourdieu reminds us of the symbolic power of certain acts (1991: 116–17).
37. Instructive in this study once again is Tilly (1990). Tilly, of course, misses the role played by the colonial rule in developing means of coercive apparatuses.
38. Terray (2003: 71).

4

The Citizen and the Subject: A Post-Colonial Constitution for the European Union?*

Sandro Mezzadra

In many of his recent interventions, Étienne Balibar has stressed the strategic importance of including the history of colonial expansionism (or the history of, what Edward Said has termed, the *colonial project*) in any critical reflection on the question of European citizenship and constitution. This inclusion, not exclusive to academic debate, is a fundamental issue of everyday life in Europe, attributed to the 'increasingly larger and legitimate presence, despite the suffered discriminations, of populations from colonial origins in the old metropolises'. Reflection on colonial history then is ridden with 'new tensions and violence' whilst potentially inscribing what Balibar calls a 'lesson of otherness' into the very code of European citizenship and constitution: the European recognition 'of otherness as an indispensable element of its own identity, its virtuality, its 'power' (Balibar 2003: 38–39).

It is precisely this *ambivalence* of the colonial legacy that lies at the core of this chapter. Starting from some conceptual remarks on the history of the discourse of citizenship in modern Europe and its relationship with the 'colonial project', I will try to highlight some characteristics of the present constitutional situation in Europe, stressing the relevance of the peculiar position of migrants in order to evaluate the whole development of the new European citizenship. These characteristics (as my main thesis suggests) are bound to influence the political development in Europe independently of the future of the 'Constitutional Treaty' which is currently being discussed and has been rejected by the referendums held in

France and in the Netherlands in the spring of 2005. While the referendums will still be important, although ambivalently open, there will be political and constitutional consequences. There is the possibility of a nationalist backlash and, what Slavoj •i•ek (2005) has termed, the return of 'proper politics' (in the shape of a radical reinvention of the European political space). The constitutional elements highlighted in this chapter are part and parcel of what we can call (following an important section of the European legal theory of the 20th century), the *material constitution* which has taken shape within the framework of the European integration process. Every political option, and especially every radical leftist option, will have to take these elements into account in the coming years.

I

Balibar's valuable considerations prompt a number of questions. First of all: what is new in the 'lesson of otherness' referred to by Balibar? In post-colonial studies, otherness is widely recognised as an essential element of European identity since the beginning of modernity. As for instance, Homi Bhabha or Gayatri Spivak taught us, a movement of contamination, transits and translation (a movement of *metissage*) contradictorily cohabits within colonial experience and anticipates the 'post-colonial' present. It is important to stress that, in light of post-colonial studies, the relationship between Europe and its 'others' is not to be reduced to a simple opposition (which could be described in terms of 'exclusion'). That relation, to borrow the Lacanian term used by Spivak (1999), must instead be reconstructed by bringing it back to a movement of *forclusion*. Let us try to simplify the somewhat esoteric language of many post-colonial critics: the image of Europe and its 'civilisation', beginning in the 16th century, takes its shape within a movement of constant comparison with the images of the 'barbarism' (but also of the 'liberty') of 'savage' peoples inhabiting the spaces which are open to the European conquest. Those peoples then, are from the very beginning, *implied* in the theoretical and practical work that in turn produces the unity of European space and the concepts which articulate that unity.

The concept and discourse of citizenship are no exception to this rule. In recent years we have learned for instance from Immanuel Wallerstein that it is not possible to understand the history of the capitalist mode of production without considering it from the very beginning as a *world-system*. Elaborating on the work of such a conservative legal thinker as Carl Schmitt, we have understood that it is not possible to make sense of the development of the *jus publicum europaeum* (that is, at the same time, of the modern European system of States) without considering the global scope conceptually inherent to it since the discovery and the conquest of the 'new world'. I think that we must apply a similar approach to the concept and the institutions of modern European citizenship, stressing precisely their *global scope* since the very beginning of their history.

Starting with John Locke in the late 17th century, a set of *borders* defined not only the legal and political experience of the citizen, but also what we can call the *political anthropology implied in the modern European discourse of citizenship*, that is, the way in which the individual was imagined and constructed as a citizen (see, for instance, Mezzadra 2002). We know the importance of the relationship between citizenship and property introduced by Locke. But it is important to underscore that the concept of property itself is, for John Locke, an 'anthropological' concept (that is, it is rooted within a determinate conception of 'human nature'). It indicates first of all the *property of the self*, that is, the capacity of an individual to rationally dominate his passions and to discipline himself in order to be able to do that labour which constitutes, in turn, the foundation of every 'material' property. Only *this* individual is able to become a citizen, and by the same time this figure produces its own borders, that is, a series of figures which are bound to be the 'others' of citizenship: the woman (who, in Locke's view, is *by nature* destined to subordinate herself to the authority of the man within the family), the atheist, the foolish, the 'idle poor', and the *American Indian*.

It is precisely this Lockean image of the individual as a citizen (with the 'epistemic' and material violence implied in it) that was for instance taken as presupposition by Emerich de Vattel in his *Droit de gens* (1758) to legitimate the European colonial expansion: the inhabitants of the spaces outside Europe were not characterised by the property of the self theorised by Locke (that is, *they were not individuals*), and this was the reason why they could develop neither a conception nor a practice of exclusive property of the land they inhabited, which could therefore be 'justly' occupied by the Europeans. Certainly, Vattel himself was quite crude in his writing, stressing at the same time that the natives could be justly 'exterminated' if they resisted the superior European right of conquest (Vattel 1758: 78). This is, of course, a crucial characteristic of European colonialism, the point in which the epistemic violence implicit in it turns out to be the origin of an absolute material violence. Ranabir Samaddar, among others, has shown us that terror and violence did not limit themselves to accompanying the moment of conquest, but rather shaped the very constitutional history of modern colonialism, defining it as the history of a permanent state of exception.

Nevertheless, terror and violence are only one side of the European colonial history and project. As Ranajit Guha has shown, working on the Indian case described by Samaddar himself, the perspective of the 'conquistador' gave way quite soon, in colonial knowledge as well in colonial governmentality in 'British India', to the perspective of the 'legislator' (Guha 1997: 77). It is this shift of perspective that creates the space in which the distinction between citizen and subject, which I used for the title of this presentation, could operate. Once again we are not confronted here with a simple relation of exclusion. If the colonial subject is the 'other' of the metropolitan citizen, their relation cannot be conceptualised in the same way in which we can understand for instance the relation between the 'barbarous' and the citizen of the ancient Greek *polis*. To put it very briefly, the 'educational' character of modern European colonialism (see, for instance, Metha 1999), which is best represented by the writings of Macaulay, implicates the very definition and experience of the colonial 'subject' in the space and in the logic of the discourse of citizenship. It is this implication which lies at the core of the European colonial project and which explains the peculiarly contradictory dimension of colonial law, colonial constitutionalism and colonial governmentality (see, for instance, Plamenatz 1960 and Thomas 1994).

While the distinction—and the contemporary existence—of the citizen and the subject corresponded to other distinctions that allowed a hierarchisation of the space of citizenship within the metropolis itself (most notably, to the distinction between 'active' and 'passive' citizen), it posed peculiar problems to European political and legal thinking. These problems, at the core the problems posed by the contemporary existence of 'representative government' in the metropolis and 'despotism' in the colonies, were solved for instance by John Stuart Mill, as it is well-known, by the development of a logic of the 'not yet' (Chakrabarty 2000). Writing at the beginning of the 20th century, the Italian jurist Santi Romano explained the necessity of colonial subjecthood in terms of a fundamental distinction in the quality of *historical time* in which the colonies were living. The specific backwardness of the peoples subject to colonial dominance made it necessary to rule them not according to the principles of 'constitutional government' prevailing in Europe but according to the principles of 'the patrimonial State existing before' it (Romano 1918: 104).

Henry Sumner Maine, the great British jurist who served for seven years in the 1860s as a legal adviser to the colonial administration in India, also referred to a difference in the quality of historical time while commenting in 1875 upon 'the spectacle of that most extraordinary experiment, the British Government of India, the virtually despotic government of a dependency by a free people' (Maine 1875: 33). Almost summarising his own experiences in 'British India', he wrote about the task of colonial administrators: 'the British rulers in India are like men bound to make their watches keep true time in two longitudes at once'. 'Nevertheless', he added, 'the paradoxical position must be accepted...' (*ibid*.: 37). It had to be accepted in order to govern *progress* as a process involving England and India in a common history while maintaining among the two an unbridgeable border, a *temporal* as well as a spatial border, which had to be ruled under the mark of pure domination.

I think this is a good definition, although on a very abstract level, of the peculiarity and contradictions of the modern European colonial project and experience, a definition which, I repeat: on a very abstract level, can be applied well beyond the British and the Indian case. The tracing of that absolute spatial as well as temporal border (a kind of 'meta-border') became the logical condition of the distinction between citizen and subject. It was at the same time conceptually as well as historically implied in the tracing of the borders among European nation-states, that is, in the production of the spaces within which the modern history of citizenship inscribed itself. If this is the case, then on a very abstract level, we can see one of the most important roots of our present condition in the challenge posed by anti-colonial struggles and movements to the very existence of that meta-border. Notwithstanding the manifold delusions and defeats that marked the history of decolonisation, that challenge was eventually successful. And this is the reason why it makes sense to call our present condition a 'post-colonial condition'—in effect, only by stressing the link to anti-colonialism (Young 2001). At the same time, however, precisely because of the ways in which the end of colonialism came about, post-colonialism denotes a situation in which the 'meta-border' between metropolis and colonies no longer organises any stable world cartography; but the possibility is given that it reproduces itself, in a rather fragmented way, within the territory of the former metropolises themselves (Mezzadra–Rahola 2005). It is in the background of such a definition of post-colonialism that I am now turning to analyse the European constitution.

II

First of all, it is necessary to highlight some very broad characteristics of the European constitution, in order to understand its relation with the concepts and the practice of modern constitutionalism. Of course there are important elements of continuity, but my hypothesis is that these elements are placed within a general framework that is significantly new in its essence and expresses a relative break from the experience of modern State. If we try to analyse the European constitution in terms of the basic concepts which were developed within this historical experience, we risk ending up with the same impression that Samuel Pufendorf, in the late 17th century, got in front of the Holy Roman Empire: the European constitution could take in our eyes the shape of a *monstrous creature*.

The first anomaly of the 'European constitution' in comparison with the traditional understanding of constitutionalism lies in the fact that we are confronted here not so much with a constitution as a formal document which determines the framework of the political and legal development within the fixed borders of a determined political unity, but rather with a constitutional *process*. I think this is a *structural feature* of the European constitution, and not a provisional situation that will be stabilised by the final approval of the constitutional treaty. To put it briefly: *The European constitution is, by definition, a constitution evolving for a body politic in the making*. The only possible comparison to be made in modern history in this respect is with the American constitution (that is, by the way, with a constitution which was deeply influenced by colonial experience), and it is not by chance that this comparison has been made quite often in the last years (see, for instance, Moulier Boutang 2003). In the European case, however, the flexibility does not concern only the borders of the political unity, it seems rather to be a key feature of the 'formal' constitution itself.

To talk about the European constitution as a constitutional process, means to take into account a radical subversion of the relation between some of the main concepts developed within the tradition of modern constitutionalism. Let's take for instance the concepts of constituent power and constituted powers (see Negri 1999). In European modern legal thinking this relation was always developed as a temporal relation: *First*, there was the expression of the constituent power, which was *then* bound to be silenced within the constitutional framework instituted by its action. In the case of the European constitution, this model doesn't seem to work. In the European constitutional process, the power of innovation, which is implicit to the concept of the constituent power, seems to be rather fragmented on a plurality of levels and seems fated to live in a permanent tension with the constituted order of powers. This means, on the one hand, that the European constitution is open to its constant transformation and that the logical possibility is given to imagine the relation between social movements and institutions in the European space in a way that is significantly different from the one characteristic of the experience of modern State. On the other hand, however, the openness of the European constitution refers to a situation in which too the working of powers gains new chances of freedom and arbitrariness. This situation enables the transition from the paradigm of government to the paradigm of governance (see, for instance, Borrelli 2004) to open up space for new forms of governmentality, that are not necessarily 'softer' than the ones connected to the traditional paradigm of government.

We can analyse the same set of questions in terms of the distinction between the concepts of 'formal' and 'material' constitution, which has been developed by an important section of European constitutional theory in the 20th century. In the European constitutional process, this relation seems to be assumed as a tension that is not bound to be inscribed within a fixed framework. And once more we are confronted here with the ambivalence of the openness of the European constitutional process: the concept of material constitution points, indeed on the one hand, to the constitutional relevance of social and political conflict; but on the other hand, it sheds light on the importance of a set of processes and actors (*administrative* processes and actors, from the point of view of classical modern legal theory) which are relatively free to operate independently of the 'formal' provisions of the constitution.

It seems that among the commentators of the European constitutional process, especially the ones who stressed the importance of the *already existing European constitution* (that, as it was stressed at the beginning of the chapter, already exists independently from the ratification through a formal constitution or 'constitutional treaty') got this point. In the analysis of such authors as Dieter Grimm, Joseph H. H. Weiler, Ingolf Pernice and Franz Meyer, what is stressed is precisely the overlapping of constitutional circles and levels of different scope which concretely shapes the European constitutional space, registering and pushing forward the disarticulation (that is, the crisis and transformation) of the classical notion of constitutional order (see, for instance, Meyer–Pernice 2003).

But how can we define precisely the kind of 'political space' which is emerging in the framework of the European constitutional process? Among recent literature on the subject, I find the book *Das kosmopolitische Europa* (2004) by Ulrich Beck and Edgar Grande, particularly interesting and thought-provocative, although I do not necessarily share the peculiar European enthusiasm that shapes their perspective. In a key chapter of their book, Beck and Grande try to apply to the European body politic the concept of *cosmopolitan Empire*. Starting from the assumption that the European Union is neither a State (be it in the form of a 'Superstate' or in the form of a federal State) nor a Confederation of States (Beck–Grande 2004: 83), they propose to apply to it the category of Empire, stressing the one, that in their eyes, is the main difference among it and the State:

> 'The State tries to solve its security and welfare problems establishing fixed borders, while the Empire solves them precisely through the variability of borders and external expansion' (*ibid.*: 91).

On the one hand, the emphasis put on the expansion (sure, through 'consensus' in Beck and Grande's analysis) as a key feature of the European Union points to the structural importance of the eastwards enlargement, in the sense that it can become the mirror in which it is possible to see the European political space reflected in some of its most important characteristics (see, for instance, Rigo 2005). On the other hand, it is important to underscore that the variability of the borders of the European Union corresponds to the internal heterogeneity of its space. The persistence of nation-states themselves within the European Union, which are not bound to be overcome in the constitutional process, but rather expand some of their powers in the framework of that process and become fundamental articulations of the 'cosmopolitan Empire' (Beck–Grande 2004: 114–19), is part and parcel of this heterogeneity. Furthermore, as Beck and Grande themselves stress in their book, either on the level of constitutional or on the level of territorial analysis it is possible to distinguish an area of 'full integration', an area of 'deepened cooperation', an area of 'limited cooperation', and an area of 'enlarged domination' (*ibid*.: 101–102). It is in the context of this heterogeneity of the political space and constitution of the European Union that it is necessary to develop the point made by Beck and Grande themselves: 'the European Union is also ... the post-colonial Europe' (*ibid*.: 58).

III

There seems to be a wide consensus in recent literature on the subject that the functions and the institution itself of the border are undergoing deep transformations in the context of 'globalisation'. Particularly important here are the transformations related to the issues of citizenship and migration. Coherent with the thesis put forward by Beck and Grande, it seems that we are experiencing an overcoming, although not a linear one, of the modern State model. While in this model the tracing of fixed borders (and the clear distinction between inside and outside) was the condition of the development of citizenship, nowadays we are confronted with a process which has been described as a 'de-territorialisation' of the border (see the literature discussed in Mezzadra 2004b and the essays collected in the first section of Mezzadra 2004c). And, it is important to point out that the concept of 'de-territorialisation' doesn't refer to a situation in which space and territory do not play a role any more in the working of border, but rather to a situation in which the latter cannot be confined to a given place, which is the territorial limit of a political unity.

The new border regime which has taken shape in Europe within the framework of the Schengen agreement seems to be a perfect case-study for this process (see, for instance, Walters 2002). To put it briefly, once again: what Beck and Grande describe as variability of borders seems to correspond to a simultaneous process of undoing and retracing of borders themselves. On the one hand, the European 'external borders' projects their shadow well beyond the 'limit' of the territory of the European Union (involving, for instance, such countries as Morocco, Tunisia, Libya, Ukraine in their management). On the other hand, they tend to trace themselves back within the European 'polis', as this process becomes particularly clear (although it is in no way limited to it) in the existence of *administrative detention centres* for migrants (that is, of a peculiar institution of the new border regime) in most European states.

This process of undoing and retracing of borders has run simultaneously into the making of European citizenship, and I think we should try to understand what the consequences of this coincidence are. My hypothesis is that European citizenship itself is being constructed as a *heterogeneous space*, and it is precisely this heterogeneity of European citizenship that creates the condition for the post-colonial re-emergence of the distinction between citizen and subject within the European constitution. The heterogeneity of European citizenship is expressed also formally in the text of the constitutional treaty, where it is constructed as 'second grade citizenship', since it depends on the national citizenship regulated by member states (Articles 1–10).

We can now go back to our starting point, picking up the analysis developed by Étienne Balibar. Just taking his departure from this specific regulation of European citizenship, Balibar has indeed stressed that the national management of the inclusion mechanisms of citizenship are now 'totalized at the European level', transforming the 'non communitarian foreigner', i.e., the migrant coming from outside the European Union, to an 'excluded (figure) from the interior'—indeed, to a *second class citizen* (Balibar

2001: 191). I would like to add that this process, in which Balibar sees the root of a 're-colonising' of migration (*ibid.*: 78), takes place in a situation in which national migration policies are increasingly developed under the pressure of European directives, and especially of the new border regime which I have briefly discussed earlier. The effect of this border regime is to produce a movement of *selective and differential inclusion* of migrants, which corresponds to the permanent production of a plurality of statuses (finding its limit in the *illegal alien* who is bound to become a permanent inhabitant of European political space), which tends to disrupt the universal and unitary figure of modern citizenship. This process is at the core of the transformations that have gone into citizenship. It does not concern only migrants but it tends to involve growing sections of 'autochthonous' populations in Europe through the neo-liberal process of politics by which rights are fragmented and become more and more precarious. Moreover, it seems to be one of the key features of the transformation of the European labour market, which is increasingly determined by what the 'European Monitoring Centre on Racism and Xenophobia' of Wien defined in 2001 as the 'ethno-racial division' of work in Europe.

The heterogeneity of European citizenship corresponds under these conditions to the heterogeneity of the governmentality regimes that rule European populations and European spaces. A growing number of people living in Europe do not seem to inhabit the social space which corresponds to the expansion of citizenship rights, that is 'civil society'. Rather, their lives are increasingly the targets of the technologies of governmentality which define what Partha Chatterjee has called the *heterogeneous* space of *political society*, and which 'often predate the nation-state, especially where there has been a relatively long experience of European colonial rule' (Chatterjee 2004: 36).

A new form of politics, which has been called *domo-politics* by William Walters, criss-crosses the rationality of liberal–political economy in the governance of mobility. 'Domo-politics' refers at the same time to the Latin word *domus* (house or home) and to the Latin verb *domare* (to tame, to domesticate, also used metaphorically to indicate the act of conquering or 'subduing men or communities') (Walters 2004: 241). It is precisely this act of conquering, with its colonial imprint and covered by the rhetoric of security in the European *domus*, which criss-crosses the making of European citizenship if we analyse it from the point of view of European migration politics. I agree with Walters (who coined the term *domo-politics* in the context of an analysis of the paper published in 2002 on migration management by the British government called 'Secure Borders, Safe Havens'), that the governance of mobility aimed at through the peculiar mixture of domo-politics and liberal–political economy (which seems to shape European migration politics) does not try 'to arrest mobility, but to tame it'. It doesn't aim at 'a generalised immobilisation, but [at] a strategic utilisation of immobility to specific cases coupled with the production of (certain kinds) of mobility' (*ibid.*: 248). It tries, therefore, to promote what I called earlier a process of selective and differential inclusion of migrants.

IV

The concepts of 'political society' and 'domo-politics' refer to specific colonial technologies of governmentality and power that criss-cross the multi-level European constitution, revealing some unpleasant consequences of the post-colonial nature of the European constitution. But on the other hand, there is another side to this very post-colonial nature. It has to do with the 'increasingly larger and legitimate presence' of migrants (of 'populations of colonial origin') in Europe, stressed by Balibar in the quotation from which I took my departure. The emphasis here must be on the adjective *legitimate*. I think that the legitimacy of the presence of migrants in Europe, independently of their legal status, can and must be interpreted in the terms suggested by a radical re-reading of the concept of citizenship. According to this radical re-reading, which I tried to develop elsewhere (cf. Mezzadra 2004a), citizenship cannot be reduced to its formal, institutional definition. There is a second face to citizenship, and this second face concerns the social and political practices that challenge the formal definition of citizenship.

According to this definition, we can see migratory movements themselves as constituted by a set of social behaviours and practices that place more and more pressure on the formal definition of citizenship. Considered from this point of view, on the level of everyday life, migratory movements are shaping European space and European citizenship into a kind which is very different from the ones we have been analysing so far: they are indicating, at least the possibility, we could say, of a global Europe that really takes into account in a positive way the 'lesson of otherness' which is inscribed in the European constitution by the colonial legacy. We have seen how this lesson of otherness can nurture heterogeneous practices of domination. Europe is nonetheless inscribed as a political space in our future, and I am convinced that there is no way back to the age of nation-states. It is a question of political agency transforming the open process of the European constitution in a space of heterogeneous practice of freedom and equality. The post-colonial migratory movements of the present are in this sense a challenge not only to the borders of European citizenship, but also to the borders of our political imagination.

Note

1. This paper was originally presented at the conference 'Conflicts, Law, and Constitutionalism' held in Paris, Maison des Sciences de l'Homme, 16–18 February 2005. I would like to thank all the participants in the conference, especially Paula Banerjee, Rada Ivekovic and Ranabir Samaddar, for their comments and criticism.

5

The Silent Erosion: Anti-Terror Laws and Shifting Contours of Jurisprudence in India

Ujjwal Kumar Singh

The repeal of the Prevention of Terrorism Act (POTA), 2002 figured prominently in the Common Minimum Programme (CMP) of the United Progressive Alliance (UPA), the coalition that replaced the National Democratic Alliance (NDA) government in May 2004.[1] On 21 September 2004, the President promulgated an Ordinance repealing POTA a month before it was to come up for legislative review. The Ordinance was approved by the Parliament in its winter session confirming the removal of POTA from the statute books. This chapter examines POTA as a terrain around which discursive practices of extraordinariness accumulate.

Specifically, this study looks at the inception of POTA as an ordinance, its enactment, amendment, and subsequent repeal, interspersed with the Supreme Court's decision that upheld its constitutional validity.[2] In the trials under POTA including the Parliament attack case, and the trajectory of POTA cases against the Marumalarchi Dravida Munnetra Kazhagam (MDMK) leader Vaiko in Tamil Nadu, and Raghuraj Pratap Singh alias Raja Bhaiyya in Uttar Pradesh, and the thousands of 'invisible cases' from Jammu and Kashmir, Jharkhand, Gujarat, Delhi, Andhra Pradesh, Maharashtra and Uttar Pradesh, both before and after the repeal, one finds that POTA unfolded in multifarious ways. This chapter will explore these diverse strands, focusing not only on law's words i.e., the nature of rules, principles and procedures, the interpretations in judgements, but also on law's deeds and effects—on the lives of people, assumptions of justice, and the legal and penal structures of the state. The latter I shall call, following Paddy Hillyard, the 'violence of jurisprudence'(Hillyard 1993), identifying thereby with a position that refuses to see law as an antithesis of violence. It rather looks at 'the awesome, physical force that law deploys' and the 'effects of legal force' (*ibid*.: 263) unraveling in the process the legitimising discourses of 'national security' and 'democracy' that shroud it. Within the broad framework of the history and practice of law, this chapter draws on the experiences of the working of previous such laws, including Terrorist and Disruptive Activities (Prevention) Act, 1985 and 1987 (TADA). It also attempts to show how the justification of security laws continues to be rooted in the *dilemma of democracy* framework,[3] reinforced by the context in which POTA was pushed through—the so-called international consensus against global Islamic terrorism—for safeguarding freedom and democracy. Extraordinary laws like POTA, it argues, maintain the hegemonic structures of the nation-state by externalising plural forms and sites of self-realisation as 'extraordinary'. All such laws— from the Preventive Detention Act (1950) through TADA and POTA, apart from the Armed Forces Special Powers Act (AFSPA) and the Public Safety Acts (PSAs) applied in parts of the North-East and Jammu and Kashmir—restrict the 'political' by determining who (group/collectivity or individual) belongs to the 'people'. By externalising parts of the population from the political community they attempt to iron out diversity, and in the process affect a greater distancing and conflict between plural collectivities and the general laws applied on them. Their unfolding in specific contexts has shown that the targeting of minority communities (TADA in Punjab, TADA and POTA in Gujarat) and tribals and peasants associated with Marxist–Leninist groups (TADA and POTA in Jharkhand and Andhra Pradesh) is a prominent feature of such laws.

Moreover, a close examination of the legal–juridical discourses after 11 September 2001, particularly the judgements in TADA and POTA cases, the Report of the Committee on Reforms of Criminal Justice System (2003) commonly called the Malimath Committee Report,[4] the repeal of POTA and the synchronous amendment of the Unlawful Activities Prevention Act (UAPA), 1967 shows the development of a complex and interlocking system of laws, so that laws pertaining to the so-called ordinary crimes and those claiming to deal with extraordinary situations intertwine and come to traverse common grounds.[5] Most recently, the POTA Repeal Act, 2004 and UAPA Amendment Act, 2004 have affirmed the shifting contours of jurisprudence in India through an intermeshing of the ordinary and the extraordinary. It is argued that the procedural changes and a separate system of dispensation of justice that extraordinary laws espouse, validated by hegemonic discourses of nationalism and a simultaneous construction of 'suspect communities', and the process of intermeshing and overlap with ordinary laws and legal practices for dealing with organised crime, erode existing legal and judicial institutions and processes, manifesting thereby, the 'violence of jurisprudence'.

Anti-Terror Laws: The Idea of Extraordinariness

Within the legal framework of constitutional democracy the political community in India gets constituted in two ways: (a) through the processes of standard application of rules and according to a uniform legal status to all citizens, and (b) through the inclusion of pluralities as special categories, or through special means, such as religious, linguistic groups, specially administered areas, or through scheduled lists, special provisions, etc. The nature of the accommodation of pluralities within the legal/constitutional framework in terms of 'cultural categories' with special rights, or as 'administrative units' requiring separate structures of administration, means that any *political* assertion of specificity is more likely to be seen as disruptive and a threat to the political community.

As a result, therefore, extraordinariness can be seen as having a dual facet. It demonstrates a process of normalisation whereby specific conditions and ideological and cultural diversities are not only included as exceptional; it is also assumed that in matters of governance, they would require special arrangements.

The examination of extraordinariness as delineated through anti-terror laws throws up the following features:

(i) These laws come with objects and intents proclaiming the need to respond to specific problems of extraordinary nature.

(ii) It follows from the fact of extraordinariness that these laws are expected to be temporary and that their lives are co-terminous with the extraordinary events they intend to overturn.

(iii) Since they are extraordinary measures in response to extraordinary events/situations, they are constitutive of extraordinary provisions pertaining to arrest, detention, investigation, evidence, trial, and punishment.

The Universalising Discourse on Terrorism and the Construction of a 'Suspect Community'

With the events of 11 September 2001, followed closely by the attack on Parliament on 13 December the same year, the discourse on terrorism in India situated itself in the burgeoning idea of global risks. The preambles of extraordinary laws worldwide are steeped in the idea of global risks, pressing for concerted and consensual efforts against global terrorism. The analysis in this section shows that this 'consensual' effort against global terrorism is rooted in a universalising and essentialising discourse on Islamic fundamentalism. The debates in Parliament from October 2001 through March 2002 show that POTA was being justified as part of the international effort to fight terrorism. The 'Statement of Objects and Reasons' of POTA clearly identifies the 'global dimensions' of challenges to 'internal security'.

The Malimath Committee Report (2003) too, while looking for ways to include permanent legal measures against terrorism, identifies 'terrorism as a global problem' and traces its origins to the decimation of the army of Middle-Eastern countries in the Sinai War of June 1967: 'The Arab World has since then been simmering with anger and rage leading to the contemporary wave of terrorism in the Middle-East' (*Report* 2003: 212). This preface on terrorism is followed a few pages later by a paragraph (19.3) on the 'Pakistani Link with International Terrorism' and another on 'Pakistan's Proxy War Against India' (19.4). This linkage not only reveals the Committee's subscription to a universalising discourse on global terrorism, it also offers the explanation for some of the reforms that the Committee seeks to effect in the Indian Criminal Justice System.

TADA judgements that have come in the last couple of years as well as the few POTA judgements that have been delivered similarly allude to Islamic terrorism. In a POTA judgement, delivered on 21 July 2003, in the case *State v. Mohd. Yasin Patel alias Falahi and Mohd. Ashraf Jaffary*, for example, the POTA Court sentenced the accused Falahi, an American national, and Ashraf, an Indian national, for five years under Section 20 (membership of a terrorist organisation) of POTA and for seven years under Section 124-A (sedition) of the Indian Penal Code (hereafter, IPC) respectively. The prosecution case was that on 27 May 2002, the two accused, who were members of the Students Islamic Movement of India (SIMI), an organisation banned in September 2001 under Section 3 of the Unlawful Activities Prevention Act, 1967, were 'present on the road near Jamia Milia Islamia University library, and were pasting stickers on the eastern wall'. The stickers carried the following notation in English: 'Destroy Nationalism Establish *Khilafah*', accompanied by a picture of a closed fist. 'In the fist', reads the judgement, 'was shown a missile with Indian sign, and flags of several countries like Russia, America, including that of India, crushed. At the bottom of the fist were several Muslim youths raising hands and thereafter was the name of the organisation—'Students Islamic Movement of India' written. In the bag the police found 33 more stickers.'

While the veracity of evidence and the procedure of investigation that followed is not the concern of this chapter, it is significant that the POTA Court also found the accused guilty under Section 124-A of the IPC that deals specifically with charges of sedition. Sentencing them under this Section, the judgement reads: 'The motive of SIMI as stated in the Constitution of SIMI is to bring into force Islamic Order and to destroy nationalism in India and other countries' (Lower Court Judgement, July 2003: 36).[6] Given that Section 124-A IPC explicitly removes 'criticism of government' from its purview, the Judgement goes on to say '… a person may affix posters criticising the Government. He can do it freely and liberally but it must be without an effort to incite the people to break the nation or to destroy the nation. Nation and government are two different things. When one criticises the government, he criticises the manner in which government functions or apathy of government to the public in general or to specific class. *But when a person attacks the very nationalism, he acts as a fundamentalist and his motives are not to criticize the government but to act against the very fabric of society*'.[7]

The fact that one of the accused Mohd. Yasin Patel, was an American national, that both the accused had received education in a *madarsa*, and had chosen India as their 'workshop' and 'hatchery', was seen evidence corroborating guilt: 'Another factor which is important in this case', the judgement reads, 'is the nationality of the accused. He is an American national. He has chosen American nationality by volition. He possesses American Passport. All his brothers, sisters and parents are settled in USA. Unless his intentions were to indulge in anti-national activities through organisations like SIMI there was no need for him to make India his workshop' (p. 35). The fact that 'he got education in a Madarsa and not in a regular college recognised by the state' and that 'both of them possess education only in Kuran and Islamic studies' were cited as further evidence corroborating their guilt. Sentencing Falahi, the judge pronounces: 'He is a person who believes in international Islamic order and wants to destroy nationalism of the people here. He instead of working in USA for his aims, of which country he is a citizen, has chosen India as his workshop. I consider that a person who chooses to become a USA national and works for destruction of other countries does not deserve leniency'.[8]

A similar spectre of an Indian nation in threat from transnational Islamic terrorism is raised in the opening paragraphs of the POTA Court Judgement in the case *State v. Mohd. Afzal*.[9] The Judgement begins by identifying terrorism with a specific religion without naming it: '…terrorism is a scourge of all humanity. It is being perpetuated and propagated by religious fanatics, to poison the minds of their followers and generate mercenaries and terrorists to kill innocent persons' (POTA Court Judgement, December 2002: 1). That the reference here is to Muslim fundamentalism is clear from the fact that page 3, paragraph 4 specifically mentions three instances of terrorist attacks—the attacks on World Trade Centre, on a theatre in Russia and on Akshardham temple: 'Strike by terrorists on World Trade Centre or at a theatre in Russia and at Akshardham temple in Gujarat and other temples in the country show the reach of terrorists to destroy innocent lives'.[10] Care is taken thereby to show that the attack on Parliament was part of a global network of terrorism that thrived on its nexus with 'underworld criminal organisation' and 'obvious technical advantage'. It is not surprising then that much of the prosecution's case projects the attack on Parliament as part of a larger conspiracy, designed and dictated by unseen forces, linking up through a network of mobile telephones and laptop computers.

More significant perhaps is the manner in which the new contexts of 'global Islamic terrorism' have been cited in a recent judgement in a TADA case pertaining to Sikh militancy. On 22 March 2002, for example, the Supreme Court judgement in the TADA case *Devender Pal Singh v. State of NCT of Delhi and Another*,[11] coming several years after the institution of the case, took recourse to the new contexts of terrorism to justify the stringent interpretation of provisions pertaining to 'confession', and sentenced the accused to death.[12] 'The menace of terrorism', the TADA Judgement states, 'is not restricted to our country, and it has become a matter of international concern and *the attacks on the World Trade Centre and other places on 11-9-2001* amply show it. *Attack on Parliament on 13-12-2001* shows how grim the situation is….'[13] The spectre of the besieged nation and the perception of global risk affirmed by an international consensus, form the context of the judgement that is temporally removed from the circumstances in which the 'terrorist act' was originally committed and brought to trial. This synchronisation, and gloss of historical specificity, moreover, feeds into the seemless, universalising discourse of global terrorism.

Earlier, in the interregnum between TADA and POTA, discussions on the Prevention of Terrorism Bill, 2000, which was expected to take the place of the lapsed TADA, constantly referred to the 'besieged' us, reiterating the 'urgent need' for a 'fresh examination' of issues of 'terrorism' and other 'anti-national' activities. It is significant that while the TADA-like Bill was being entrusted in 1999 for the perusal of the Law Commission of India, the latter expressed its concurrence with the government that India perhaps required a *permanent anti-terrorist law*, 'without any further loss of time'.[14] Within Parliament, however, questions were being raised about TADA having been used discriminately against minority communities, and the prolonged judicial process it entailed. However, suggestions for making extraordinary laws more foolproof, poured in.

The Law Commission in its *173rd Report*, while examining the issue of a 'suitable' anti-terror Bill, continued to mark out the dangerous 'outsiders' within the country. Showing remarkably selective memory, the Commission claimed that 'religious fundamentalist militancy', '*first* raised its head' with bomb explosions in Mumbai, and since then 'continued to make its presence felt'. The latest incident (February 1998) were the blasts by Al-Ummah, 'the principal fundamentalist militant outfit' of southern India, in different regions of Coimbatore. Other aspects of the security threat persist—as 'militant and secessionist activities' in Jammu and Kashmir, 'insurgency-related terrorism' in the North-East and 'extremist violence' in Andhra Pradesh and Bihar. Significant about the Commission's assessment of the security situation and the chronology of events that made an anti-terrorist law immediately imperative, was the manner in which it disregarded Hindu fundamentalism, particularly that of the Shiv Sena and other components of the Sangha Parivar, which predated the violence cited in the Commission's Working Paper.[15]

It is interesting how in the course of debates, champions of extraordinary laws singled out the Bombay blasts (which occurred in the aftermath of the Babri Mosque demolition in December 1992) for both criticising those who opposed such laws, and also for launching an appeal for a fresh 'anti-terrorist' law. Arun Shourie, for example, blamed the 'weak political class', the 'rights-mongering civil libertarians' and 'leaders' looking for 'issues', for impeding the country's 'life and death struggle against terrorist invasion'.[16] Launching a diatribe against their campaign leading to the lapse of TADA, which is, ironically, glorified as *the* 'vital instrument' (of democracy), Shourie wonders: 'How did this [the lapse] happen?' Claiming privileged knowledge, he informs the reader: 'I was in touch those days with officials in the Home Ministry as well as with persons who were in direct combat with the terrorists, and I remember the sequence vividly'.[17] It is surprising, however, considering his proximity with those in charge, and his own admission of vividness of memory, that while reconstructing this *sequence* (of lapsing of TADA), Shourie only ventures to 'surmise'. Almost predictably, Shourie's sequential reconstruction begins with the Bombay blasts:

> I surmised that the sequence had been as follows. After the Bombay blasts TADA at last began to touch those who wield real influence in India. They activated their agents. A din was created. 'Leaders' and civil libertarians on the look out for issues, saw an opportunity. A campaign in the name of Islam and human rights was launched.[18]

The selective identification of the 'enemy within' resonates in the manner in which TADA was used in contexts of communal conflict predominantly against the Muslim community.

A significant distinction between TADA and POTA/POTA (indicative of the political context within which POTA was enacted) is that unlike TADA, POTA carries the Hindutva image of the nation and national security. TADA was enacted in May 1985 in the context of militancy in Punjab, specifically a series of bomb explosions in Delhi. POTA, on the other hand, does not mention specific states or regions as problem areas. The Statement of Objects and Reasons refer to the 'upsurge in terrorist activities', 'intensification of cross-border terrorist activities' and 'insurgent groups in various parts of the country'. The challenge the nation especially faced, it states, was from 'global dimensions' that terrorism 'had now acquired'—'the modern means of communication and technology using high-tech facilities available in the form of communication systems, transport, sophisticated arms and various other means'.[19]

Moreover, while identifying 'terrorist activities', TADA specifically referred to 'threatening harmony between communities' as an act of terror.[20] Following widespread allegations of its targeted use against religious minorities, POTA removed 'threatening harmony between communities' from the ambit of 'terrorist activities', purportedly as 'a safeguard'. Far from being a safeguard, the removal, in practice, translated into a deflection of attention from the communal activities of Hindu fundamentalist organisations, while the Act continued to be used selectively against the Muslim minority. Perhaps the most prominent selective use of POTA has been in Gujarat, where out of 250 persons against whom POTA had been imposed, 249 were Muslims. The majority of POTA cases in Gujarat have resulted from its application in the Godhra Case involving the burning of a coach of the Sabarmati Express, in which 125 Muslim men are chargesheeted.[21] Curiously, while the circumstances of the tragic train-burning incident are still being pieced together, the Chief Minister of Gujarat, Narendra Modi, declared it a 'terrorist act' immediately after it occurred. In the midst of the unbridled brutalities unleashed against Muslims in different parts of Gujarat, on 2 March 2002, Prevention of Terrorism Ordinance (POTO) was applied in the train-burning case.[22] Contrary to popular perception, POTO was not subsequently 'withdrawn', but only 'kept in abeyance', or deferred, till more suitable circumstances presented themselves. The fact that POTO, still an ordinance, was to come up before the Parliament for approval before it became an act, was an important consideration. POTA got enacted in an extraordinary joint session of Parliament on 26 March 2003, and almost simultaneously, the Act was re-invoked in the train-burning case. The entire pattern of invocation, abeyance and deferral, followed by re-invocation, shows the exclusionary nature of the politics these acts represent, and thrive on. While POTA detainees in the train-burning case still await trial while they languish in jails, most cases pertaining to the riots that followed (all under the ordinary criminal law) threatened to peter out, until the Supreme Court took note of them.

Extraordinary Laws: Exceptions or Norm?

The justification of extraordinary measures, as pointed out at the beginning, rested on the assumption that such measures are unavoidable and necessary responses to specific crimes of an extraordinary nature. They are, therefore, temporary; their lives co-terminous with the extraordinary events they intend to overturn. The section that followed showed how the discursive practices surrounding extraordinary laws, while designing a separate system for dealing with extraordinary events, have emphasised, alongside assurances of temporal controls and legislative oversight, the indispensability of such laws. In this section we shall see how extraordinary laws have not been transitory, either in terms of their temporality or their outcome on the legal system. Moreover, it shall show, how through a subtle process of symbiosis, laws pertaining to so-called 'ordinary crimes' and those claiming to deal with extraordinary situations, intertwine in specific contexts. Not only is this interlocking evident in the letter of the laws and unfolds in judicial pronouncements, it is also (as the Malimath Committee Report (2003) would show), evident in their effect on ordinary laws, so much so, that much of the 'extraordinary' gets accepted in jurisprudence, ideologically and procedurally.

(a) An Unending String of Extraordinary Laws

An unending string of extraordinary laws have existed in India, enacted after independence or having continued from the colonial period.[23] The Preventive Detention Act, 1950, used against the communists in Telengana, was the first detention law after the

Constitution was enforced. The Indo–China War of 1962 provided another occasion for the vigorous use of preventive detention by the government. The declaration of emergency due to the war enabled the government to promulgate the Defence of India Ordinance, 1962 and to frame rules under it. The Defence of India Act, 1962, which replaced the Ordinance, empowered the Central government to make rules, ostensibly for securing the defence of India, civil defence, public safety, public order, the conduct of military operations, or for maintaining supplies and services essential to the community.[24] The official state of emergency persisted till subsequent wars with Pakistan in 1965 and 1971, and the government continued to detain people under the Defence of India Act, 1962. In 1967, the Unlawful Activities (Prevention) Act was passed. Under this Act, any organisation could be declared illegal and any individual imprisoned for questioning India's sovereignty over any part of its territory. The Preventive Detention Act, renewed seven times, lapsed in 1969 owing to lack of support for Prime Minister Indira Gandhi in the Parliament. There were no central laws of preventive detention for two years. The states, however, continued operating their own preventive detention laws.[25]

The 1971 general elections gave Indira Gandhi sufficient strength in the Parliament to pass the Maintenance of Internal Security Act (henceforth MISA).[26] MISA had been modelled broadly on the Preventive Detention Act, 1950, containing provisions giving broad application to Article 22(4), and 22(5) of the Constitution, pertaining to disclosure of the grounds of detention and opportunities to make representation against the order. The Defence of India Act, 1971, introduced some changes in MISA, making it more stringent. The National Emergency of 1975 suspended the right of access to the courts for the restoration of the fundamental freedoms of the people. Under such conditions, MISA assumed formidable proportions. Certain amendments were subsequently made by the government, virtually rewriting the Act. The Constitution (39th Amendment) Act placed MISA in the ninth schedule of the Constitution, taking it beyond judicial review. On 29 April 1976, the Supreme Court upheld the validity of MISA as amended and refused the writ of *habeas corpus* under Article 226 of the Constitution, which had withstood suspension owing to a state of Emergency.[27] The Constitution (42nd Amendment) Act, 1976, further strengthened the powers of the Central government by providing that no law for the prevention of anti-national activities could be declared invalid on grounds that it violated the fundamental rights in Part III of the Constitution. In 1977, MISA was repealed by the Janata Party government. The Janata Party government, however, did not repeal the other extraordinary laws that were also enacted by the earlier governments, including the Armed Forces Special Powers Act, 1958[28] and the Unlawful Activities (Prevention) Act, 1967. Preventive detention laws were, however, enacted by different political parties in power in the states of Madhya Pradesh (henceforth MP), Jammu and Kashmir, Bihar and Orissa. A subsequent attempt made by the Janata government to bring in a mini MISA in the form of a Criminal Procedure (Amendment) Act proved futile.[29] When the Congress returned to power, the National Security Act (henceforth NSA), 1980 was brought onto the statute books. The NSA was followed by Terrorist and Disruptive Activities (Prevention) Act, (henceforth TADA), 1985 and 1987, through efforts to bring in the Criminal Law Amendment Act and Prevention of Terrorism Bill after TADA expired in 1995, to POTO and POTA, 2002, which was repealed in September 2004.

(b) Procedural Continuities: Self-Perpetuating Provisions

Extraordinary laws come with self-perpetuating provisions. The life of the Preventive Detention Act, 1950 was extended by consecutive amendments till 31 December 1969, so much so that it became a normal feature of Indian political life, with the number of persons detained every year under this Act gradually decreasing each year (Bayley 1962: 25). TADA provided for its extension every two years, and continued to exist on the statute books through extensions till 1995. In 1993, when TADA was extended for what turned out to be the last time, the extension had became so *routine* that only eight Members of Parliament participated in a discussion that lasted barely an hour and 10 minutes.[30] It is significant that the period after which parliamentary review of the Act could take place was increased in POTO to five years. Following criticisms, the second Ordinance promulgated in December 2002 reduced the period to three years. The increased period for which such Acts can remain on the statute books, without being subjected to legislative review, is indicative of the longevity that is sought for them. This quest for a longer life is frequently justified by articulating the risk of running into a 'legal vacuum' in the absence of effective anti-terrorist laws. In its 173rd Report, for example, the Law Commission of India, alluded to the request it received from the Home Ministry to 'undertake a fresh examination of the issue of a suitable legislation for combating terrorism and other antinational activities', a subject of 'utmost urgency', in view of the fact that 'while the erstwhile Terrorist and Disruptive Activities (Prevention) Act, 1987 had lapsed, no other law had been enacted *to fill the vacuum* arising therefrom' (Law Commission of India 2000: 1). The Malimath Committee in its turn, proposed a *permanent solution* recommending that 'a comprehensive and inclusive definition of terrorist acts, disruptive activities and organised crimes be provided in the Indian Penal Code, 1860 *so that there is no legal vacuum* in dealing with terrorists, underworld criminals and their activities after special laws are permitted to lapse, as in the case of TADA, 1987 (*Report* 2003: 294).

(c) Anti-Terror Laws: 'Life After Death'

Extraordinary laws, moreover, come with the provision that the expiry of the law shall not affect 'any investigation, legal proceeding', etc., that may have been initiated when the Act was still in force, which shall continue 'as if this Act has not expired'. The experience with TADA showed that the continuation after expiry imparted a prolonged 'life after death' to the Act. Cases under TADA continue to be tried in various designated courts and the Supreme Court several years after it expired. A 1999 newspaper report noted that 3000 to 7000 cases still remained to be decided.[31] By one account, three years after TADA was revoked, the state of Assam had nearly 1000 TADA detainees in prisons. Since 1991, only 14 persons have been convicted under TADA in the state, despite a total of 26,000 arrests having been made. Considering that only four out of 1237 TADA-related cases have ended in conviction, it is quite possible that the majority of those still languishing in jails may probably be acquitted.[32] The delay in judicial proceedings, resulting in many cases in acquittal from charges after a long-drawn judicial procedure, has meant wasted lives. This is brought out most poignantly in the case of the release of 44 TADA détinues from Mysore Jail, in October 2001, who had been picked up by the Special Task Force in 1994 on the suspicion of providing food to the dacoit Veerappan. Among these 44 were entire families, including daughters, mothers, mothers-in-law, and a 14 year old boy Muruga who was picked up while returning from school. Twenty years old at the time of release, Muruga now feels too old to pursue his studies.[33]

The unending string of extraordinary laws, provisions which assure decreased legislative review, and self-perpetuation so that such laws continue to cast their shadows long after they have ceased to exist in statute books, have made such laws part of the lives of people. The idea that they are a system of laws that exist alongside and independent of ordinary laws is not true anymore. As the next section shows, almost imperceptibly, much of the extraordinary is creeping into ordinary law as a result of the development of a complex and interlocking system, so that laws pertaining to the so-called 'ordinary crime' and those claiming to deal with extraordinary situations intertwine in specific contexts.

The Ordinary and the Extraordinary: From Parallel to Interlocking Systems

Ever since the enactment of the Preventive Detention Act in 1950, as Upendra Baxi points out, the Preventive Detention System (PDS) existed in the Indian Legal System as a parallel legal system in aid of the Criminal Justice System (CJS) (Baxi 1982: 30). The most striking distinction that Baxi identifies between the two systems pertains to the object, models of justice, and the patterns of power-sharing that they espouse. The Criminal Justice System is based on the assumption of (a) the primacy of social defence as the object of law; (b) the maximisation and optimisation of due process as its strategy; and (c) the pre-eminence of courts that are legalistic and pro-accused in their disposition. The Preventive Detention System, on the other hand, is primarily geared towards repressing (primarily, political and ideological) opposition, thrives on minimal due process, and gives pre-eminence to executive decision-making and 'satisfaction' in the initiation and affirmation of extraordinary proceedings. The prioritisation of the executive becomes instrumental in relegating the pro-libertarian aspects of adjudication and the predomination of a 'jurisdiction of suspicion'.

While laws like TADA and POTA are not preventive detention laws, the principles of justice they espouse correspond with

Upendra Baxi's illustration of the preventive detention system. In fact, it is in the insidious nature of such laws that they masquerade as substantive laws, bypassing thereby the constitutional and procedural safeguards, the latter provided by the Supreme Court for the accused pertaining to arrests, detention and trial. Investigating agencies and prosecution also bypass the procedures and safeguards provided under ordinary law, and subject the accused to special procedures prescribed under extraordinary laws. Thus, confessions made to a police officer (Section 32) and telephone interceptions (Sections 36–48) were considered valid and reliable evidence under the Act. Under Sections 25 and 26 of the Evidence Act, as ordinarily applicable, confessions to police are not admissible as evidence because they can be easily extracted by torture. Similarly, under the ordinary legal procedure, telephone interceptions may not be produced as primary evidence against an accused, unless they have been collected under the Indian Telegraphs Act, 1885, which assures procedural safeguards. Also, several clauses under POTA do away with the personal safeguards that are normally available to an accused. Once a person is detained, s/he is denied bail for a minimum of one year (Section 49). Moreover, bail cannot be sanctioned if the prosecution opposes it, and unless the court is satisfied of the accused person's innocence. This withdrawal of existing safeguards and dilution of evidence decreases the threshold of proving guilt, encourages shoddy investigation, and tilts the trial disproportionately in favour of the prosecution.[34]

A distinctive pattern has, however, emerged in the operation of extraordinary laws, lending to its normalisation—that of an interlocking between the ordinary and the extraordinary laws. While extraordinary laws in several countries amend specific statutes of ordinary law, bringing about, what Hillyard calls, a symbiotic relationship between ordinary criminal law and emergency legislation, and a general tightening up throughout the statutory law (Hillyard 1993: 263), the functioning of extraordinary laws in India reveals a distinctive pattern of concurrence and interlocking between the extraordinary and the ordinary.

Extraordinary laws, for example, often carry specific provisions whereby the accused may be simultaneously chargesheeted and tried for violation of other (ordinary) laws in a common trial. The parallel structure of courts set up for the dispensation of justice under extraordinary laws gives effect to such interlocking systems. Special or designated courts with expansive and overriding powers try cases under the ordinary law simultaneously in a common trial, and hand out enhanced penalties on the basis of evidence that is considerably diluted under extraordinary laws. While identifying terrorist acts for punishment, POTA (Section 3[1(b)]) brings under its purview the UAPA 1967, the Arms Act, 1959, the Explosives Act, 1984, the Explosive Substances Act, 1908, the Inflammable Substances Act, 1952, for trial under POTA with enhanced penalties (Section 5). In the Parliament Attack case which was the first POTA case to be decided, the accused were charged and found guilty by the Special POTA Court under various sections of POTA, IPC, and Explosive Substances Act.

Like other anti-terror laws, POTA worked on the principle that terrorist acts cannot be proved in the normal course and they require extraordinary measures. POTA, therefore, permitted the inclusion of evidence that could not otherwise be admitted under the ordinary law, e.g., confessions to a police officer and telephonic interceptions. In the Parliament attack case, telephonic interception formed a crucial part of the evidence against the accused. The defence for the accused successfully challenged the admissibility of this evidence in the High Court on the ground that the safeguards laid down in POTA were not followed. Significantly, the judgement by the POTA court, while submitting to the decision of the High Court, concluded that its admissibility could be considered for offences under other acts. It subsequently considered the interceptions under the Telegraph Act, and admitted them (along with confessions) as evidence against the accused, sentencing three of them to death under Section(s) 302 read with 120 B of IPC and 3(2) of POTA read with 120 B of IPC.

This brings us to yet another instance of interlocking in the Parliament attack case. It is important to note that while one of the accused, S.A.R Gilani, had made no confession, the confessional statements of two other accused Afzal and Shaukat had been collected under POTA. While admitting that confession by co-accused was not 'evidence against Gilani' the POTA Court Judge nonetheless used it against the latter giving the following grounds: 'u/s 30 of the Evidence Act the court can look into this confessional statement to lend assurance to other circumstantial evidence' (POTA Court Judgement: 253). While confession by the co-accused can be used as evidence under TADA, POTA has a safeguard whereby a confession by the co-accused cannot be used as evidence against the accused.

Yet another instance of interlocking, and consequent occlusion of safeguard relates to Section 3(4) of POTA. While specifying the punishment for terrorist acts, Section 3(4) of POTA states:

> Whoever voluntarily harbours or conceals, or attempts to harbour or conceal any person knowing that such person is terrorist, shall be punishable with imprisonment for a term which is not less than three years but which may extend to imprisonment for life and shall also be liable to fine:
> *Provided that this sub-section shall not apply to any case in which the harbour or concealment is by the husband or wife of the offender.* (emphasis added)

Overriding the safeguard against implication through association (by marriage) that was provided in this provision, the judgement found Afsan Guru alias Navjot, the wife of Shaukat Hussain Guru (an accused in the case), guilty under Section 123 of IPC which makes concealment of design to wage war against India as an offence. Outlining the case against Afsan Guru under IPC, the judgement pitted her matrimonial duties against her patriotic duties to the State. Significantly, while finding Afsan Guru guilty under the ordinary law, the Special POTA Court took recourse to the evidence produced in the court relating to the conspiracy under POTA, specifically the telephonic conversation between the husband and the wife that was intercepted under the extraordinary procedures provided under POTA.

More significant is the manner in which this interlocking has allowed the expansion of the scope of POTA, reflecting the ideological contexts within which the Act was unfolding. We may recall here that TADA was widely criticised for the communal use of Section 3 which included acts that 'alienate any section of the people' and those that 'adversely affect the harmony amongst different sections of the people' in its definition of terrorist activities. While these grounds for defining terrorist activities were removed from POTA as a safeguard against possible abuse, the targeting of Muslims continued. As the following illustration will show, this targeting has been facilitated by an interlocking between POTA and UAPA 1967.

Section 3[1(b)] of POTA lays down that 'whoever is or continues to be a member of an association declared unlawful under the Unlawful Activities (Prevention) Act, 1967', commits a terrorist act. In the POTA case *State v. Mohd. Yasin Patel alias Falahi and Mohd. Ashraf Jaffary* (discussed earlier) one can see how this interlocking allowed the discarded ground of 'disturbing peace and communal harmony' to sneak almost imperceptibly into POTA, broadening thereby the scope of the Act. On 21 July 2003, the Special POTA Court in Delhi sentenced the two accused Mohd.Yasin Patel alias Falahi and Ashraf Jaffary for five years under Section 20 of POTA and for seven years under Section 124-A of IPC. Section 20 of POTA is part of Chapter III of the act titled Terrorist Organisations. It deals with the procedures through which an organisation may be declared terrorist, and lays down the offences and punishments relating to membership in such an organisation. The two accused in the case were members of SIMI, an organisation banned under UAPA. The government notification banning SIMI stated that the latter had been indulging in activities that were prejudicial to the security of the country, had the potential of disturbing peace and communal harmony, and disrupting the secular fabric of the country. It needs to be noted that the accused were arrested on 27 May 2002 under UAPA. Since SIMI was also a banned organisation under Section 18 of POTA, four days later the accused were booked under POTA. Investigations against them were conducted under POTA, and they were subsequently sentenced under Section 20 of the Act. The proceedings against SIMI under POTA effectively made communal disharmony a punishable offence under POTA.

The Report of the Malimath Committee and the Fudging of Boundaries

With the Malimath Committee Report one sees the most explicit manifestation of the process of normalisation of the extraordinary. The Committee's recommendations, as its terms of reference indicate, intended to reform the criminal justice system so as to bring it 'in harmony with the aspirations of the people', which included, 'simplifying judicial procedures and practices', 'closer, faster, uncomplicated and inexpensive' delivery of justice to the common man, '… making the system simpler, faster, cheaper and people-friendly' and 'restoring the confidence of the common man' (*Report* 2003: 3–6).

Significantly, efforts at meeting the aspirations of the people show a distinct shift towards incorporating in ordinary law, legal–juridical principles and practices that are associated with extraordinary laws. Declaring at the outset, its dislike for a law that 'should sit limply' (while those who defied it went 'scot-free'), the *Report* sets out to make recommendations that allow the provisions that are specific to laws catering to extraordinary situations, and theoretically limited in their scope and temporality to creep into ordinary law. In the process, it not only makes a case for a reversal of the philosophical premises of criminal jurisprudence, but also suggests the inclusion in the Criminal Code, through amendments and additions, some of the most controversial and contested extraordinary procedures for crimes of 'ordinary nature'.

A direct offshoot of the proactive role for the judge envisaged by the Committee is the truncation of the 'Right to Silence' of the accused, guaranteed under Article 20(3) of the Constitution. This Right, the Committee felt, was an impediment in the quest for truth, as the accused in most cases, was 'the best' and 'critical source of information', which the judge was bound to tap (*Report* 2003: 267). It is interesting that this 'tapping' is envisaged as *a non-coercive* exercise despite the fact that the failure to answer in a convincing way is to be seen as an evidence of guilt, allowing the court to draw inverse reference against the accused. The inquisitorial role of the judge to elicit information from the accused is sought to be augmented by the Malimath Committee by bringing it in line with Section 27 of POTA that authorises the Special Court to take (from the accused) finger prints, foot prints, photographs, blood, saliva, semen, hair, voice sample, etc.

This induction of the inquisitorial role of the court is accompanied by recommendations enhancing the role of the police. Suggestions under the head 'Investigations' ask for the inclusion of provisions which are specific to extraordinary laws and have drawn criticism for circumscribing the right to life and liberty of citizens. The Committee recommends, for example, that 'Section 25 of the Evidence Act may be suitably amended on the lines of Section 32 of POTA, 2002 [so] that a confession recorded by the superintendent of police or officer above him and simultaneously audio/video recording is admissible in evidence subject to the condition that the accused was informed of his right to consult a lawyer' (*Report* 2003: 276).

In most trials under POTA, as well as some TADA judgements that have come recently, confession before the police have constituted the primary prosecution evidence and proof of guilt. It is significant that nowhere does the Committee express the slightest apprehension about abuse of powers by the police and the likelihood of the increase in custodial violence with the inclusion of this provision in the Criminal Code. On the contrary, the Committee goes a step further to expand police powers by suggesting an amendment in Section 167 of the Criminal Code, which fixes 90 days for the filing of chargesheet, failing which the accused is entitled to be released on bail. The modified section under the Committee's recommendation would empower the court to extend the same by a further period of 90 days 'if the court is satisfied that there was sufficient cause', in cases where the offence is punishable with imprisonment above seven years. This suggestion again seeks to bring the Criminal Code in line with the stringent bail conditions that exist in extraordinary laws like POTA (*Report* 2003: 275). Apart from confessions before a police officer, laws like POTA consider electronic interceptions as valid and reliable evidences under the Act. The Malimath Committee recommends that 'a suitable provision be made on the lines of Sections 36 to 48 of POTA, 2003 for interception of wired, electric or oral communication for prevention or detection of crime' (*Report* 2003: 276).

Terrorism and Organised Crime: Spot the difference

Before POTA was brought onto the statute books, debates surrounding it identified the failures of TADA to point out either the futility of anti-terror laws, or conversely, to work out a law that was more effective than TADA. The quest for *effective* law meant an imbrication with laws brought for dealing with organised crime. Subsequently, POTA came with extraordinary provisions that were hitherto part of acts like The Maharashtra Control of Organised Crime Act, 1999 (MCOCA) which boasted of 76 per cent conviction rate, as opposed to the paltry conviction rates in the ordinary law and the lapsed TADA. It may be pointed out that the provisions of the Act that made it *efficient* and a model for emulation were precisely the ones that also made it draconian and extraordinary. Significantly, these were provisions that were in focus in the debates in the joint sitting of Parliament on 26 March 2002, convened to consider the Prevention of Terrorism Bill after it was rejected by the Rajya Sabha.

NDA members consistently cited the success of MCOCA, especially its high conviction rate, pitting it against those arguing against the Bill on the ground that such laws are ineffective, as manifested in the abysmally low conviction rate under TADA which expired in 1995. The trappings of a tough law came from MCOCA, a law first enacted and applied in the state of Maharashtra, extended later to Delhi, and replicated in other states like Andhra Pradesh, Karnataka and Arunachal Pradesh, to deal with organised crime.

In the course of his speech initiating the motion for the consideration of POTA, the then Deputy Prime Minister and Minister for Home Affairs, Lal Krishna Advani declared:

> it is also true that one single provision which has been incorporated in MACOCA that intercepts or intercepted communication would be deemed admissible evidence, has changed the whole perspective....

In a replication of Sections 13 to 16 of MCOCA that authorised interception of wire, electronic or oral communication, POTA came with detailed provisions pertaining to interception of communication. Both MCOCA and POTA, through their relevant sections, lay down the procedure of authorisation, the appointment of competent authority to authorise interception, procedure of application for authorization, authority competent to carry out interception, protection of information collected and the procedure of submission of interception orders to a review committee.

The distinction between POTA and MCOCA, however, as emphasised in the debates in Parliament lay in the definition of 'organised crime':

> The definition of organised crime has nothing to do with the definition of terrorism. *These are two different concepts.* ... 'Organised crime' under MCOCA means 'any continuing unlawful activity by an individual'. *Before anything becomes an organised crime, the prosecution has to show*

continuing unlawful activity, which is also defined under the Act but there is no such definition under POTO because you do not have to do any continuing unlawful activity if you have to be a terrorist.[35]

While the concept of terrorism is indeed different from organised crime, the definitions of the two remain equally diffuse, leaving open possibilities of slippage. Even if the distinction made above was taken into account, there are ample grounds of slippage, permitting the use of the Act against 'terrorism'. Section 2(e) of MCOCA defines 'organised crime' as 'any continuing unlawful activity by an individual, singly or jointly, either as a member of an organised crime syndicate or on behalf of such syndicate, by use of violence or threat or intimidation or coercion, or other unlawful means, with the objective of gaining pecuniary benefits, or gaining undue economic or other advantage for himself or any other person or promoting insurgency'. Moreover, in its 'Statement of Object and Reasons', MCOCA includes in its fold—'terrorist gangs', 'narco-terrorism', 'cross-border connections and networks', directly facilitating its applicability in certain cases of 'terrorism': '... It is seen that the organised criminal syndicates make a common cause with terrorist gangs and foster narco-terrorism which extend beyond the national boundaries'.

A careful reading of a Supreme Court Judgement of 2002 in a TADA case (*Jayawant Dattatrya Suryarao v. State of Maharashtra*) is illustrative of how such overlapping may occur: the case involved an incident of shoot-out in Mumbai's J. J. Hospital campus on 12 September 1992. According to the prosecution:

> ... the accused persons *belonging to a criminal gang, engaged in organised crimes, extortion of money, smuggling, drug trafficking* and *eliminating or injuring persons* who do not follow their dictates, having made preparation, such as procuring sophisticated weapons like AK-47 rifles, pistols, revolvers, dynamites and hand grenades and by firing the shots through the said weapons, *committed murder of a person belonging to a rival gang* who was admitted in the hospital for undergoing treatment as well as two policemen who were on guard duty there.[36]

The five accused in the case were charged under Sections 3(1) [striking terror in the people, overawing the government] and 3(4) [harbouring terrorists] of TADA and Sections 302 (murder) and

212 (harbouring offender) of the IPC. The counsel for defence attempted to distinguish the offence of the accused from 'terrorist activities' questioning the appropriateness of the application of TADA: '... there is nothing on record that the accused intended to create any terror', 'at the most, intention to commit murder could be inferred', 'there was no question of creating any terror in the mind of the public at large'.[37] In their judgement, however, the judges held to the position that the offence amounted to 'terrorist activity' and TADA was indeed applicable in the case. The judges put forward the position that it is not possible to define 'terrorism' by precise words; what constituted terrorist activities had to be 'inferred from facts and circumstances of each case' since there would generally be no direct evidence [of terrorist activity].[38]

Thus, what could have also been construed as 'organised crime' under MCOCA, defined as 'use of violence', 'threat', 'intimidation', 'coercion', or 'other unlawful means' by 'mafia gang members' 'amounted to terrorist activity' in this particular case. The purpose of this discussion is to show that the possibility of one slipping into the other in specific cases is not remote.

Repealing POTA and Amending UAPA

MCOCA, we have argued, was largely seen as providing a modular template of efficiency for POTA, slipping into anti-terror laws, provisions that were part of laws dealing with organised crime. In this section we shall see how the repeal of POTA was accompanied by the importation of POTA provisions into the Unlawful Activities Prevention Act (UAPA) 1967, thereby giving permanence to measures that were brought in as temporary. On 21 September 2004, the President promulgated two ordinances, repealing POTA a month before it was to come up for legislative review, and amending the provisions of the UAPA 1967, respectively. In its winter session, both Houses of Parliament gave the ordinances their approval confirming the removal of POTA from the statute books and the replacement of UAPA 1967 by UAPA 2004. The simultaneous promulgation of both ordinances and their subsequent enactment have to be viewed against the immediate backdrop of UPA government's Common Minimum Programme (CMP) and the election promises by most of its constituent members, primarily the Congress, to repeal POTA. A careful reading of the promise to repeal POTA in the CMP shows that the UPA government also cautioned that it will not compromise with its fight against terrorism. It is no wonder then that the repeal of POTA came alongside the amendment of an existing law to include specific POTA provisions pertaining to the definition of terrorist activities and banning of terrorist organisations.

Considering that it was the first time that an anti-terror law was being repealed (TADA was allowed to lapse in 1995), by bringing the two ordinances together the government sought to send across the message of having kept its poll promise of repealing POTA, and at the same time of having adhered to the CMP that pledged both to repeal POTA and simultaneously strengthen 'an existing law' for a continued 'fight against terrorism'. It may be recalled here that the spectre of a 'legal vacuum' in dealing with terrorism had been raised persistently after TADA lapsed in 1995. The repeal of POTA alongside the passage of the UAPA 2004 (incorporating POTA provisions) has confirmed a dangerous trend: of making temporary and extraordinary measures part of the ordinary legal system, evident in the recommendations made by the Malimath Committee. The inclusion of extraordinary provisions into the ordinary law of the land not only gives permanence to measures that are otherwise brought as temporary measures to deal with specific situations, it also ends the periodic legislative review that extraordinary laws go through for their extension. The latter is important not only as a safeguard against an overbearing political executive but for democracy in general, because legislative reviews are expected to bring contested issues into the domain of public discussion and debate.[39]

A close reading of the CMP further shows that the basis of repeal of POTA is not because the UPA government thinks that the law is inherently undemocratic; rather, because the law has been 'misused'. The determining logic behind the repeal, therefore, appears to be that while the Act itself is fine, it has been, as the CMP says, 'grossly misused over the last two years'. This has led to a situation where POTA has been repealed but not rolled back, which is to say that while the Act may not be invoked anymore, cases already registered under the Act have been sustained and put through a time-bound review process. The short text of the Prevention of Terrorism (Repeal) Act, 2004 consists of two sections:

one specifying its title and commencement, and the other announcing the repeal of POTA 2002, along with four saving clauses. The saving clauses attempt to provide a way of dealing with the numerous POTA cases that have accumulated over its short span of life. This has led to a situation where while POTA has been repealed and most of its provisions done away with (reminiscent of TADA's life after death), cases under the Act have been sustained. An especially empowered Review Committee has been provided for, to identify *appropriate* POTA cases for continued trial. While the repeal of POTA has meant the elimination of the system of parallel justice that the Act had set up, the fact that the Act has not been repealed with retrospective effect has led to a situation where a new and complicated procedure will supplant the existing review process. The unfolding of POTA cases after its repeal has shown that irrespective of the review process under the provisions of the POTA Repeal Act, the fate of a POTA case would eventually be decided within the framework of the Act, which continues to live through existing cases.

A careful reading of the guidelines for dealing with the cases that have accumulated over POTA's short life span reveals two premises: one, laying down the *norm of continuity*, whereby punishment, liability, rights and privileges, as well as investigations and legal proceedings instituted under the Act would continue to apply in all POTA cases *as if the* Act *has not been repealed.* Two, Section 3 of the Repeal Act directs that the legal–judicial process set in motion in cases under POTA shall be *put on hold* until the Review Committee gives its approval. Under its new and enhanced powers, the Review Committee is entrusted with the task of *reviewing all cases registered under the Act*, to see whether or not a *prima facie* case for proceeding against the accused can be made, *whether or not an appeal for review has been made* to the Review Committee under Section 60(4) of the Act. The task of review has to be completed within a year. While reviewing cases, the Review Committee has the powers of a Civil Court, and can order the production of specific documents or requisition public records from any court or office. If the Review Committee feels that there is no *prima facie* case against the accused, then even if the court has taken cognisance, such cases shall be deemed to have been withdrawn. Similarly, cases that are still in the process of investigation shall be closed. Further, in cases in which trial has not begun, the Act provides that no court can take cognisance of an offence under the repealed POTA one year after the commencement of the Repeal Ordinance. Thus, while the repeal of POTA has meant the elimination of the system of parallel justice that the Act had set up, and the reinstatement of the due process laid down in the Criminal Procedure Code, 1973 in matters of arrests, bail, confessions, and burden of proof, the fact that the Act has not been rolled back, i.e., not repealed with retrospective effect, has led to a situation where a new and complicated procedure has supplanted the existing review process.

As discussed earlier, cases that still continue under the lapsed TADA have led to a situation where the Act lives after its death. With the continuity of cases under repealed POTA and the provision giving the Courts the power to take congnisance of offences under the Act for a year after repeal, a similar spectre of life after death presents itself. The unfolding of specific cases under POTA in different stages of investigation and trial continue to raise a quandary, which has deepened after the setting up of the Central Review Committee under the Repeal Act, opening up zones of contest. In the past, the high-profile cases of Vaiko and Raghuraj Pratap Singh *alias* Raja Bhaiyya have shown that trial and review procedures laid down in the Act have conflicted. Moreover, the state governments, the Central government, the Special Courts, the High Courts and the Supreme Court have figured in this conflict as contending parties. The tussle on the one hand, over the relative primacy of the executive and the judiciary, especially in cases which have gone beyond the stage of executive sanction for initiation of legal proceedings to trial under the law, and on the other hand, resistance by respective state governments against interference in 'their' POTA cases by the Central government, has continued to exist. The post-POTA repeal development in the Godhra case has shown that the decision of the Central Review Committee that no *prima facie* case under POTA existed against the accused, and that POTA charges against them should be dropped, has met with resistance. The Gujarat government rejected the observations and recommendations of the Central POTA Review Committee; and on 31 May 2005, the Special Public Prosecutor, while placing the opinion of the Central POTA Review Committee before the designated court in Ahmedabad, argued that the prosecutor was not compelled to agree with the findings of the Review Committee. Moreover, the primacy that the Central government had sought in matters pertaining to invocation and withdrawal of POTA in specific cases continued to be resisted, as the government's counsel reiterated the position that 'the review committee cannot interfere in the judicial process…. It can address the state government that the case is fit to be withdrawn and its role is limited only that far'.[40]

The Unlawful Activities Prevention Act, 2004: The Silent Erosion

As pointed out earlier, the promulgation of the Unlawful Activities Prevention Ordinance (UAPO) on 21 September 2004, alongside the POTA Repeal Ordinance, allowed the UPA government to obviate apprehensions of a legislative vacuum in dealing with terrorism following the repeal of POTA. The promulgation of UAPO, while easing the repeal of POTA, almost imperceptibly siphoned some of its extraordinary provisions into an existing law, making them permanent. At the same time, it also smothered periodic legislative review which was a substantive safeguard in temporary laws dealing with terrorism.

The UAPA 2004 substituted four new chapters (Chapters IV, V, VI, and VII) for Chapter IV of UAPA 1967 to include 'terrorist activities' alongside 'unlawful activities', specifying different procedures to deal with each. With this substitution, specific provisions of POTA pertaining to the definition, punishment and enhanced penalties for 'terrorist activities', and specific procedures including the banning of 'terrorist organisations' and interception of telephone and electronic communications were inducted into UAPA. The inclusion of POTA provisions pertaining to 'terrorist activities', and 'terrorist organisations' ensured that the amended UAPA like POTA and TADA before it replicated offences already listed under the ordinary law as 'terrorist'. The use of explosives, disruption of community life, and destruction of property are, for example, already punishable offences under the law. Similarly sedition and waging war are also offences under Sections 124-A and 121 of the Indian Penal Code. We may recall that POTA had replicated offences, which were already part of the UAPA, 1967. This replication ensured that a range of activities could be converted into terrorist crimes, subject to special procedures of investigation and trial, and enhanced punishment. The Parliament attack case showed that charges under ordinary law when augmented by charges under POTA brought them the maximum possible punishment (under POTA) in the Special POTA Court judgement. The augmentation or 'strengthening' of UAPA 1967 as UAPA 2004 has inversed the process whereby POTA has flowed into UAPA changing the character of the Act. Alongside the process of interlocking, which involved intermingling and knitting together of the ordinary and extraordinary laws at a specific moment, there can now be seen a trend whereby emergency provisions come to be incorporated into ordinary criminal law which then becomes the standard which future extraordinary laws must adhere to or surpass. Through a cyclical process of interlocking and strengthening, a standardisation of ordinary law takes place which not only softens people's sensibilities towards extraordinary laws, but also raises the threshold of extraordinariness.

The consequences of this strengthening and the standards made acceptable in ordinary law are not hard to gauge. Apart from the fact that the permanence given to extraordinary provisions have removed them from periodic legislative review, their induction into UAPA has not been accompanied by the induction of commensurate safeguards. Thus, whereas POTA provisions that were especially insidious viz., confessions to a police officer and the period of a police and judicial remand (before a bail could be given) have been dropped, the provision giving evidentiary value to telephone tapping has been retained, without the elaborate safeguards that were provided in the repealed POTA. What is to be especially noted is that unlike POTA, UAPA 2004 does not provide for a Review Committee under UAPA 2004 to see if, *prima facie*, a case under provisions pertaining to terrorist activities can be made out.

Apart from replication, the UAPA also comes with an innovation, i.e., extra-territoriality. A careful reading of the definition of terrorism in POTA and UAPA shows that the latter comes forth with provisions that show an enhanced scope for the territorial jurisdiction of the Act, extending the law to terrorism in foreign territories. The scope of terrorist activities is no longer confined to acts that strike terror or disrupt supplies of essential services, in the Indian people or in the territory of India, or done with the intention of 'compelling' the Government of India. In each case, 'terrorist activity' is widened to include people and life of the community in India *and* in any foreign country, and the Government of India *or* the government of a foreign country. This insertion of extra-territoriality may appear to suggest partnership in and a commitment to the United Nations resolution calling for international cooperation against 'global terrorism'. In actual practice, however, this is bound to affect the law of extradition and refugee protection.[41]

The process of replication and augmentation in the UAPA 2004 has, however, given rise to a strange contradiction within the Act. The UAPA 2004 imports the provisions prescribed in POTA for banning terrorist organisations, adding a separate chapter on 'terrorist organisations' and specifying the procedure for their banning. Thus, the UAPA (as amended now) has two different kinds of banning—a simple one for banning 'terrorist organisations' (imported from POTA), and a relatively complicated one for banning 'unlawful organisations' (persisting from UAPA 1967). This basically means that while banning an organisation for unlawful activities has inbuilt mechanisms of control, such safeguards are absent while banning an organisation as 'terrorist'. Considering the interlocking between the UAPA 1967 and POTA (as discussed in an earlier chapter where organisations banned as unlawful under UAPA came under the purview of Chapter III of POTA consisting of Sections 18 to 22 pertaining to offences relating to membership in terrorist organisation), it is likely that in future more organisations would be banned as terrorist than merely unlawful. Moreover, the procedure for de-notification of terrorist organisations as laid down in Section 19 of POTA and retained in UAPA 2004 (Sections 36–37) are equally tedious. It must also be noted that the provision of a Review Committee in UAPA 2004 under Section 37 is only for the purpose of de-notification of a terrorist organisation and not for the review of cases pertaining to 'terrorist activities'.

Conclusion

Democracy in India is rooted in liberal constitutionalism and the doctrines of rule of law are accepted as the guiding principles of government. The definition of extraordinary situations and the response to these situations through a separate set of laws are justified as *necessary* exceptions to the rule of law. Terrorism has provided the most plausible justification for enhancing the powers of the state through extraordinary laws. These laws greatly enhance the coercive powers of the State, which makes itself manifest in the daily lives of the people, effects changes in the structures of governance, and ushers in a politics of suspicion and distrust.

POTA, as stated at the outset, unfolded in a way so that competing visions of politics are marked out as antagonistic. The resolution it seeks is not through deliberation or recognition of difference, but through elimination and externalisation of difference. Extraordinary laws thus are manifestations of a politics of negation. Processes that prolong the lives of such laws, and procedural interlocking and intermeshing that seek to give them permanence are symptomatic of a deepening of the politics of negation. Thus, as the boundaries between the ordinary and extraordinary become blurred, the boundaries of suspicion and antagonism within society get ossified.

Anti-terror laws in India as elsewhere in the world have generally been associated with specific contingencies or circumstances that are presented as justification for the extraordinary procedures and enhanced penalties that the Acts sanction for crimes that are also punishable under the ordinary law of the land. The ongoing and proposed changes in the criminal justice system indicate a pattern whereby the coercive aspects of the State are being progressively strengthened. The arming of the State with greater powers of surveillance and control over citizens prepares the ground for authoritarianism, albeit through the democratic path. This pattern shows that a 'strong' State is not necessarily the outcome of an Army takeover. More dangerous perhaps is the donning of 'authoritative control' by the State, sustained by claims of preserving democracy and representing the will of the people. While the repeal of POTA is welcome, the UAPA by including POTA provisions has confirmed a dangerous trend of erosion— that of making temporary and extraordinary measures part of the ordinary legal system. The manner in which the repeal of POTA has been conceived, as well as the normalisation of 'extraordinary' situations and measures through their incorporation into ordinary law, is dangerous for democracy. They pose a permanent threat to the personal liberties of ordinary citizens and clear the way for an invasive, intrusive and hegemonic State.

Notes

1. The NDA alliance was led by the right wing Bharatiya Janata Party (BJP). The UPA, a coalition led by the Congress party formed the government with the support of the left parties. The left parties, however, remained outside the coalition government.
2. The Prevention of Terrorism Ordinance was promulgated on 24 October 2001 followed by the Second Ordinance on 30 December 2001. The Act to replace the Ordinance was passed in an extraordinary joint sitting of the two Houses of Parliament on 26 March 2002, after the Upper House (Rajya Sabha) representing the states, rejected it.
3. Within this framework, 'extraordinary situations' are seen as emerging due to the openness and freedom, which democracy allows. Through successive laws, this dilemma seems to have moved into an *impasse* where individual rights and human dignity are pitted against notions of national security, sovereignty and integrity.
4. The Committee on Reforms of the Criminal Justice System was constituted in November 2000 to identify areas for reform in the Criminal Justice System. The Committee started working in January 2001 and submitted its report on 21 April 2003 with 158 recommendations for changes in the Code of Criminal Procedure (CrPC) 1973, the Indian Evidence Act, 1872, and the Indian Penal Code (IPC), 1860.
5. For a detailed discussion of the theme, see Singh (2004a).
6. Unlike the Supreme Court and the High Court Judgements and orders which are published, the lower court judgements can only be procured through court registry.
7. *Ibid.*: 37. Emphasis added.
8. *Ibid.*
9. The case is commonly known as the Parliament attack case. On 13 December 2001, five armed men drove into the precincts of the Parliament House, killing nine members of the Parliament watch and ward staff and injuring 16 others, before they fell to the bullets of the security men. This attack was widely portrayed as an attack on Indian democracy. The investigation into the attack was handed over to the Special Cell of the Delhi Police on the day of the attack which implicated four persons: (1) Mohammad Afzal, a former JKLF militant who had surrendered in 1994, (2) his cousin Shaukat Hussain

Guru, (3) Shaukat's wife Afsan Guru (Navjot Sandhu before marriage), (4) S.A.R. Gilani, Lecturer of Arabic at the University of Delhi. In addition to the four accused there were three others charged in the case including Jaish-e-Mohammed chief Maulana Masood Azhar (who had been released by the NDA government in response to the hijacking of the Air India plane IC 814), Azhar's aids—Ghazi Baba and Tariq Ahmed. The latter were declared proclaimed offenders and were not part of the trial. The accused were tried under Sections 121 (Waging War), 121A (Conspiracy), 122 (Collecting arms, etc. to wage war), 123 (Concealing with intent to facilitate design to wage war), 302 (Murder), 307 (Attempt to murder) read with 120B (Death sentence for waging war). The charges under POTO (added later) pertained to Sections 3 (Punishment for terrorist acts), 4 (Possession of certain unauthorised arms), 5 (Enhanced penalties for contravening provisions or rules made under the Explosives Act 1884, Explosive Substances Act 1908, Inflammable Substances Act 1952, or the Arms Act 1959), 6 (Confiscation of proceeds of terrorism) and 20 (Offences dealing with membership of a terrorist organisation). The case was brought before a Special POTA Court in Patiala House, Delhi, under Justice S. N. Dhingra on 22 December 2001. The trial started on 8 July 2002 and continued on a daily basis. Arguments concluded on 18 November 2002; the conviction took place on 16 December 2002 and on 18 December three of the accused were sentenced to death, and the fourth (Afsan Guru) was given five years of rigorous imprisonment. After their conviction by the Special Court, the accused went on appeal to the High Court. The High Court gave its verdict on 29 October 2003, upholding the death sentence on Mohammad Afzal and Shaukat Hussain and enhanced their punishment under Section 121 of IPC. It exonerated S. A. R. Gilani and Afsan Guru. The Supreme Court Judgement delivered on 4 August 2005 (on the appeals by the prosecution and Shaukat Hussain and Mohammad Afzal against the exonerations and sentence respectively) dismissed the former, sustained Afzal's death sentence, and commuted Shaukat's death sentence to 10 years of rigorous imprisonment. The review petitions filed against the order by the Delhi police and Afzal were dismissed by the Supreme Court on 22 September 2005.

10. *Ibid.*: 3.
11. In this case, an explosion of a car bomb on 11 September 1993 near a place from where the car of the then President of the Indian Youth Congress (I) was passing, resulted in the death of nine persons and injury to several others. The investigations implicated five persons— all members of the Khalistan Liberation Front (KLF), in a conspiracy to assassinate the Youth Congress leader. Devender Pal Singh was

awarded the death sentence by the Designated TADA Court on 24 August 2001, which was upheld by the Supreme Court by 2:1 majority, in the above judgement. See *Supreme Court Cases* (2002: 978–1014).

12. Like POTA (Section 32), Section 15 of TADA permits certain confessions made to police officers to be taken into consideration. Unlike POTA, however, TADA allows under Section 21(c) that a confession made by a co-accused that the accused had committed the offence, shall be considered as 'Presumption as to offences under Section 3 (Punishment for terrorist acts)'.

13. *Devender Pal Singh v. State of NCT of Delhi, Supreme Court Cases* (2002: 978; emphasis added).

14. 'The Necessity for a Permanent Anti-Terrorist Law'. Working Paper on Legislation to Combat Terrorism, Annexure I. See Law Commission of India (2000: 32).

15. For a fuller exposition of this theme, see Balagopal (2000).

16. The political class is blamed in particular for not preventing the demise of TADA, in spite of the judiciary having upheld its constitutional validity (2000: 246).

17. *Ibid.*: 240.

18. *Ibid.*: 244.

19. 'Objects and Reasons', POTA 2002.

20. TADA Section 3: Punishment for terrorist acts: (1) Whoever with intent to overawe the government as by law established or to strike terror in the people or to alienate any section of the people of to adversely affect the harmony against different sections of the people does any act or thing by using bombs, dynamite or other explosive substances or firearms or other lethal weapons or poisons or noxious gases or other chemicals or by any other substances (whether biological or otherwise) of a hazardous nature in such a manner as to cause, or is likely to cause, death of, or injuries to, any person or persons or loss of, or damage to, or destruction of property or disruption of any supplies of services essential to the life of the community, or detains any person and threatens to kill or injure such persons in order to compel the government or any other person to do or abstain from doing any act, commits a terrorist act.

21. On 27 February 2002, coach S6 of the Sabarmati Express was burnt in Godhra, Gujarat, leading to the gruesome death of 59 persons, some of whom were 'karsevaks' returning from Ayodhya. This was followed immediately by a communal onslaught against Muslims in several districts of the state for over more than three months. The Godhra case is being investigated and tried under POTA, with 125 Muslims already chargesheeted. Significantly, the Review Committee, set up by the Central Government under the POTA Repeal

Act 2004, recommended to the Gujarat government that no *prima facie* case under POTA could be made in the case.

22. A confidential government order No. S.B.V/POTA/202003/477, dated 11 March 2003, Government of Gujarat, Home Department, Sachivalaya, Gandhinagar, authorised the Godhra Railway Police Station under Section 50 of POTA to carry on its investigations in ICR no. 9/2002 under the provisions of POTA. The grounds for invocation of POTA were that the accused, *with an intent to threaten the unity and integrity of India and to strike terror in the people*, had used 'inflammable substance' and 'lethal weapons', causing the death of 59 persons and injuries to 48 persons, 'damaged public property and disrupted essential services' like the movement of trains. The accused committed, thereby, a 'terrorist act' under the provision Section 3, sub clause 1(a) of POTA. The order elaborated that 'a criminal conspiracy was hatched' during two meetings held on the night of 26 February 2002 (*Terror by Proxy* 2003: 2).

23. The essential form of the two main codes of law—the Code of Criminal Procedure (1898) (amended in 1978) and the Indian Penal Code (1860)—drawn up during colonial rule, continue to operate in independent India. The Official Secrets Act of 1923 (an amendment in 1967 enhanced most of the offences punishable under the Act with greater sentences of imprisonment) and the Dramatic Performances Act (1876) are other examples. For a detailed study, see Banerjee (1991: 226–35).

24. Section 3(1), Defence of India Act (1962). Section 30(I)(b) dealt with preventive detention. The Act and the rules were modelled on the lines of the Defence of India Act, 1935. The Supreme Court declared the Act *intra vires* in the *Mohan Singh v. State of Punjab* case. *All India Reporter* (henceforth *AIR*), 1964, SC 381.

25. On 10 August 1970, the West Bengal government applied the Bengal Suppression of Terrorist Outrages Act of 1936—a colonial law used against the revolutionaries—giving the police extraordinary powers of arrest and detention for terrorist activities, possessing arms or literature propagating such thoughts. In November 1970, the Prevention of Violent Activities Act, directed towards debilitating the mass organization of the CPI(ML) and CPI(M) was promulgated.

26. On 7 May 1971, the President promulgated the Maintenance of Internal Security Ordinance, 1971. Two months later, the Parliament passed the Maintenance of Internal Security Act, 1971 which became effective from 2 July 1971, authorising the Central government to order the detention of a person, if satisfied, that such person is acting in a manner prejudicial to: (1) the defence of India, the relations of India with foreign powers, or the security of India, or (2) the security of the State or the maintenance of public order, or (3) the maintenance

of supplies and services essential to the community. See MISA, Section 3(I)(a).

27. *Additional District Magistrate, Jabalpur v. Shekhavat Shukla, AIR Manual*, 1979 (4th edn) SC 1207.

28. The Armed Forces (Special Powers) Regulation, 1958 was specifically promulgated in April 1958 to suppress the Naga movement. The Regulation gave special powers 'to officers of the armed forces in disturbed areas in the Kohima and Mokokchung districts of Naga Hills–Yuensang Area' while making the officers at the same time immune from 'prosecution, suit or other legal proceedings in any court of law' in respect of anything done in any part of Kohima or Mokokchung district of the Naga Hills–Tuensang Area with a retrospective effect from 23 December 1957. A similar act was passed for the states of Assam and Manipur (The Armed Forces (Assam and Manipur) Special Powers Act 1958 No. 28 of 1958 (11 September 1958). A legislation for disturbed areas was enacted for Punjab in December 1983 (The Punjab Disturbed Areas Act, 1983 amended in 1989) to put down the movement for a separate state.

29. The Bill introduced by the Janata Government on 24 December, 1977, sought to make detention without trial an integral part of the ordinary law by adding a 19 clause-chapter in the Code of Criminal Procedure, 1973.

30. See *Lawless Roads* (PUDR: 1993).

31. Ziya Us Salam, 'Caught in the Crossfire', *The Statesman*, 25 June 1999.

32. Talukdar (1999: 4).

33. 'Dawn of a New Life After Years of Struggle', *The Hindu*, 2 October 2001.

34. See *Trial of Errors* (2003: 4).

35. Kapil Sibal, responding to criticisms leveled at the Congress for its stand against POTA, while continuing the operation of MCOCA in Maharashtra (*Parliamentary Debates* 2002: 105; emphasis added).

36. *Supreme Court Cases* (2002: 898); emphasis added.

37. *Ibid.*: 924.

38. *Ibid.*: 925. For arguments given by judges in response to similar contentions by counsels of defence may be found in other cases, for example: *Hitendra Vishnu Thakur v. State of Maharashtra* SCC (Cri) 1087, and *Girdhari Parmanand Vadhava v. State of Maharashtra*, SCC (Cri) 159.

39. It must be remembered that POTA came with a provision that required that the Act be reviewed by the Parliament every three years. For TADA this period was two years. By inserting specific provisions of POTA into the amended UAPA, the government has managed to give permanence to these provisions. While POTA and TADA came up for periodic review before the legislature, opening

them to political debate and public scrutiny, the inclusion of POTA provisions in UAPA has removed them from such periodic scrutiny.

40. 'On Godhra, Gujarat rejects POTA review panel report', *Indian Express*, 10 June 2005.

41. In 2002, the Government of India deported several Nepali students and journalists to Nepal despite the fact that they were likely to be politically persecuted in their home country. The Delhi High Court upheld the deportation on the ground that the Indian government was simply exercising its legitimate sovereign authority. What it overlooked was the fact that under the extradition treaty with the Nepalese government, the Indian government was obliged to hand over all 'wanted' Nepalese to the Nepalese government, but it retained with it the right not to deport a person who was wanted for a political offence. The right not to be deported, of persons likely to face torture and political persecution in their home country, translates into a responsibility of the State to offer protection to such persons. This responsibility is augmented if read alongwith the convention of non-refoulement in Article 33(1) of the 1951 Convention on the Status of Refugees which states that 'no refugee should be returned to any country where he or she is likely to face persecution or torture'. While the Nepali students were not refugees in India, the fact that they would face persecution on their return to Nepal brought them under the purview of non-refoulement. With the inclusion of extra-territoriality, it would be easy to label an act as 'terrorist', filter it out of the category of political, and the protection it was thereby entitled to.

6

The Post-Communist Revolution in Russia and the Genesis of Representative Democracy

Artemy Magun

While many notions in contemporary politics stem from the early modern period or even from the Middle Ages and antiquity, the compound phrase 'representative democracy' was born at the end of the 18th century, during the course of the American Revolution. The system of representative democracy was then theorised and instituted during the French Revolution. Interestingly, in North America, it was Alexander Hamilton who first advanced the notion in 1777 (Podlech 1984: 525)—the same Hamilton who later, in *The Federalist Papers*, advocated limiting the new republic's democratic element. In France, Emmanuel Sieyès modified Rousseau's teaching and transferred the 'general will' to the nation's representatives, thus making it workable and tangible. Representative institutions had existed in the old regime: the king himself convoked the Estates-General, after all. Thus, Sieyès's main task was to supply them with a democratic, unitary, 'national' interpretation.

'Representative democracy' was an oxymoron at the moment of its emergence. Representation (especially, representation by election) had always been considered an aristocratic institution. Rousseau saw it as a 'modern'—that is, a medieval, feudal—form of government, linked to the institution of estates (Rousseau 1988: 95). Even for Locke, representation referred to the estates; for Hobbes and Bossuet, it referred to the incorporation of both God and society in the figure of the monarch. The model of Sieyès merged the two (contradictory) senses of representation: the representatives of the estates were to become a constituent power, representing the sovereign nation. Both terms in this oxymoronic formula point toward something else altogether—namely, to the contradiction in the phrase itself. Far from being 'sublated' since the term's initial appearance, the contradiction has been perpetuated and may at any time display either its restorationist–conservative or its radical utopian side. Furthermore, this formulaic tension is, in fact, a sign of an *event* that exceeds the concept. Simultaneously, the event opens up this internal contradiction, thus determining the tendency that will prevail for some time to come.

In general, one may argue that representative democracy as such is the creation of *revolution*. Revolution is an event in which a society turns against itself—a moment of internal conflict. It is also, however, an internal fold in which society aspires to constitute itself from within. The *re-* in 'representation' is of the same nature as the *re-* in 'revolution': both words refer to the internal *fold* in modern society, which, in its political structure, *turns* toward and against itself (Nancy 2002: 148). In this context, 'representative' democracy implies an ambivalent attitude to (direct) democracy: democratic politics proves wary of democracy as such. In fact, representative democracy may mean a restraint on democracy, as for Hamilton; or democratisation of a hitherto estates-based representation, as for Sieyès.

It has long been noted that the task of the revolution—the self-constitution of a State—is self-contradictory. By definition, revolution is ambivalent, allowing opposite interpretations. If any form of legitimacy comes into being only as a result of this self-constitution, who is entitled to constitute a new state? Who is the 'self'—the people, the nation—that must constitute itself before it even exists at all?[1] Will the old people constitute the new one, or will the new people retrospectively recreate their own origins? In *Qu'est-ce que le Tiers Etat*, written just before the French Revolution, during the elections to the Estates-General, Sieyès suggests solving this problem by distinguishing between the *constituent* power and the *constituted* power. The former does not have a legal status or form, but depends on a *fact*. This fact, however, is that of *representation*. If the deputies of the Third Estate have come to Paris from all over France, the rule by which they were elected or the legitimacy of their status is not that important. Therefore:

Whatever is the manner in which they are delegated, in which they assemble, and in which they deliberate—if one cannot ignore (and how could the nation that commissions them, ignore them?) that they act in virtue of an extraordinary commission of people, their common will shall mean (*vaudra*) the will of the nation itself (Sieyès 1970: 180–81; translation mine).[2]

The deputies do *represent* the *nation*, albeit imperfectly, and there are no formal criteria that apply in this case. The nation is, by definition, constituent and sovereign. It can give a constitution to a new republic, even through the few people who claim to represent it. Here, representation does not mean substitution or identity. Rather, it means the *fact* of the mere presence of the deputies, and the *event*, in which these delegates to the king become sovereign legislators. Any such emphasis on fact indicates a desire to suppress history, forget the past, and deal with the datum. There is then, paradoxically, something deeply revolutionary in the appeal to the fact. This kind of appeal should be distinguished from any notion of 'positivism', since here 'fact' means an eventful change of perspective—the possibility of what had been previously deemed impossible. (Hence, also, the oxymorons and paradoxes in revolutionary discourse, which thus conveys surprise.) Indeed, it has been shown that the very term 'revolution' in reference to a political turmoil was censored, in the 18th century, because it connoted a *fait accompli* (Rachum 1999). The moment that Louis XVI admitted, in his well-known exchange with the Duke de Liancourt, that the events of 14 July were a revolution, he actually admitted that they had *happened*.

Let me now turn to the facts of the anti-communist revolution in Russia. Russia's representative democracy was established not simply as a copy of the western model but as the result of a revolutionary development. One can argue, as I have elsewhere (Magun 2003a: 1; 2003b: 2; 2006) that the post-communist transformation in Russia was a *revolution* not only in name but also in essence.[3] Thus, its anthropological consequences—stagnation, melancholia, apathy, and internal struggle—closely resemble the situation in French society during the French Revolution (1789–99). These consequences follow from the primarily *negative* thrust of any revolution—the negative thrust that survives what it negates and turns the society against itself after its victory over a transcendent absolutist authority. The recent events in Russia draw our attention to a revolution's negativity, particularly because in the Russian case the revolution was almost purely negative, almost entirely non-productive. They even allow us to redefine the concept of revolution, retrospectively, as something that is focused not on the utopian breakthrough, but on the fundamental process of destroying and dissolving the old regime. This entirely negative process has its own substance and result because the negative energy remains even after its work is done. Thus, if Claude Lefort (Lefort 1988) has suggested that we view the results of the French Revolution as the void in the place of power that delegitimates any-one who holds it, we can add that, in the case of post-communist Russia, the delegitimation of power went even further, leading to the abandonment and disavowal of its 'place'.

I will now discuss the strange moment of this revolution—the transformation of Soviet representative bodies. In the 80s and 90s, the revival of the revolutionary democratic institution—the Soviets (councils)—at first played the role of the constituent power that would create the new regime. This revival ended in a disaster however: the Soviets buried themselves along with the new Russian revolutionary democracy. The revived Soviets became a representation of *protest* against the communist regime, an institutionalisation of the negative energy of the society. As such, they were truly democratic, but after their victory over the Party and a short period of political creativity, they reverted to the expression of protest and resistance, now against the politics of the Russian president and his government. An analysis of their short history is instructive, especially given the attention that the revolutionary councils or Soviets often receive as an alternative form of democratic representation (Arendt 1965: 232–75).

A Brief History of Soviets in Russia

The Soviet Union, as is widely known, maintained the institution of revolutionary councils or Soviets (which, however, had lost all real power to the Communist Party in the early 20s).[4] Soviets of workers' deputies first emerged in 1905, during the first Russian revolution, on the basis of strike committees, and they often took on the task of local self-government. Although the Soviets certainly had some roots in the communal culture of the Russian peasantry, no less important was the revolutionary reversal of a form that was created purposefully by the Moscow police.[5] In *Scenarios of Power*, Richard Wortman recounts how the Russian tsarist State created the workers councils as part of its project to unite the Tsar with the people and thus solve the social question from above. As Wortman writes:

> Finally, the police began to organise unions in the industries of Moscow. They arranged for elective district assemblies, and a workers council (*soviet*) for the entire city of Moscow. In the first years of the twentieth century the experiment of the police spread to other cities. Thus the tsarist administration, in resisting the appeal of revolutionary groups among proletariat, sanctioned workers' grievances and gave them their first lessons in political participation. (Wortman 2000: 370)

Obviously, this policy was based upon a corporate under-standing of society, as ultimately embodied in the Tsar—a model similar to the one that stimulated the medieval concept of repre-sentation.

In February 1917, when the second Russian revolution began, its leaders decided to reproduce these councils or Soviets. The newly founded Soviets of workers' and soldiers' deputies became an alternative centre of power to that formed by the former State *Duma* (the so-called Provisional Government). After a period of diarchy, the Bolshevik Party carried out a coup against the government in order to give 'All Power to the Soviets!' (*Vsia vlast Sovetam!*), as the slogan of the time encapsulated their aims. For a while, it seemed to many people, including the Bolsheviks themselves, that the Soviets were a viable form of democracy that could become the basis for a new workers' state. The Soviets were, in many ways, different from the regular 'parliamentary' type of representation. Unlike the parliaments, the Soviets were thought of as bearers of *all* power (in Russian, *vsevlastie*). In technical terms (that were not employed), this meant that they were *sovereign*. At the same time, only the deputies to local Soviets were directly elected. These Soviets sent their delegates to Congresses of Soviets. The system was built as a continuous chain of delegation whose foundation was based on direct democracy. The Congresses of Soviets did not work permanently but gathered several times a year. The rest of the time, a permanent organ formed from their ranks (the *ispolkom*, or executive committee) assumed the supreme (not just executive) power. All voting was open. Except for *ispolkom* members, deputies served in the Soviets on a non-professional, non-permanent basis.

Such an institution is clearly attractive not only because it emerges spontaneously and relies on the active segment of the people, but also because it provides a diffused continuity—not a hierarchy—in the relations between deputies and their electorates. Arendt suggests that the reason the Soviets failed was their involvement in actual management (Arendt 1965: 273). What doomed the Soviets more directly, however, was their organisational weakness. The irregularity of their meetings, the non-professional character of the members, and open voting made the Soviets easy to control and manipulate, particularly through their small but permanent *ispolkomy* (which were subordinate both to the Soviets and to the central government of the Russian Republic). The 'all-power' (*vsia vlast*) accumulated in the Soviets was used by the Bolsheviks to gradually establish the total, supreme power of their own party; they subsumed the Soviets to the Party's dictate. The 'Stalinist' constitution of 1936 introduced the secret ballot and direct elections to the so-called Supreme Soviet of the USSR. Soviets were now called 'Soviets of the working people' (*Sovety trudiashchikhsia*)—not Soviets of workers', peasants', and soldiers' deputies, as they had been before. The Congresses of the Soviets were abolished. But this step in the direction of 'parliamentarianism' simply meant that the Soviets had lost all their meaning as organs of power. In 1977, the new constitution renamed the Soviets once more: this time, as the *Sovety narodnykh deputatov* (Soviets of People's Deputies). This meant that the Soviet State went even further in absorbing the ideology of parliamentarianism—although, of course, nothing changed in the actual (decorative) functioning of the institution itself.

In 1988, as a part of his more general programme of democratising the socialist regime, Mikhail Gorbachev, the new general secretary of the CPSU, decided to revive this institution. He made elections competitive ensuring that votes were honestly counted. He forced the true power holders, the Party secretaries, to run in these elections, and he revived the Congress of People's Deputies (Shablinskiy 1997). Gorbachev and his liberal supporters also revived the slogan of 1917: 'All Power to the Soviets!' They strove, first, to revive the mobilisational energy of the October Revolution, and second, to bring the system closer to the Western political system, with its 'rule of law' (*pravovoe gosudarstvo*). The same slogan was then taken up as a weapon by the pro-Western deputies of the new Congress—this time to challenge the rule of the Communist Party itself.

The new system was clearly an attempt to create a Soviet analogue of the Western parliament. However, it preserved many features of the revolutionary (later powerless) Soviets: a huge, rarely convoked, unprofessional Congress; a mixed system of elections to the Congress (a portion of the deputies were chosen by 'social organisations'); the indirect election of a Supreme Soviet that met in permanent session; an imperative mandate with the right to recall deputies (*otzyv*); and, most importantly, an aspiration to the plenitude of power (Gorbachev's revival of the Leninist motto 'All Power to the Soviets!'). All of these features made the new Congress a classic example of a *constituent power*, although hardly a stable parliamentary body. As subsequent events showed, this constituent organ would not give up its sovereign power easily.

Ironically, Gorbachev's plan worked better, in a sense, than he could ever have imagined. The revived system of Soviets became a channel for expressing popular *anger*. This anger united the deputies—most of whom otherwise tended to focus on the problems of their home regions—in the good old tradition of estates-representation. The Congress, then, became truly democratic and truly representative of society: it not only represented its different groups but also aspired to constitute its political unity. TV coverage of the Congress provoked mass rallies in the downtowns of big cities and nationwide political mobilisation at all levels. Using the system of Soviets in the Russian Republic (reformed after the Soviet model), Boris Yeltsin, Gorbachev's reformist opponent, ultimately succeeded in rising to power and, after the failed August 1991 coup, in dissolving the Soviet Union and unseating Gorbachev. However, soon after this victory, there developed a conflict between Yeltsin and the Russian Supreme Soviet. The latter had broad authority under the constitution ('All Power!'). It used this authority to consolidate its power against the president and the economic and political reforms he advocated, trying instead to build a parliamentary republic and to unseat the president. In 1993, the country faced a situation of diarchy similar to the one that had developed between the Russian Soviets and the Provisional Government in 1917. The Supreme Soviet of the newly 'independent' Russia, and particularly its leader, Ruslan Khasbulatov, sometimes called themselves a 'parliament'. Sometimes, however, they emphasised that they were a 'soviet'. They, thus, tried to show the deeply national Russian roots of this institution (Khasbulatov 1993). However, the general line of the Congress and the Supreme Soviet was their reactive opposition to the reformist policies of the president and his government.

Yeltsin and his advisors blamed the conflict on the imperfect structure of the Soviets: inherited from the USSR; this structure did not fully correspond to the Western model of democracy. The pro-Western liberal media called for 'desovietisation', for a turn toward the 'normal' parliamentary system, and for the separation of powers: they thus interpreted the new democratic Soviets as the last trench of the 'old regime'. After a major clash between Yeltsin and the Congress of Soviets in 1993, which ended in the armed dissolution of the latter, a new constitution was approved by referendum on 12 December 1993. The system of Soviets was destroyed and a contemporary Western-type parliamentary system with very limited authority was erected in its place. Ironically, the lower house of the new parliament was called the State Duma, after the powerless government-controlled 'parliament' of the post-1905 period, which had been overthrown by the revolutionary Soviets. In the 1993 Russian constitution, many features of the Soviet system were suppressed: the very institution of the Congress itself; the non-professional status of most deputies; and the relative ease in revoking the mandate of a deputy who did not fulfil his promises. The new constitution created a professional parliament that was perhaps more efficient at making laws but much easier for the presidential administration and the government to control and bribe. Soon after the Duma began to meet, in 1994, the Yeltsin administration started a war in Chechnya, whose militarised, separatist regime had originally stemmed from the revolutionary democratic mobilisation of the *perestroika* era. As the new Russia evolved, the Duma was successfully subordinated to the president and transformed into a bureaucratic, lobbyist organ.

The Question of 'Spontaneity'

In *On Revolution*, Hannah Arendt criticised the classic concept of political representation for alienating and demobilising the subject. Instead, she pointed to the phenomenon of revolutionary councils, which 'spontaneously' emerged in all large European revolutions, particularly during the French Revolution of 1789–99 (the so-called Parisian sections), the Paris Commune of 1871, the Russian revolutions of 1905 and 1917, and the Hungarian Uprising of 1956. According to Arendt, the councils provide an opportunity for self-government that is not direct democracy but that preserves continuity among the levels of representation, or delegation, and thus stimulates active political participation.

In the Russian post-communist revolution, the democratic institutions emerged out of the Soviet communist regime's frozen, relict forms of representation. In the same way, the Soviets themselves emerged in 1905 out of artificial, police-inspired organs for achieving social consensus. Likewise, the actors of the French Revolution came to power via the Estates-General, a medieval form of representation. This paradoxical development allowed a diffused, network-like, mobilisational form of representation. The effect of this representation was largely *negative* and at times even paralyzing rather than constructive; this only means, however, that its primary function was to represent society's internal rupture. The *temporal knot* formed by this revolution of representatives indicates that we are dealing with a fold in which the society turns towards and against itself. As events developed, this form of representation was suppressed and replaced by parliamentary representation, which created an abrupt divide between the representatives and the represented. After this critical watershed in the 90s, political democracy in Russia has been limited and even minimal, since the balance between too much and too little democracy has not been attained (at least at present). One might claim, however, that revolutionary representation's potential for diffused resistance remains (as may be shown) a hidden ground of legitimacy for the regime.

For Arendt, the councils, or Soviets, were the truly revolutionary mode of government—an alternative to representation or a better species of it.[6] Arendt's councils are an analogue to what Sieyès called 'constituent power'—*the formless, pre-legal sovereign democratic authority that precedes the constitution and the government, and operates to create them.* Arendt chooses the Soviets because they provide a mode of signification based on contiguity—metonymy—rather than on metaphoric substitution. Similarly, Sieyès insists that the constituent representatives of the nation represent it simply by making its *part*, a part that just happened to be in the right place at the right time. Thus, neither the superior qualities of the representatives nor the procedures of the nation's 'reproduction' have any meaning. In French, this kind of 'partial' representation was indicated by the partitive form: *Il y a de la nation*. Clearly, partial representation is more democratic and more tightly linked to the specific situation (the event) that requires representation than is the procedure-bound election that aspires to reproduce society correctly.

In Arendt's account, the Soviets emerge 'spontaneously' (she repeats this word many times) through the 'organizational impulses of people themselves', in a climate of the 'swift disintegration of the old power' (Arendt 1965: 257).[7] For her, this means that in spite of the existing tradition of such councils, which dates to the Middle Ages, their emergence has never been planned in advance. But 'spontaneity' also implies unconditional freedom, creation *ex nihilo*; and this meaning seems to be important for Arendt as well, since she speaks of the 'miraculous' emergence of the Soviets. However, this accent on 'spontaneity' seems problematic in view of the critique of political subjectivity that Arendt powerfully develops in *The Human Condition* (Arendt 1958) and *On Revolution* (Arendt 1965). In *The Human Condition*, she argues against a view of the subject as author and owner of his actions, proposing instead the concept of action as *irruption* into the pre-existing chain of events. In *On Revolution*, she shows that revolutionaries face the paradoxical double task of (negative) destruction and (positive) foundation: this allows them to create a fleeting space of freedom that is difficult to permanently preserve. In many ways, deriving the revolutionary power from 'spontaneity' amounts to begging this paradoxical question and presenting the task of auto-constitution as a simple positive fact.

Arendt's apology of the Soviets has found a more recent follower in Antonio Negri, particularly as he develops his argument in *Insurgencies* (Negri 1999). For Negri, the Soviets are the only truly immanent political institutions: they synthesise political creativity with economic creativity (i.e., productive work) and destroy the juridical divide between State and civil society. Soviets are the constituent power in Sieyès's sense of the term, but a power that lasts continuously and does not disappear with the act of constitution. They are part of an alternative history of modernity, which is divided between emancipatory (immanent) and repressive (transcendent) currents that do not allow for any mediation between them. For Negri, as for Arendt, the Soviets are sites of true 'spontaneity', 'invention', and 'activity'. According to him, the working class 'invents' the Soviets in the course of the class struggle. Both Arendt and Negri thus transpose the fiction of an absolute beginning from the formal constituted power to the formless constituent power. History shows, however, that the organs of constituent power do not emerge from a void. They usually build, in one way or another, upon the already existing institutions of the old regime. It is simply that the meaning and function of those institutions are radically reversed.

The constituent power often emerges not out of nothing, then, but rather out of the representative institution of an autocratic regime subsequently overthrown by it. This was the case with the Estates-General in France, the Russian Soviets of 1905, and the degraded Soviets in the USSR. The turn to these institutions often appears to be a restorationist, archaic gesture, since they are clearly outmoded, no longer corresponding either to the absolutist state or to the bureaucratic communist regime, respectively.

There is much in common between the revolutionary workers councils and the estates-based representation of the *ancien régime*: semi-imperative mandates; the non-professional character of representatives; an indirect, chain-like structure of delegation; and the right of recall. While the French *Constituante* emerged directly from the Estates-General, the 'municipal revolution' that gave birth, among other things, to the Paris Commune also relied to a large extent on the *electors* to the Estates-General—a chain in the indirect mechanism of medieval representation (Furet and Richet 1973, 80–81). The Soviets of 1905 had their roots partly in the attempts of the police to incorporate and regulate the workers. Even in the year 1917–18, the Soviets were conceived as vehicles of estates—or class-based representation. The city Soviet was a council of 'soldiers and workers' since its members were elected proportionally only from these groups, in factories and army barracks. The All-Russia Congress of Soviets was also a congress of soldiers and workers, and the Soviets of the peasants formed their own congress. Only after the Bolshevik victory, and not without a struggle against the Socialist Revolutionary Party that had prevailed in most peasant Soviets, the Soviet congresses began to reunite the deputies of workers, soldiers, peasants, and Cossacks. Some ideologues of the 1993 Yeltsin constitution even call the Soviets an 'estates institution' (Shablinskiy 1997: 19), ignoring the constituent democratic function of these bodies. The institution of Soviets in the communist Soviet Union partly played the role of a king's court since it was a regular reunion of the country's elite, but it also gave deputies a real chance to address local, regional or professional problems that the country's leaders could be expected to resolve. In this latter sense, it was not all that different from estates-based institutions or other representative bodies in autocratic countries.

History shows that the estates and the councils can be transformed into each other. Both of them are alternatives to parliamentary representation with its mask-like substitution of the representative for the represented. Instead of this logic of substitution, estates and councils are based on a loose contiguity of delegation. However, the medieval estates are manifestations of complaint and protest, while the councils are organs of *rule*. The transformation of estates (or even ritualised communist Soviets) into revolutionary councils means that a negative and passive stance is converted into a positive, active one. This conversion is, however, easily reversed. What is important here is the very link between representation and the revolutionary *event* that changes (converts) its meaning to its opposite: a descendant model of power is turned into an ascendant model; an analytic representation of social groups into a 'synthetic' representation of unity; the passive representation of complaint and interest into the active representation of constitution and foundation.

The prefix *re-* in 'representation' designates opposition, repetition, and temporal reversal. Where there used to be an absolute, transcendent authority, now there is a *fold* or a *knot*—a site where self-government (or subjectivity) arrives at a temporalised paradox or aporia. Revolution—this is well demonstrated by Arendt (Arendt 1965: 45)—essentially implies a turn to the past, a will to 'restoration' that aspires to self-constitution but cannot help stopping and subverting the present by this very turn. Moreover, revolutionary representation generates a topsy-turvy world, a world stood on its head (this is Hegel's figure for the French Revolution; Hegel 1956: 447). This sense of a topsy-turvy world illustrates the resistance to representation or symbolisation implied by the revolutionary moment.

Conclusion

We thus need a historical concept of representative democracy, instead of a formalist, legalist concept. Democratic legitimacy is derived from revolution; it is therefore finite and historically concrete.[8] The formalist concept of representative democracy does not work because it is a logical contradiction, the site of an aporia (like many other modern political concepts such as natural law and popular sovereignty). Democratic legitimacy is based on the *event* of liberation, on a negation and, even, inversion of the past. (In the Russian case, this has meant imitating the West while at the same time drawing on our own liberating experience that repeats it.)

We cannot fully separate the positive, constructive side of representation from its negative, passive aspect. On the contrary, political power is acquired only through protest and resistance, which may (or may not) gradually crystallise into the structures of rule. The negative side of revolution precedes its positive side, and it therefore should not be disavowed or rejected. Thus, the 'spontaneity' that Arendt detects in the councils is intimately linked to the 'swift disintegration of the old power' (Arendt 1965: 257)—a link she shrewdly mentions but does not develop. In the earlier chapters of *On Revolution*, Arendt persuasively shows the clash of violent, destructive tendencies in the French Revolution with its creative, foundational aspects. The same was true of the Soviets. Thus, Oscar Anweiler speaks of their 'double function': self-government *and* continuous political work aimed at overthrowing the existing powers. Soviets were organs both of self-organisation and of political dissolution (Anweiler 1972: 68). After their victory, the Bolsheviks did not manage to undo the insurrectional essence of the Soviets, which led to the 1921 Kronstadt Rebellion and the suppression of the Soviets' independence.

It is important that democratic representation follows not only the *spatial* logic of gathering provincial deputies in the centre, but also the *temporal* logic of referring to a past (but not entirely past) event. Time is the sphere of loose, indeterminate, internal borders, which corresponds better to the representative model of councils than to the hierarchical representation of the parliamentary type. The reference to the past, which is inscribed in the revolutionary constitution of representative democracy, introduces a creative indeterminate asynchrony into this representation. For example, Yeltsin's clash with the Russian Supreme Soviet in 1993 was a clash of forces elected at two different moments in the development of the post-communist revolution. Unfortunately, the current Russian political regime has contrived to hold the legislative and presidential elections within half a year of each other, which facilitates the subordination of the Duma to a popular president.

The *form* of representation is never self-sufficient. The most wonderful institutions can reverse their meaning entirely; organs of democratic mobilisation can become instruments of hierarchical rule, and vice versa. Therefore, we should always keep an eye not only on the form but also on the *fact*. When one institution ceases to be democratic or representative, there may be another institution that is representative but not democratic; or there may be yet another, which is democratic but not politicised, which does not represent the unity of the country. In fact, there is need for both—democratising representation and representing democracy. Today's mass media are organs of representation and therefore of political power; in this sense, they are much stronger than most parliaments. Why not democratise them? And meanwhile, why not further politicise the Internet, which is already quite democratic? A fact can thus be constituent of representative democracy without being sufficient for its realisation, since it has yet to be *reoriented* through a revolutionary event.

Notes

1. On this question, see Arendt (1965: 161–64); Derrida (1984); and Honig (1991).
2. Similarly, Martin Nilsson notes that the ritual of purification and expulsion of the abject things not subject to sacrifice also does not require 'ideality of execution'. This act is truly constituent of the

society that affirms its limits through it. As such, it cannot follow a strict procedure (1964: 87). Cf. Iampolskii (2004: 698).

3. On the revolutionary essence of post-communism in Russia, see also Mau and Starodubrovskaya (2001); and Sogrin (1999).

4. On the history of the Soviets during the so-called Soviet period, see Korzhikhina (1995).

5. This is Alexander Skirda's argument in *Vol'naia Rus': ot veche do sovetov* (Skirda 2003). This book, an anarchist apology of the Soviets, is yet another attempt to construct an eventless continuity of political institutions throughout Russian history.

6. Arendt hesitates over whether to call the councils a form of representation or not. Thus, she actually speaks of the structure of councils as ultimately 'representing the whole country' (1965: 267).

7. Arendt derives her emphasis on 'spontaneity' from Oscar Anweiler— her main source on the history of Soviets (Anweiler 1958, rpt. 1972).

8. Jacques Derrida rightly notes that the question of representation is essentially tied to the constitution of a historical epoch, to its 'mission' and 'destiny' (1987). It is not by chance that for Sieyès, representation is also a matter of a particular *epoch* (1970: 178–79).

7

The Acts and Facts of Women's Autonomy in India

Paula Banerjee

Any discussion on women's autonomy in India has to begin with the 19th century because it was at this time that by a conjuncture of events the question of women's rights assumed centre stage in debates on social reforms both in England and India. Although social reformers recognised that something needed to be done to improve the condition of women in India, their actions were often not driven by any notion of gender justice or equality. That story is too well known for reiteration, but what needs to be remembered is that these debates led to some changes in the situation of women both in England and in India. More importantly, however, these debates led to the specific social construction of women primarily as members of a community than as individuals. This ensured that questions of women's autonomy were to be historically subsumed within religious and personal law. Thus they were hardly ever treated within a context of either individual rights or justice. Even to this time, women's autonomy remains hostage to personal and customary law.

This chapter addresses questions of women's autonomy in India and analyses its location within the legal discourse. Women's movement has primarily tried to analyse such questions through exploring women's position in law. Among other indicators, women's position in society is often analysed through marriage, divorce and property acts. This chapter seeks to analyse the evolution of these acts and to critique as to whether that has indeed led to women's autonomy or whether it has merely subsumed questions of autonomy, resulting in further marginalisation of women in polity. The chapter begins with the assumption that locations do matter and that laws affect different women differently, particularly in the context of India, where civil law is constantly pitted against personal and customary law. Therefore, to understand the situation of women in India, an understanding of the evolution of laws seems necessary, because laws are considered as primary markers of autonomy.

I

Discourses on women's autonomy have always remained associated with other discourses such as those on rights and representations because Indian society, even until the recent past, did not treat women as autonomous subjects. Therefore, legal provisions on women's rights and representations are some markers to understand women's position in the Indian society. The official discourse on Indian women in the post-colonial period is often shaped by the colonial discourse on Indian women and 'the way it entered into the nationalist discourse in the pre-independence period'.[1] To understand the colonial discourse we need to analyse some of the 'pro-women' enactments undertaken in the 19th century by social reformers, who were largely men. In the 19th century, gender was far from being marginal to the new world and was constantly being re-articulated through social reforms, beginning with the Abolition of the Sati and not running its course until the Age of Consent Bill in 1892.

It all started with the abolition of Sati in 1829 but that only affected Hindu women. Around the same time as the Abolition of Sati Act, there emerged a division between public law and personal law. It is said, 'public law was designed to encourage and safeguard the freedom of the individual in the marketplace, and was established by statutes, personal law was intended to *limit* the extent of freedom'.[2] Where women's issues were concerned, even statutory Acts were considered to be part of the personal realm. This is clearly revealed by the passage of the Indian Marriages Act. In 1864, the Indian Marriages Act was enacted but it scrupulously avoided any modification of the Hindu and Muslim personal laws, thereby creating procedures for Christian marriages alone. Other Acts such as the Hindu Widows Remarriage Act and the Age of Consent Act did affect notions of marriage, at least among the Hindus, but they made no effort to put issues of marriage within the realm of the civil. The Indian Succession Act of 1865 was one of the first efforts to systematise civil law in India. It declared that no person 'shall by marriage acquire any interest in the property of the person that he or she marries', thereby challenging husbands' right over their wives property but it did not stipulate any maintenance for the wives, which would later lead to the destitution of many women. Even this Act was not applicable to the Hindus, nor to Muslims, nor even to the Parsis who had a separate legislation for their community.

In the 1850s, the first divorce acts came into legal usage in England. Although the Bill was introduced because of pressures from women's groups, it treated men and women differently; women could obtain divorce only on grounds of 'aggravated' adultery and men needed to prove 'simple' adultery. The first Indian Divorce Act came into effect in 1869. The underlying reason for the enactment of this Act was not to ensure equality of sexes, but to make provisions so that marriages legalised in England can be dissolved in India if needed. It needs to be said that notions of equality of sexes had already appeared in political and legal discourses of the time. For example, Sir Henry Maine, who was one of the chief architects of these Acts, was said to have commented sarcastically of the Parsi partial civil code that allowed the daughters to inherit only one-fourth of what the sons were allowed to inherit. However, no effort was made to translate these sentiments into legal provisions for any community in India. Even the Age of Consent Bill that raised the marriageable age for women from 10 to 12 was severely criticised by Hindu leaders who considered it as a severe encroachment into their 'personal' domain, thereby relegating questions of women's autonomy into the domain of the personal, that later came to be defined as group rights.

Legislative Assembly Debates during the first half of the 20th century also concerned itself with discussions over the position of women. Both during the 1920s and 1930s, there were heated discussions over the situation of Hindu women in the Assembly debates. In 1939, two crucial bills in this regard were introduced. One of these was the Hindu Women's Right to Divorce Bill and the other was the resolution to set up a committee to investigate the position of women under existing laws. Discussions over both these resolutions portrayed how questions of women's autonomy were addressed. G.V. Deshmukh, who introduced both resolutions, was often at pains to explain that he had consulted the orthodox religious opinion. No one challenged the concept that for any legislation on women's position in society, the orthodox religious opinion needed to be not just addressed but consulted as well. There were others belonging to the orthodox opinion such as M. Ananthasayanam Ayyangar, who were totally against encouraging any changes in the lives of women. He, for instance, opposed wives receiving maintenance in the case of divorce because that meant they would be provided for even when they lived away from their husbands. In fact, he said that if wives lived away from their husbands even when their husbands meted out 'ill-treatment' he saw no reason for women being allowed to claim maintenance. He loudly complained that:

> So far as the wife is concerned, when does her right of maintenance accrue? It is only when she wants to live away from her husband that the question of maintenance comes in. Is there any Member of this House including the Leader of the House who is unconditionally prepared to allow any woman to live separately from her husband even though there may have been ill-treatment?... Therefore, all this is moonshine and let no ladies be tempted by it.[3]

There were some members even in the Congress party such as Bhulabhai Desai who were concerned that if position of women changed to any great extent it will result in chaos, as among the Parsi community, he claimed: 'recently, my friends, the Parsis, have gone just as far as they could and some 300 odd Parsi ladies who were waiting for it, got themselves divorced as soon as the Bill was passed'.[4] Therefore, most of the members were against any large-scale changes that might have substantive effects in the lives of women as individuals. Herein was the crux of the problem. Women were to be treated as part of their family or community, but not as individuals. Hence the Hindu Women's Right to Property Act of 1937 recognised the right of the widow, but not of the daughter because a daughter's community remained undecided as women largely belonged to the community that they married into. Even this concession was considered as extremely radical.

Therefore, the debate over the resolution for appointment of a committee that was meant to investigate the position of women soon changed the terms of reference and became a debate on the formation of a committee that would investigate only the legal position of women. Also, only Hindu women were to be their focus of investigation. These debates portrayed that any change in the situation of women could only be possible through legal means. That there can be other ways of addressing questions of women's position in society was never even considered. Further, such changes were never considered as part of women's rights. Finally, even the right to discuss changes in the position of women hardly ever included women's own voices; rather, it was considered to be a matter for the community leaders to debate upon. Therefore, in the official discourse women's autonomy was hardly ever discussed. The issue of women's autonomy was then subsumed within questions of legal change. Such changes, however, were imagined after the sanctity of marriage; integrity of religion and what was perceived of as stability of society were supposedly left intact.

II

The Constituent Assembly Debates 1948, addressed the question of women's autonomy by taking up questions regarding women's rights. Even while the Constitution was being formulated women's questions were being subsumed within the group questions. Women's issues were never seen independently of the issues of the community. The Hindu Code Bill envisaged major changes in the situation of Hindu women. When the Bill was introduced in the Constituent Assembly it was done so ostensibly to 'amend and codify certain branches of Hindu Law'.[5] The Bill dealt with those aspects that were usually taken up by the personal law and that particularly affected women's lives. It examined questions of succession, maintenance, marriage, divorce, adoption and guardianship among the Hindus. For the first time, the Bill suggested that married daughters should get half of what the sons were getting. According to B. R. Ambedkar, who proposed the Bill, the change 'which the Bill makes so far as the female heirs are concerned is that the number of female heirs recognised now is much larger than under either the *Mitakshara* or the *Dayabhaga*'.[6] Further, both the *Mitakshara* and the *Dayabhaga* discriminated against women on the basis of whether they were rich or poor and married or unmarried, which the present Bill was meant to do away with.

The Bill converted women's limited rights over her estate into her absolute possession. Until then the practice was that a woman could enjoy the profits of her estate in her lifetime but after her death it reverted back to her husband's family. This Bill, however, recognised that she had the same rights over an estate as other men and she could keep it or dispose of it. It abolished 'the right of reversioners to claim the property after the widow'.[7] The Bill also abolished caste as the basis of marriage and adoption. Most importantly, it recognised the principle of monogamy. It also made it possible for concubines to claim maintenance. Over the question of maintenance, it again raised the contentious issue of women's right to maintenance even if she lived away from her husband. While explaining this provision Ambedkar said:

> Generally, under the provisions of the Hindu law, a wife is not entitled to claim maintenance from her husband if she does not live with him in his house. The Bill, however, recognises that there are undoubtedly circumstances where if the wife has lived away from the husband, it must be for causes beyond her control and it would be wrong not to recognise the causes and deny her separate maintenance.[8]

Consequently the Bill provided that women were entitled to claim separate maintenance if their husband suffered from 'loathsome disease', if he kept a concubine, if he was guilty of cruelty, if he had abandoned her for over two years, if he converted to another religion and 'any other cause justifying her living separately'. This was, perhaps, the most far-reaching of all the measures suggested. As has been pointed out, even a decade before, wives' claim to maintenance, especially if they lived away from their husbands, raised virulent protests from many of the legislative assembly members. This Bill, however, was bold enough to not just take up the same question, but also move forward to claim that if a wife could justify her decision to live away from her husband, she had a right to do so and could claim maintenance. It recognised a woman's right to divorce on multiple grounds, including cruelty. As pointed out by Pattabhi Sitaramayya, the Bill was 'a progressive measure of reform, comprehensive in outlook, far-reaching in its result, radical in its nature … [as it] embraces the rights of women in regard to inheritance, in regard to marriage, in regard to property, in regard to divorce, in regard to personal freedom'.[9]

The women members of the Constituent Assembly were jubilant. Hansa Mehta encapsulated this mood in her speech by congratulating Ambedkar for bringing forward this Bill. She said that although the Uniform Civil Code abolished sex discrimination with regard to inheritance, it only gave the daughter half the share of the son. 'This violates the principle of equality on which we have again and again said that our new Constitution is going to be based'.[10] On the question of marriage she claimed to be gratified that the principle of monogamy was recognised: 'and if the Code comes into being then the principle of monogamy will be established'.[11] The women members of the Assembly, who were most affected by the Bill, clearly supported it but that was not reason enough to accept it.

Protest came first from the orthodox quarters and it raised a storm. Naziruddin Ahmad, who said he was speaking for some of his friends, was among the first people to start a virulent critique. It is interesting to note that Ahmad was not part of the Hindu community. He said he was opposed to the Bill as it was opposed by the 'the orthodox section of the community'. He clarified that he did not wish to 'spoil the cause of orthodox Hinduism'. The Hindus opposed women's right to inherit land because it would lead to fragmentation of land. It should be mentioned here that, in any case, agricultural land was outside the purview of this Bill. Ahmad ended his recriminations by saying that unlike the authors' aims of creating public opinion in favour of women's rights, legislation should rather follow public opinion, and not try to create it. He said that only 'some of the ultra-modern sections are behind it, but the masses, most of whom are ignorant, are indifferent to it'.[12] It has to be stressed that voices such as Naziruddin Ahmad's were not the exceptions but the norm. Not surprisingly then, the Bill was first sent to a select committee. On 31 August 1948, there was a motion to postpone the consideration of the Bill in the then current session. It was finally shelved and placed within the Directive Principles. According to Aparna Mahanta, the 'failure of the Indian state to provide a uniform civil code, consistent with its democratic secular and socialist declarations, further illustrates the modern state's accommodation of the traditional interests of a patriarchal society'.[13]

Even while fundamental rights were being discussed, there was a demand that discussing discrimination on the basis of sex was not necessary as women were presumed to be discriminated only as members of a certain community and not because of their gender. For the Congress party, right to equality was one of its long established platforms. The leadership had adopted a resolution during the Karachi Congress in March 1931 that there should be right to equality and non-discrimination for all. But during the Constituent Assembly Debates the same leadership consistently refused equality to women. This was nothing new. Even Gandhi, while promising equality to minority communities during the second session of the Indian Round Table Conference in October 1931, completely overlooked the situation of minority women by saying that personal laws of all these communities will be allowed to continue unchanged.[14] In the Constituent Assembly Debates, therefore, most of the orthodox members even while discussing the fundamental rights of men made sure that no mention may be made of 'sex'. It were the women members who insisted that where fundamental rights were concerned, the term 'man' could not stand in for both 'male' and 'female'. Hence, discrimination on the basis of 'sex' was barred by the Constitution. However, even this debate could not liberate the women's question from questions of community. Since the Constitution was recognised as the point of origin for post-colonial legal discourse, women's question remained hostage to questions of community.

It is interesting to note that the debate on status of women appeared in unprecedented forms during the Constituent Assembly Debates, and for a while it centred on Article 31 which focused on the question of people's right to livelihood. Article 31, clause (i) as proposed read: 'the citizens, men and women equally (should), have an adequate means of livelihood'. The first amendment that was suggested was that 'men and women equally are unnecessary and redundant'. When the member proposing this amendment was questioned as to why he thought the clause was unnecessary he replied, 'the masculine, as it is well-known, embraces the feminine'. He went on to explain that 'if we are to make it clear that any law shall apply to men and women equally and if we are forced to declare it everywhere, then this expression has got to be used unnecessarily in many places'.[15] In answer to such declarations, even well-known leaders such as Mahavir Tyagi said that what the amendment proposed was merely an 'improvement in language or change in words'.[16] Although Ambedkar opposed the amendment, Tyagi asserted that the amendment was actually about semantics, thus, disregarding the political implications of such rhetoric. Such disregard for issues central to women often cuts across religious and ethnic lines. This was made clear during the debate on the Hindu Code when it was decided to be placed in the list of Directive Principles ensuring that it would probably never see the light of the day even though, as pointed out earlier, Rajkumari Amrit Kaur and Hansa Mehta supported it vociferously. The Constituent Assembly Debates then has maintained the tradition of ignoring women's voices when women's issues are being discussed.

The Indian State's attitude to women was further revealed over the question of abducted women. The partition of the Indian subcontinent in 1947 witnessed probably the largest refugee movement in modern history. About eight million Hindus and Sikhs left Pakistan to resettle in India while about six to seven million Muslims relocated to Pakistan. Such a transfer of population was accompanied by horrific violence. Some 50,000 Muslim women in India and 33,000 non-Muslim women in Pakistan were abducted, abandoned or separated from their families.[17] Women's experiences of migration, abduction and destitution during partition, and the State's responses to it is a marker of the relationship between women's position as marginal participants in state politics and gender subordination as perpetrated by the State. In this context, the experiences of abducted women and their often forcible repatriation by the State assumes enormous importance today.

The two states of India and Pakistan embarked on a massive Central Recovery Project during which about 30,000 women were recovered by their respective states. Some incidents relating to these abducted women exemplify the politics of gender during partition. Even when the two countries decided on little else they decided that the abducted women must be restored to their families. Problems arose over the process and progress of recovery. An Abducted Persons (Recovery and Restoration) Bill was brought in the Indian Parliament. Boys below the age of 16 and women of all ages were brought under the jurisdiction of this Bill that gave unlimited power to police officers with regards to abducted persons. If a police officer detained any woman, under this Bill the officer could not be questioned in any court of law. What such a situation meant was that the women themselves lost the agency over their own person. Their voices were often not heard, and when heard not taken into cognisance. Although numerous amendments were proposed in the House, the Bill was passed unchanged on 19 December 1949.[18]

According to Rameshwari Nehru, Adviser to Government of India, Ministry of Rehabilitation, many abducted women showed extreme unwillingness to leave their 'captors'.[19] Ritu Menon and Kamla Bhasin observe that women were:

> abducted as Hindus, converted and married as Muslims, recovered as Hindus but required to relinquish their children because they were born of Muslim fathers, and disowned as 'unpure' and ineligible for marriage within their erstwhile family and community, their identities were in a continuous state of construction and reconstruction, making of them... 'permanent refugees'.[20]

These women were forcibly repatriated though refused rehabilitation by their families. The reason for such forcible repatriation lies in the attitude of the young Indian State towards its women.

Many explanations are given for this forcible repatriation of women. Menon and Bhasin point out how national honour was bound to women's bodies. Even Jan Jindy Pettman reconfirms the crucial issue of how repatriation was made a nationalist project because women's bodies became markers of male honour. As in any other nationalism, women's bodies became 'part of other people's agendas'.[21] India made claims of moral superiority over Pakistan or the *other*, and this claim was based on the State's ability to protect/control female bodies. This control was essential for the self-definition of the male identity that was in a state of crisis. Recent feminist research has demonstrated how 'citizen' is a gendered category by examining how women are treated unequally by most states, especially post-colonial states, even though most of these states give constitutional guarantee for women's equality.[22]

Abducted women were not considered as legal entities with political and constitutional rights. All choices were denied to them and while the state patronised them verbally by portraying their 'need' for protection, it also infantilised them by giving the decision-making power to their guardians who were defined in the Act by the male pronoun 'he'. By insisting that the abducted women could not represent themselves and had to be represented, the State marginalised them from the decision-making process and made them non-participants. For the abducted, it was their sexuality that threatened their security and the honour of the nation. Thus, their vulnerability was perceived to be rooted to their bodies. Their bodies made all women susceptible to such threats and so they had to be protected/controlled. By denying agency to the abducted women, the State made it conceivable to deny agency to all women under the guise of protecting them. This Act, therefore, frontally challenged the notion of women's autonomy. It has to be remembered that the Act was passed in 1949, by when the needs of designing correctives for women's vulnerability to abduction had all but disappeared. This Act therefore was more a mechanism to control women rather than to protect them. In fact, the family of these women often refused to accept the forcibly repatriated women, but still they had to be brought back. What was repeatedly stressed was that women belonged to their family, the kin, and the nation but never to their own person. In the context of increasing women's militancy and activism in Tebhaga, Telengana and their further assertions of person-hood in the Constituent Assembly Debates, this Act was necessary to symbolise their subject position, and not just challenge but summarily deny their growing expectations of autonomy.

III

The Abducted Persons Act remained in operation until 1956. The State's initial actions against any recognition of women as equal partners in state-formation and then granting these women some legal correctives seem to have contained women's activism for a long time. The militancy that was visible in the working women's movement and the Tebhaga and Telengana movements remained a thing of the past, and the legal correctives reiterated women's social positioning as wives and mothers. These legal correctives or measures did not go beyond what one analyst calls the 'typecasting

[of] women as wombs to bring forth babies, lips to utter sweet nothings, and laps to cuddle infants'.[23] The Hindu Law Code contained in it the Hindu Succession Act came into force in 1954–56. This Act stated that, 'property of the intestate shall be divided among the heirs .... The intestate's widow, or if there are more than one, all the widows together, shall take one share. The surviving sons and daughters and the mother of the intestate shall each take one share'.[24] For the first time, the Act recognised the daughter's right to inherit parental property.

Soon however, motions were on to curtail women's right to inherit agricultural land particularly in Punjab, the agricultural heartland of India. Many women leaders met the Chief Minister of Punjab to press their views against such a measure. Likewise, the Hindu Marriage Act, 1955 gave women and men equal right to divorce on such grounds as adultery, but the implementation of this Act remained skewed. Also, not all Indian women were beneficiaries of this Act, and women from other communities remained under their own personal laws. For example, Muslim women continued to be guided by Shariat Laws of 1939 that decreed that women cannot inherit agricultural land. Even legal correctives could not change women's marginal position in society and there was rampant social discrimination. For example, in The Special Marriage Act, 1956 both husbands and wives were given equal rights to divorce on the ground of cruelty, but in its implementation the courts did nothing to revise the patriarchal paradigm of a 'good wife'.

According to one observer:

> The recognition of cruelty as a ground for divorce was significant as it expanded the grounds on which women and men could exit from a difficult marriage. However, the courts have interpreted this ground against the norm of familial ideology. When applied to women, this amounts to a moral evaluation of her conduct, and whether it conforms to the norm of a good mother and wife. A wife who fails to perform her marital obligations, which are primarily concerned with caring for and obliging her husband, is vulnerable to a charge of cruelty.[25]

Women also could not effectively challenge the paradigm created by the state of a *good woman* until much later. That The Hindu Law Code did not in any way challenge that paradigm is evident from the new educational policy set up by the Government of India under a National Committee on women's education in 1959. This Committee argued that the courses likely to interest women were home science, music, drawing, painting, nursing, etc. As such, these were no different from the courses stressed in the 1930s when the main role for women was seen to be makers of good homes by the colonialists and as helpmates to their husbands by the nationalists. The new laws in no way gave women equity. Their biased implementation also portrayed that as long as women's rights remained hostage to community rights it could easily be subverted. The only way out was to rescue women's rights from being placed in opposition to group rights; but as yet women's groups had not developed strategies whereby women's rights could be negotiated not in opposition but in tandem with other rights such as minority rights or ethnic rights.

The Citizenship Act of 1955 dramatically reiterated the male-centrism of the Indian project of state-formation. As its title suggests, the Act dealt with modes of acquiring, renunciation, termination and deprivation of citizenship. Although the Act was meant to give rise to the category of universal citizen, in reality, it did not. It continued the gender dichotomy evolved by the colonial state. The section on citizenship by registration stated that 'women who are, or have been, married to citizens of India', were to be given citizenship if they applied for it. No such stipulations were made for men marrying women who were Indian citizens. Thus, citizenship by registration was largely transferred through the male line. In the section on the termination of citizenship, it was stated that where a male person 'ceases to be a citizen of India under sub-section (1), every minor child of that person shall there-upon cease to be a citizen of India'.[26] This reiterated that citizenship was transferable largely through the male line giving women a second class citizenship. Although in later acts women could transfer citizenship rights to their spouses and to their children, it did not alter the 'maleness' of Indian State as conceived in the formative years. This Act also entrenched women's location within essentially patriarchal sites such as the family or the community. The one thing that the State consistently refused to consider was a Uniform Civil Code that could have challenged women's location within a kin and a community. Therefore, demands for women's autonomy were successfully contained by the State until the 1970s when these demands resurfaced. The context was both internal and international.

The United Nations declared the decade 1975–85 for women, and Indian women activists found the occasion to explore the actual situation of women in India. They soon confronted the fact that despite legal victories over the years, political, economic and social disparities between men and women had continued. There was extensive evidence of increasing violence against women despite such measures as the amended Factory and Mines Act of 1953 and The Dowry Prohibition Act, 1961 and its amendment in 1964. These gaps between women's formal legal rights and their substantive inequality in practice could no longer remain unnoticed. Dowry deaths continued unabated, and there was no evidence that violence against women had in any way diminished. The Towards Equality Report of 1975 dramatically brought women's marginalisation in society to popular perception. It was made clear that women's political and socio-economic inequalities persisted in the face of a broad range of legislation intended to improve women's status. As a result of these developments, the Equal Remuneration Act, 1976 was passed. Even these legislations, however, proved that changes in women's lives could be made only up to a point. That legislation might also be a double-edged sword was further portrayed by events following the Shah Bano Case.

Shah Bano aged 73 was divorced by her husband after 40 years of marriage. She filed a petition for maintenance from her husband under Section 125 of the Criminal Procedure Code of 1973. In April 1985, the Supreme Court held that she was entitled to a maintenance of Rs. 179.20 per month. This judgement created a furore in the country. For Shah Bano, the victory came after 10 long years of struggle. Shah Bano was not the first Muslim woman to apply for and be granted maintenance under the Criminal Code 1973. But, the repercussions of this judgement surpassed any other perhaps because the Supreme Court called for the enactment of a Uniform Civil Code. When some by-elections took place in December 1985, a sizeable Muslim vote that traditionally voted in favour of Congress-I, turned against it. From Kishengunj Constituency, the Muslim candidate Syed Shahbuddin of the opposition came to power. Soon an independent Muslim Member of Parliament introduced a Bill to 'save Muslim Personal Law'.[27] The Congress-I, which was the ruling party, issued a whip to ensure the passage of the Bill. The women's movement and a section of Muslims vigorously campaigned against the Bill. The Hindu right-wing also campaigned against it. 'The government, initially supportive of the Supreme Court decisions, reversed its position, and supported the enactment of the Muslim Women's (Protection of Rights on Divorce) Act in May 1986, which provides that Section 125 of the Criminal Procedure Code does not apply to divorced Muslim women'.[28]

The Shah Bano Case strongly brought forth the question of the sanctity of Personal Law. A Member of Parliament in the Lok Sabha during the initial debate argued that since this issue pertains to Muslim religion, 'only a Muslim judge should decide such cases because in such cases only a Muslim have the right to do *iztihad*, that is, the right to give opinion where there is a conflict between the order of the law and that of the Prophet'.[29] Such claims asserted that the right of the cultural/religious community was greater than the political community. Meanwhile, in a dramatic turn around even Shah Bano dissociated herself from the Court judgement. She proclaimed 'I, Shah Bano, being a Muslim reject it (the Supreme Court judgement) and dissociate myself from every judgement which is contrary to the Islamic *Shariat*'.[30] Her rejection of the Supreme Court judgement symbolised women's capitulation to the cultural community when arrayed against patriarchal forces that work across cultural and political communities. In a recent interview, Sona Khan who acted as Shah Bano's lawyer commented that 'one cannot make a Shah Bano of a rich woman. It is only the poor and uneducated that get taken in by what religious fundamentalists say. Also, it is not fair to criticise the discriminatory personal laws of one community while discriminatory laws of other communities are not paid attention to'.[31] Women's apprehensions that the new law was retrogressive proved correct the next year. The Minister for Social Welfare, Rajendra Kumari Bajpai reported in March 1987, that the Wakf Board did not grant maintenance to a single woman in India in 1986.[32] But yet the controversy helped the women to organise themselves into a movement as never before. The motion that was started by the *Towards Equality Report* gathered momentum because of the Shah Bano Case. This can be gleaned from the debates led by women Members of the Parliament exactly at the time when the Shah Bano Case was on.

It all started with the Lok Sabha Debates on 'Progress of Indian Women in Social, Educational, Political and Economic Fields in the International Women's Decade'. This Debate created an occasion for the women members to place before the apex law-making body of the State the situation of women in India. It was revealed that the number of illiterate women in India increased from 215.3 million in 1971 to 241.6 million in 1981.[33] The number of women cultivators was in the decline and women agricultural labourers on the increase, proving that land was progressively being taken away from the hands of women. In India, although 'more boys are born than girls but more girls die than boys and the expectation of life is lower for girls. The death rates of females particularly in the age group of 0 to 4 is much higher'.[34] More girls suffer from malnutrition than boys. Members also pointed out that the 'number of women workers is decreasing every year', even in traditionally women-dominated industries such as cashew, tobacco, bidi, matches, tea, etc.[35] In jute and textile industries, 30 to 60 per cent women workers were displaced.[36] In India, it was said, 43.5 per cent of all marriages were marriages of girl children. Also, members reported the link between 'commercialisation of agriculture and nutrition deprivation of females'.[37] This was perhaps the first time that there was an effort to make a holistic audit of women's position in society in the Indian Parliament. Even the legal status of women came under fire. Women activists felt that within the Indian context the 'main problem is that there (are) many laws but women are dominated not by secular laws, not by uniform civil laws but by religious laws'.[38] Thus even before the controversy over the Muslim Women's (Protection of Rights on Divorce) Act, 1986 women had identified personal laws as a problem for women's empowerment.

With the Shah Bano Case, another insidious trend was noticeable that entrenched women within their own communities. While the debate over Muslim Personal Law was continuing, there were calls from some women candidates such as Abida Ahmed who argued that the 'Government should frame a law which should prohibit interference with Personal Law time and again and may end the disturbed atmosphere that has been created in various quarters as a result of the Shah Bano Case'.[39] Leaders such as Jaffar Sharief even argued that 'today, in the Shah Bano's Case, I am finding that many people are more sympathetic towards Muslim women than for *their own women*. This is very very strange'.[40] The whole question of women's rights was subsumed within the question of group rights. It became a question of 'our women' versus 'their women'. Once again, the State failed to protect women's rights and capitulated to the patriarchal definition of women being part of their communities.

In fact, the State played a partisan role in this controversy. While debating on the Muslim Women's (Protection of Rights on Divorce) Act 1986, in the Lok Sabha, the Congress government clearly took the side of Muslim orthodoxy against women's rights. Instead of advocating neutrality in matters of religion, the law minister, in one of the debates dwelt at length on the equality of all religion in the political lives of citizens. He said: 'Tolerance of diversity and differences should be the hallmark of governance in a multi-cultural society. Secularism demands that everybody should not be tarred with the same brush'.[41] The upshot of all this meant that women's rights were to be guided by personal law that often reflected the views of the orthodoxy. As Zoya Hasan contends, 'Women's status was a very secondary consideration in government policy'.[42] The government rather wanted to appease the Muslim leadership who were largely against the Supreme Court verdict. In the process, the government once again portrayed that women's lives were to be guided by their own communities. Hence the position of the government echoed that of the All India Muslim Personal Law Board. The politicisation of the question led to a realignment of politics. The left and the Hindu right were aligned together and the Congress and the Muslim conservatives were on the other side. No one paid heed to what the women's movement was seeking to convey. Maintenance became a matter of compensation and not part of women's rights as such. Gender justice and equal rights for women once again became a victim of rights of communities where women were placed by the State. The new political realignments reflected that patriarchal forces cut across party politics where women's self-definition was consistently marginalised. Movements for women's autonomy once again centred on parliamentary reforms, which due to a number of new legislation had become one of the most contested sites for the issue of women's rights.

Demands for the reservation of seats for women began in the early 1970s and culminated in the 1980s. According to one observer, 'Ramkrishna Hegde's government in Karnataka started the process in 1983 before Central legislation mandating representation for women was passed. It provided for 25 per cent reservation for women at village panchayat levels. This was before any powerful women's lobby emerged in Karnataka to press for this move'.[43] After the Shah Bano Case, women within political parties seized on the issue of representation as the only way to change the situation of women. A backlash against the women's movement seemed to be imminent.

That a backlash against demands of the women's movement was imminent was portrayed by the legislation on the family courts. The Family Courts Act, which was passed in 1984, was a procedural statute that carved out separate and innovative adjudications for family disputes. The Act shifted matrimonial litigations from the district courts and maintenance litigations from magistrates' courts to family courts. Ironically however, the principle of gender justice, which was the primary motivation of the women's rights movement for the demand for special courts for family matters, was not clearly spelt out in the enactment. Instead the Act emphasised on the preservation of the family as its primary aim and intent for the enactment. In a study on the workings of family courts in West Bengal, noted women's rights activist and lawyer Flavia Agnes commented:

> The primary concern of the campaigns seems to have been lost at the official level, in the process of transforming the demand from a campaign into an enactment. An impression seemed to have been conveyed to all official functionaries that 'preservation of the family' is synonymous to 'protection of women's rights'. Legislative history of matrimonial law, however, is counter to this premise.[44]

The workings of the family courts portray the lack of state priority given to such instruments which are meant to improve women's access to justice.

The Family Courts Act proved to be the writing on the wall that was slowly becoming visible. However, one of the first legislative instruments for the protection of women's rights in the early 1990s was indeed progressive. This was the 73rd Amendment of 1992 that reserved 33 per cent seats for women at the Panchayat level. This led to the introduction of the September 1996 Bill that called for the reservation of one-third seats for women in the Parliament. Debates over this issue continue even until today. Women's demand for equitable representation started with the *Towards Equality Report*. The *Nairobi Declarations* in 1985 also called for increased representation for women. Therefore, the 73rd Amendment responded to women's long-standing demands for representation. The question of representation became one of the important demands for the women's movement too. Once the 73rd Amendment was passed, however, women's movement felt a severe backlash that had been present in the horizon from the 1980s onwards. The ostensible reason was the view that only the female relatives of political leaders benefited by reservations made in the 73rd Amendment. Hence, few states embraced this Amendment. States such as Meghalaya, where there are overwhelming numbers of matrilineal tribes have not embraced this Amendment as yet. In other states it took years to take action on this Amendment. In a recent Action Aid project that presents the case of Assam one researcher comments 'although 73rd and 74th Amendment ensures political voice to women, autonomy [for women] or independent decision-making is still a far cry'. She is of the opinion that it has neither led to a more gendered analysis of the issues confronting government and nor has it increased the profile of women's needs in the political agenda of the state. She, however, agrees that the sheer number of women in the formal political space contains within it potential for change that is as yet unrealised.[45] The reason for this lies in State's attitude to women in general and women's socio-economic position within the society in particular.

Even on other issues regarding women's rights, the backlash was increasingly being felt. The family court system became a victim of this backlash. There was little initiative to implement the Family Courts Act. A recent report portrays that even in a 'progressive state' such as West Bengal there are only two such family courts today and the budget allocation for such courts is a paltry sum of Rs. 14,88,000. In 2003, there were 6390 cases of matrimonial litigation of which family courts handled only 270.[46] The capacity of these courts to provide speedy redress to women is now being questioned.

The backlash against activism for women's rights caused the majoritarian women's movement, which was substantially weakened by legislative reversals due to the controversy generated by the Uniform Civil Code, to all but dissipate. Women's resistance to patriarchal systems in India did not end with this; instead it found newer avenues, but law was no longer the most important of these.

IV

This chapter was intended to discuss how the Indian State on the one hand has legislated towards the enhancement of women's autonomy, yet on the other hand has whittled away from women's autonomy because of their reliance on religious dictums and paradoxically also on dictums of modernisation that continued to locate women within patriarchal groupings. In the process, women's autonomy though often sanctioned by law remained a distant and an ambivalent dream in reality. By exploring how a process that had its origin in the colonial times continued to be sanctioned by the Constitution (that is, women's location within the personal realm and not within the civic), I show that even though there are 'acts', there are far stronger 'facts' of citizenship. This chapter I hope reflects the light and darkness around the notion of citizenship—a term which at once connotes a reality and a reminder of the fact that equality for women, though promised, remains like a forever distant dream. There are many groups of women who still remain at the periphery of citizenship. To state but one example, despite the 73rd Amendment, it is clear that even in the 1990s the situation of women from the scheduled castes and the scheduled tribes remained extremely precarious. Dowry deaths among land- less women continue unabated. Among the tribal people who are giving up *jhum* cultivation, women are the poorest of the lot. Pauperisation of a community always means further impoverishment of the women of that community. Neither legal rights nor representation have brought women their desired autonomy. The majoritarian women's movements seemed, even if willing, still unable to liberate women from their own patriarchal legal systems epitomised by personal and customary laws that often discriminate against them. Women remain located within the personal or the customary, the tribal or the ethnic. According to Ritu Menon and Kamala Bhasin: 'Family, community and state emerge as the three mediating and interlocking forces determining women's individual and collective destinies'.[47] Among these three denominators the Indian State has had a complicitous relation with family and community where women's rights are concerned. Therefore, although civic laws have gone only up to a point in supporting women's subject-hood and autonomy, it has not given women their due. After all, civic law is an instrument of the State.

This chapter is not intended to convey the impression that women have given up their efforts to be recognised as autonomous subjects. Now women activists realise that legal activism is neither the only course of action and nor the only solution. From the 1980s, women have no longer restricted themselves within a majoritarian women's movement, but have started a number of autonomous movements. They have recognised that women's rights are always posited against community rights, and then subverted. These autonomous movements have therefore started forming coalitions with other civil society groups within their own communities, thereby making a stronger claim for recognising women's rights as human rights. From recent developments in Northeast India, it seems that these women's groups have found a way forward but that calls for another account. As far as the legal system is concerned, it continues its ambivalence in recognising women as citizens. Women remain guided by different sets of laws that are often discriminatory. Feminist scholarship and women's struggles alike have drawn attention to the incomplete nature of certain political projects, such as, women's citizenship and autonomy. Autonomous movements also fail to locate women's autonomy as a priority area. The Constituent Assembly Debates that shaped the process of state-formation also shaped the Indian State's attitude to women. Through its provision, the newly drafted Constitution in 1950 made women permanent exceptions by locating them not within the Constitution but within community laws. The legal system in India is yet to get out of this bind created by the makers of the Constitution. This is notwithstanding certain progressive legislations that different governments undertook, often as a response to the demands made by the women's movement. The basic dichotomy, however, between questions of women's autonomy and their location within their communities' personal and customary laws remains.

Notes

* I am grateful to Deepti Mahajan for her assistance.
1. Mahanta (1994: 88).
2. Susie Tharu and K. Lalita (1991: 157).
3. M. Ananthasayanam Ayyangar (*Legislative Assembly Debates* 1939: 3674).
4. Bhulabhai Desai (*Legislative Assembly Debates* 1939: 3662).
5. 'Hindu Code' (*Constituent Assembly Debates* 1948: 3628).
6. The Mitakshara and the Dayabhaga are the two schools of Indian legal thought. See B. R. Ambedkar (*Constituent Assembly Debates* 1948: 3630).
7. *Ibid.*
8. *Ibid.*: 3631.
9. Pattabhi Sitaramayya (*Constituent Assembly Debates* 1948: 3635).
10. Hansa Mehta (*Constituent Assembly Debates* 1948: 3643).
11. *Ibid.*: 3643.
12. Naziruddin Ahmad (*Constituent Assembly Debates* 1948: 3640–42).
13. Mahanta (1994: 95).
14. Ansari (1999: 114).
15. Naziruddin Ahmad (*Constituent Assembly Debates* 1948).
16. Mahavir Tyagi (*Constituent Assembly Debates* 1948).
17. For a scholarly account of gender in the politics of partition, refer to Menon and Bhasin (1998) and Butalia (1998).
18. Banerjee (1998: 8–9).
19. *Rameshwari Nehru Papers*.
20. Menon and Bhasin (1993: 13).
21. Pettman (1996: 194).
22. Yuval-Davis, Anthias and Campling (1989: 6).
23. Mahanta (1994: 94).
24. The Hindu Succession Act, 1956 (Act No. 30 of 1956) [as on the 1 June 1982] Section 10, Rules 1 & 2, Government of India, New Delhi, p. 5.
25. Kapur and Cossman (1996: 110–11).
26. S.C. Consul, Citizenship Act, 1955, The Law of Foreigners, Citizenship and Passport (Allahabad: 1962), pp. 179–85.
27. This phrase was used by a number of scholars writing on the Shah Bano case including, for instance, Zakia Pathak and Rajeswari Sunder Rajan in 'Shah Bano' (Butler and Scott 1992: 257).
28. Kapur and Cossman (1996: 63).
29. Abdulwahed Owaisi (*Lok Sabha Debates* 1985: 399).
30. Shah Bano's open letter of 2 November 1985, quoted in Jayal (1999: 120).

31. Interview of Sona Khan with Deepti Mahajan, 6 July 2004, New Delhi.
32. Jayal (1999: 135).
33. Geeta Mukherjee (*Lok Sabha Debates* 1985: 288).
34. Jayanti Patnaik (*Lok Sabha Debates* 1985: 307).
35. Hannah Mollah (*Lok Sabha Debates* 1985: 312).
36. *Ibid.*
37. Kishori Sinha (*Lok Sabha Debates* 1985: 318).
38. Hannah Mollah (*Lok Sabha Debates* 1985: 314).
39. Abida Ahmed, 'Code of Criminal Procedure (Amendment) Bill' (*Lok Sabha Debates* 1984: 333).
40. Jafar Sharief (*Lok Sabha Debates* 19 November 1985: 7); italics added.
41. *Lok Sabha Debates* (1986: 313).
42. Hasan (2001: 75).
43. Kishwar (1999: 135).
44. Agnes (2004: 2–3).
45. Hazarike (2005).
46. Agnes (2004: 6–7).
47. Menon and Bhasin (1998: 255).

8

The Limits of Constitutional Law: Public Policies and the Constitution*

Virgilio Afonso da Silva

In spite of having a strong economy, with a GNP among the 15 highest in the world,[1] Brazil suffers from flaws in the social area, common to all developing countries. Its widespread social inequality[2] worsens the problem even more, since it makes a great majority of the population depend completely on the implementation of public policies, especially in the areas of education, health and housing.

In the legal field, the combination of some factors made the picture even more complex, especially after the present constitution was passed in 1988. This complexity is due to the following reasons: on the one hand, the public policies implemented by governments have never been sufficient to satisfy the immense demands of a population in need of public services in acceptable quantity and quality. On the other hand, the present Brazilian Constitution has concretised much of what has always been seen as reserved for politics, such as minimum wage regulation, the establishment of interest rates and rights to education, health, work and security.

In view of this background, the role of law and especially that of lawyers has been put to the test, considering that in the liberal tradition the implementation of public policies has never been the concern of law-professionals. The consequence of this can be perceived when court decisions and law-literature are analysed. What has generally happened is a simple transposition of a reasoning from the liberal legal tradition, based on nearly exclusively bilateral relations—normally between a creditor and a debtor, or analogous models—into the area of social rights. As will be shown further on, a large number of lawyers have faced the problem of social and economic rights, which derive from the scenario exposed shortly above, in the following way. The constitution guarantees, for example, the right to health. If a person has no access to a determined medical treatment or a determined medicine, it is the duty of the judiciary to make sure that this person receives the treatment or the medicine needed.

In this chapter, I intend to treat this kind of question starting from two assumptions which may seem trivial at first sight, but which oblige the lawyer—and above all the judges—to reflect deeply upon their role in this area of constitutional law. On the one hand, the prescription of social rights in the Brazilian Constitution (or any other constitution) cannot be regarded as simple 'constitutional poetry'—it is not possible that there should be no consequence resulting from this provision. On the other hand, it is not possible that (for reasons which will be explained further on) social and economic rights are treated as if they had the same structure as the so-called individual (civil and political) rights. The role of the judge cannot be envisaged as limited to conceding remedies, health treatments, school placements, etc. to all needy and deprived individuals. At first sight, the two assumptions seem incompatible. It is exactly this impression of incompatibility which has divided lawyers, at least in Brazil, into two opposing fields, each one of which claims that it is correct.

The aim of this chapter is to try to resolve this apparently irreconcilable dichotomy, and to show that it is possible—and necessary—for both starting points to be respected, and that a discussion about the relation between the law—especially constitutional law and public policies would only become productive from the moment at which the need for such a resolution is taken seriously.

The Myth of Montesquieu

One of the main arguments supporting one of the sides of the discussion outlined above is the reference to the theory of the separation of powers. In Brazil, as in many other countries of Latin America, this theory is regarded in a stringent way. In a classical liberal model, in which judges might be considered the 'mouth of the law',[3] it is impossible to imagine that the judiciary might intervene, correct, and sometimes even define public policies. But what is understood as the theory of the separation of powers is, however, a distorted comprehension of Montesquieu's ideas applied to presidential regimes[4] in a society which is infinitely more complex than the one Montesquieu had as a paradigm. Therefore, the argument based on the pure and simple separation of powers does not seem worthy of any in-depth analysis in this work.[5]

There is, however, another argument—somehow linked to the idea of the separation of powers, to the role of judges within this separation and to the dichotomy of liberal state/welfare state—which deserves, due to its greater sophistication, special attention. This argument is based on the distinction between negative and positive duties, and it intends to draw attention to a structural difference between so-called individual rights and social rights.

Individual (Civil and Political) Rights and Negative Duties

The so-called individual rights of the first generation, known in France as 'public liberties' and in Germany as 'rights of defence', are usually defined as rights which are meant to guarantee an autonomous sphere to individuals with which governmental powers may not interfere. It is said, therefore, that such rights, e.g. the freedom of the press, religious freedom, the right to assembly, etc. impose a negative duty on the State. The State is usually forbidden to undertake measures which would interfere with those freedoms, such as imposing censorship, giving preference to a religion, forbidding a free and peaceful assembly, etc.

These types of rights usually do not cause serious problems to judges or to the relation between political and judicial powers, especially in countries accustomed to some kind of judicial review. Whenever the executive or legislative powers go beyond the barrier of 'not-doing', it is the judge's duty to guarantee individual rights and declare such measures invalid.

A more important consequence of this negative structure of classical individual rights, at least for the purposes of this work, is the assumption that negative duties do not imply the allocation of State resources. In other words, 'not-doing' is costless. In this sense, the judicial activity which controls the limits of this 'not-doing', arguably, does not interfere with budgetary issues or public policies and does not, thus, raise costs. This view is flawed and will be criticised below.

Social and Economic Rights and Positive Duties

The so-called social rights, however, particularly the rights to health, education and housing, have a different structure: their implementation does not require abstention by the State. It is necessary among other things, that hospitals, schools and houses be built, that doctors and teachers be hired and that hospital material be acquired. Quite obviously, this costs money.

Unlike what happens with respect to the implementation and protection of individual rights, the implementation of social rights, being dependent on enormous public expenses, depends on decisions which go beyond formal legal reasoning. In a scenario of scarce resources, in which there is certainly not enough money to solve all the problems of health, education and housing of individuals—and this is the reality of nearly all countries in the world—it is necessary that the decision about how and where the resources are allocated be taken by someone.

At this point, two important questions usually arise: (1) Do judges have the legitimacy to decide in the area of public policies? (2) Are judges capable of taking those decisions?

The first question will not be considered deeply in this chapter. As a matter of fact, the answer to it depends on how separation of powers is conceived in a given constitution. As already stressed earlier, keeping the judiciary out of this issue based solely on a anachronistic idea of separation of powers is a strategy that will not be considered here. The same can be said about the argument based exclusively on the lack of judiciary's democratic legitimacy. Both arguments—separation of powers and lack of democratic legitimacy—tend to be used in a very manicheistic way, which I want to avoid. Therefore, and for the sake of the argumentation, it will be assumed that judicial review is an unquestionable issue and that, in this sense, it must be acknowledged that judges are legitimate to interfere in legislation and executive issues.

The second question will be treated further on. Before that, however, it is necessary to discuss an important argument which aims at mitigating the difference between individual (civil and political) rights and social rights, and also the difference between negative and positive duties.

The Cost of Rights I

Among the recently published works on judicial enforcement of social rights in Latin America, one of the most important is undoubtedly the work of Abramovich and Courtis.[6] Even though the book abounds in arguments in favour of the judicial enforcement of social and economic rights, the most interesting argument, at this point, is the one regarding the so-called 'cost of rights'.[7]

Generally speaking, the argument is fairly simple: the implementation and protection of rights always costs money for social and economic rights as well as for civil and political rights. In this sense, public resources are also necessary to protect the freedom of press, the right to property, the right of assembly, etc., for resources are needed above all for the administration of political, judicial and security institutions.[8] According to the statistics presented by Holmes and Sunstein, just a part of the US–American operating system of justice (including the federal prison system) costs, annually, US$ 5,224,000,000.[9]

Thus, contrary to the common belief—according to which negative rights do not imply costs—it is not possible to exercise any of these rights without enormous State expenses. Protecting civil and political rights such as the due process of law, access to jurisdiction, right to marriage, right of assembly, right to vote and to be elected 'presupposes, thus, the creation of the respective institutional conditions by the State (existence and maintenance of courts, the establishment of norms and registers which make the nuptial decision or the act of associating legally relevant, the convocation of elections, the organisation of a political party system, etc.)'.[10]

Besides, while expenses with civil and political rights are not few, there are social rights which do not imply great expenses, because they do not require a 'doing', but rather a 'not-doing'. Abramovich and Courtis mention, for example, that the right to health implies a State duty that of not harming the health of individuals.[11]

Therefore, there would be no way, according to Abramovich and Courtis, to differentiate between civil and political rights on one end and social and economic rights on the other on the basis of the 'not-doing'/ 'doing' dichotomy. At the same time, one might ask if there is any sense at all in differentiating between those rights if both require State expenses for their implementation and protection. Still according to Abramovich and Courtis, there might be some meaning in this distinction, but this has nothing to do with the possibility of judicial enforcement.[12]

Why do Social and Economic Rights Lack Effectiveness?

In view of the efforts which many authors make to demonstrate that there is no difference between so-called classical basic rights (civil and political) and social and economic rights, one cannot help wondering why it is that at least in the more consolidated democracies of the developing countries, civil and political rights are carried out and guaranteed effectively while social and economic rights are often no more than a mere constitutional promise?

In such countries it is very common to hear in answer to this question that 'the government lacks political will' to implement social and economic rights. The great problem of this answer lies in the fact that even if there were a lack of political will of governments, it would be enough if there were a 'judicial will' on the part of the lawyers and judges in order to solve at least some of the problems. This is because, if there is no structural difference between civil and political rights on the one hand, and social and economic rights on the other, it would be enough if courts fulfilled their role and contributed to a wider implementation of the rights to health, education and living than they actually do.

Even though many authors make an effort to demonstrate 'stories of success' in the implementation of social rights in developing countries through the judiciary,[13] it is apparent that such stories are as overestimated as the role that the judiciary can play in this area. Just as the conquest of civil and political rights was a conquest of civil society, historically implemented with political means, the implementation of social and economic rights will not take place in a different way.

It seems to me, therefore, that in the field of social and economic rights the dichotomy between liberals on the one hand, and republicans on the other, is even sharper than it generally is.[14] However, it needs to be understood in slightly different terms for the 'liberal' side no longer defends the idea that the judiciary and the declarations of rights function as guardians of individual autonomy, but rather as implementers of collective necessities. In spite of this difference, a common characteristic still exists, which is the belief that declarations of rights and the activity of judges are the best way to protect the rights of citizens. The republican side, however, can be characterised by what has been said in the previous paragraph: the implementation of economic and social rights depends, for republicans, on the political process, and not on the judges. In a certain way, this implementation should not even depend upon the laying down of rights in a constitutional document.

As is common in such dichotomist scenarios, the solution can frequently only be found midway between the two opposed poles.[15] The great problem, in the area of social and economic rights, is the fact that this midway solution is usually regarded, at least among lawyers, as the following. The government has priority in the implementation of public policies which carry out social and economic rights, but it is the duty of the judges to control it, complement it and correct it whenever necessary. The majority of the above mentioned 'stories of success' follow this pattern. As will be seen in the following, this is not, however, a middle way. It represents, rather, the first version of the problem and its solution, that is to say, the one based on the belief that declarations of rights and the activity of judges are the best ways to protect social and economic rights.

Higher Cost of Implementation of Social and Economic Rights

The idea that judges will always help to carry out social and economic rights when correcting or complementing the public policies implemented by the government is in fact equivocal because it is based on a simple but wrong premise, according to which 'correcting' or 'complementing' are always positive concepts. This could have been true if the implementation of social rights did not imply, in all cases that matter, public expenses.

But contrary to the claims of Abramovich and Courtis, social and economic rights *do differ* from civil and political rights due to the amount of expenses their implementation requires. Although the thesis that the implementation and protection of any right costs money is true, it is also true that the implementation of social and economic rights often costs *more money*. This is due to two main reasons:

First of all, the same expenses which, according both to Abramovich/Courtis and Holmes/Sunstein, are necessary to protect civil and political rights, are also necessary to protect social and economic rights, particularly those expenses which Abramovich and Courtis call expenses for the administration of political, judicial and security institutions.[16] The administration of political institutions, for example, is not an expense to be counted only to protect political rights. To think otherwise would be problematic, for it would mean presupposing that both political institutions and political rights are ends, not means. Therefore, expenses for the administration of political institutions are expenses to be credited to the accounts both of political and civil rights, and of social and economic rights. The same is true for judicial institutions. Therefore, the 'institutional expenses', which are spread out for the implementation of any kind of rights, should not be counted when comparing the costs of social and economic rights on the one hand with costs of civil and political rights on the other.

Besides, when Abramovich and Courtis claim that civil and political rights presuppose the existence and the maintenance of a judicial system, this is only true as far as the protections of these rights is concerned, but not for their exercise. Exercising freedom of speech or the right of assembly, for instance, does not cost citizens or the State anything. Costs arise only when these rights are disrespected. The case of social and economic rights is quite different, for costs arise both in order to create conditions for these rights to be *exercised* and to *protect* them.

Starting from these conclusions, it is not difficult to recognise the difference which exists—in terms of the allocation of public resources—between judicial decisions which aim at protecting civil or political rights on the one hand, and decisions which aim at implementing or protecting social or economic rights on the other. To use an example of a case study which will be given further on, it is enough to compare the costs arising from decisions which impose on the State a duty to pay for medicine for the treatment of HIV patients, with decisions which impose on the State a duty not to interfere with the freedom of expression or of assembly of an individual or a group of individuals. To pay for medicine, to build hospitals, schools or houses in fact *does cost more money* than demanding a 'not-doing' from the State (provided that we presuppose that institutional expenses are expenses for the protection of all kinds of rights).

Case Study: Medicine for AIDS Treatment

In 2004, students of the Faculty of Law of the University of Sã Paulo carried out empirical research involving all decisions of the State Court of Sã Paulo regarding plaintiffs requesting medicine for the treatment of AIDS between January 1997 and July 2004.[17] The general result showed that in 85 per cent of the cases the plaintiffs received the medicine they had asked for. At first sight, this could be regarded as one more of the 'success stories' in the judicial enforcement of a social right. But there is some important information which remains hidden behind the numbers.

The first is the fact that according to the World Health Organisation, Brazil has the most advanced national HIV/AIDS treatment programme in the developing world—which includes free distribution of medicine, among other measures.[18]

A second important piece of information refers to those who put this policy into practice. Also according to the World Health Organisation:

> the viability of the Brazilian HIV/AIDS programme, including treatment distribution, owes much to effective *social mobilisation*, including *representation of affected communities in government, non-governmental organisations*, and other fora. The distribution of free anti-retrovirals in itself prevented the problems associated with the black market or substandard regimens.[19]

As can be seen, and as has been said above, the implementation of social and economic rights which depends on the implementation of public policies is a task for which those responsible are the government and the mobilised civil society.

Finally, the last important information behind the numbers of the case study refers to the rationale which underlies the decisions of the judges and to its consequences.

With regard to the rationale, the study stated that 'in the cases of granting (the demand), in 93 per cent of the decisions, the judges considered the right to health as an individual right.'[20] Besides, the judges generally were not worried about the existence of a public policy (effective or not) already put in practice by the government. The study states:

'Although some decisions recognise the existence of specific public policies for STD/AIDS, none of them approaches in detail the institutional design of the public policies practiced by the State.'[21]

In regard to the economic consequences of the decisions, the study concluded that only in 4.7 per cent of the decisions which granted the demand for medicine for AIDS had the judges made some considerations concerning possible damage to other public policies derived from isolated fund allocation by judicial decisions.[22]

One conclusion which can be drawn after the short exposition of this case study, which—despite isolated shows well the focus which lawyers in general give to judicial enforcement of social and economic rights is that judges apparently ignore the collective character of social rights by treating problems as if they were equal or similar to problems related to individual rights. This collective character requires policies that are thought collectively, which is something judges, as a rule, do not do.[23] With this statement I want to stress that the issue discussed in this chapter is not about choosing between *judicial activism* or *judicial restraint*, even though it is often presented as such. Although it is obvious, on the one hand, that for those who advocate judicial restraint as an ideal for judicial activity judges should be kept away from decisions concerning public policies, it does not follow, on the other hand, that judicial activism always requires judges deciding about public policies. It is thus possible to defend a sort of judicial activism, that is, to sustain that judges can legitimately discuss issues of public policies and, nevertheless, to state that this activism is constrained for a number of structural reasons.[24] This means that although judicial activism is a possibility, it depends on several structural changes in legal education, courts organisation, and above all on judicial procedures in order to avoid the individualisation of collective rights.

Several examples of the consequences of what I call 'unprepared judicial activism'[25] can be found in the judicial activity of many Brazilian courts. For instance, by distributing medical treatment individually (that is, without considering government policies),[26] judges may be harming other public policies in the area of health (or other areas), even if they manage to 'solve' some isolated cases. This is because in a scenario of scarce resources, money has to be necessarily withdrawn from other areas.

In this sense, Alberto Kanamura affirms that:

> In a country in which people die of malnutrition, of lack of potable water or of pure ignorance of basic sanitary rules, it is difficult not to question (judicial) decisions which give priority to health expenses for the sake of a treatment of single cases, while the same resources could benefit millions who live diseases as a rule. Diseases which do not exist in the developed world any more and are very simple to treat. It does no harm to remember that, in this moment, the government is trying to fight endemic hunger by treating the affected persons medically with a subsidy of BRL 50 [USD 20] per family monthly, maybe less than BRL 100 [USD 40] per person annually.[27]

The author uses the example of a genetic disease called Gaucher. In the state of São Paulo, there are about 100 carriers of this disease who, due to judicial decisions, receive free treatment. The treatment costs US$ 9.620 per person monthly. For these 100 persons, the annual costs are more than US$ 10 million. According to the numbers quoted above, this sum would be enough to help annually 250,000 people suffering from hunger. Even though it is not correct to discuss which of the two it is more important to combat, based solely on the number of people helped, one thing is certain: judges do not have in mind the whole dimension of the health policy, as they should have when they grant the financing of the treatment of this or that disease. If there are not enough resources for everything and if the judge's decision has to be executed, the money needed for this has to be withdrawn from other areas. It becomes clear, therefore, that even though the intention behind the decisions might be good, the stories of individual success are not always stories of collective success.

Conclusion

In the introduction to this chapter I defended the idea that the provision of social and economic rights in the Brazilian Constitution (or in any other constitution) cannot be regarded as if it were simply 'constitutional poetry'. That is to say, it is not possible not to have any consequences of this provision, for, as Michelman correctly argues, social rights are no less legal rights than any other declared by a Bill of Rights.[28] However, the fact of 'being no less legal rights than any other' does not entail, in my opinion, that we 'treat social and economic rights as if they had the same structure of the so-called civil and political rights' or 'as if they should be enforced in the same way as these rights are'. In other words, it might not be possible to assume that the judge's role is to grant medicine, medical treatments, school placements, etc. to all those who have no access to them, even though a right to health is guaranteed by the constitution.

Bearing in mind what has been said, what could be the role of judges (and lawyers in general) in the process of implementing social and economic rights? Although there are surely many answers to this question, I argue that all of them should depart from the premise that social and economic rights cannot be treated, except in extreme cases maybe, as if they could follow individualistic patterns similar to a relationship between a creditor and a debtor.

If this is correct, and if the judiciary is not able to think about health, education, housing, etc. in a collective and global way, they should leave this kind of task to the political process. It would be naïve, however to ignore it—individual plaintiffs will not cease to exist and judges will have to decide about them. If, for the reasons discussed, judges should not distribute medicine or similar benefits to individuals, they should be able to channel individual claims and, in a kind of constitutional dialogue process, demand objective and transparent explanations about the allocation of public resources through public policies so that they can discuss and challenge such allocations with the political power whenever necessary.

However, it is obvious that for this purpose the role of judges has to be reconsidered. Even more, in a country where the separation of powers is interpreted as a synonym of non-dialogue between powers, as is the case of Brazil, this is a task hard to implement. As it was shown, however, easy solutions, like the distribution of medicine in a disorderly and irrational way, will not contribute at all to the real implementation of social rights in the country.

Notes

* I am grateful to Diogo R. Coutinho for his helpful comments on prior drafts. I also would like to thank all participants to the international seminar on 'Conflicts, Law, and Constitutionalism', held in February 2005 at the Maison de Sciences de l'Homme, Paris, for their constructive criticisms on the thesis defended in this chapter.

1. According to the Human Development Report (HDR) of the United Nations Development Programme, Brazil has the ninth highest GNP (Gross National Product) in the world when measured in PPP (Purchasing Power Parity) dollar. If measured in absolute values, Brazil has the 13th highest GNP. Statistics available at *http://hdr.undp.org/statistics/data/pdf/hdr04_table_13.pdf*.

2. Again, according to the HDR of the United Nations Development Programme, Brazil has the fourth highest rate of social inequality (Gini Index—Ratio of the richest 10% to the poorest 10%). Statistics available at *http://hdr.undp.org/statistics/data/pdf/hdr04_table_14.pdf*.

3. See Montesquieu (1951: 6).

4. It should not be forgotten that the so-called 'theory of the separation of powers', attributed to Montesquieu, is based mainly on one chapter in *The Spirit of Laws* in which Montesquieu 'describes' the British political system around the middle of the 18th century, which had little in common with contemporary presidential democracies (1951: 6).

5. Michelman also stresses the inadequacy of thinking of the problem of social rights solely as a matter of separation of powers. See Michelman (2003: 13–15).

6. See Abramovich and Courtis (2002).

7. See, for all, Holmes and Sunstein (1999).

8. See Abramovich and Courtis (2002: 23).

9. See Holmes and Sunstein (1999: 234).

10. Abramovich and Courtis (2002: 23).

11. See Abramovich and Courtis (2002: 25).

12. According to these authors, the distinction between civil and political rights on the one hand, and social and economic rights on the other, may be useful for other aims, such as, for example, 'to situate, in a

historical context, the form according to which the various rights were conceptualized and laid down'. See Abramovich and Courtis (2002: 48).

13. See, above all, Sunstein (2001: 221–37) and Abramovich and Courtis (2002: 132–248).

14. For this counter-position between the liberal and republican paradigms, see, above all, Habermas (1994).

15. In a certain way this is also the position that Habermas assumes in the debate between the liberal and republican versions. See Habermas (1992: 361–66).

16. See Abramovich and Courtis (2002: 23).

17. This research received a prize from the IPEA (Institute of Applied Economic Studies, Brazil) in 2004 and was co-ordinated by Prof. José Eduardo Faria (General Co-ordinator of the group) and Prof. Diogo R. Coutinho (Research Co-ordinator). I would like to thank the students involved in the project—Camila Duran Ferreira, Ana Carolina Carlos de Oliveira, Ana Mara Franq Machado, AndréVereta Nahoum, Brisa Lopes de Mello Ferrã, Evorah Lusci Costa Cardoso, Leandro Alexi Franco, Marcele Garcia Guerra, Marco Aurßo Cezarino Braga, Rafael Diniz Pucci, and Vinćius Correa Buranelli—for having allowed to me the access to the data and the results of the research. The study will be always quoted as Ferreira *et al.* (2004).

18. As a result of this programme, there was a reduction by 50 per cent of the mortality rate in consequence of AIDS, a reduction of 26 per cent in the number of registered cases and of 80 per cent in the necessity of admissions to hospitals caused by the disease. Thus, it was possible to avoid 358.175 admissions in the period between 1997 and 2001, causing a reduction of resources of US$ 1.036.603.072,14. [Source: Ministéio de Sade do Brasil (Ministry of Health of Brazil)]. See, on these results, Oliveira-Cruz, Kowalski and McPake (2004: 292) and Hofer, Schechter and Harrison (2004: 967–71).

19. Emphasis added; see World Health Organization, 'Treatment Works', at *http://www.who.int/3by5/en/treatmentworks.pdf*.

20. Ferreira *et al.* (2004: 24).

21. *Ibid.*: 23–24.

22. *Ibid.*: 25–26.

23. They do not think collectively not necessarily because they do not want to, but because, among other things, the courts have no adequate structure to act in this form and because judges have no access to the complex information which is the basis of the implementation of public policies.

24. For example: because judges are not prepared for such tasks (as a consequence of structural problems in Brazilian legal education),

because courts are not structured, and because the judicial procedures were not conceived for that sort of task.

25. JoséReinaldo de Lima Lopes calls this 'irrational voluntarism'. See Lopes (1994: 113–42).
26. And this does not only happen in cases of medicine for the treatment of AIDS.
27. Alberto Kanamura, 'O dilema do gestor da sade', (10.07.2003) *Folha de São Paulo* at 3.
28. See Michelman (2003: 14).

9

Regulation of the Particular and Its Socio-Political Effects

Rastko Močnik

The introduction of a certain type of democracy was a prelude to war in the Yugoslav Federation. In Iraq, and before that in Afghanistan, war was a prelude to democracy. Should we rectify our perhaps archaic notion of 'democracy'? Should we reconsider it in the light of statements such as that made by President Bush who claimed that while elections in Iraq might not have been up to our democratic standards, it was nevertheless a miracle that they had happened at all?[1] Or, should we let our reflection be led by indications closer to social realities and start from the observation that, in all the three cases mentioned here, the establishment of democracy has been accompanied by the emergence of supposedly traditional social divides along the lines of ethnicity and religion?

The creation of new states in Central and Eastern Europe and in the area of the former Soviet Union has been justified as the exercise of the right to self-determination by the acts of 'national sovereignty'. The result, however, has been the imposition of the 'sovereignty' of the majority ethnic group, which immediately triggered analogous claims by the minority ethnic and/or religious groups now deprived of an adequate constitutional status, and actually exposed to various practices of ethnic cleansing. It was as if the establishment of democratic constitutional arrangements produced, as its immediate effect, the destruction of the very presuppositions of such arrangements—the autonomous political sphere and its complement, the 'abstract individual' emancipated from her or his personal circumstances (like those of ethnicity, religion, etc.). Instead, a new logic has been instituted which, although consistently articulated to the proto-juridical frame of human rights, imposed a *matryoshka*-like[2] structuring of the social field where bigger ethnic groups contain smaller groups and those contain even smaller groups~~all~~ of them struggling, with the same arguments and within the same ideological horizon, for recognition and for their collective rights.

Identity and the 'Politics of Recognition'

All social groups~~from~~ those who have formed a state to provide for their needs down to those who, for the same purpose, request (from this very state) special arrangements~~struggle~~ for their 'identity'. Their identitary strategies likewise affirm *particular cultural* elements within a *universalistic, juridical,* institutional frame.[3] Hence the internal tension of identity constructions: on the one hand, their cultural contents are of 'contingent', 'arbitrary' and particularistic nature, on the other hand, they are constituted by their articulation into a universalistic construction.

Identitary strategy consists in bringing a culturally-backed particularistic group 'claim' under some general principle. In this sense, it is not different from any standard rhetorical procedure which presents a particular proposition as compatible with, or even deducible from, a principle or, rather, a *topos* presumed to be 'general' (not specifically dependent on any particular situation) and 'shared' by the audience and the speaker. However, the specific feature of the identitary strategy is that the subsumption under a general principle is performed in the name of 'identity', and that the addressee's consent as to the adequacy of the subsumption is required in the form of *recognition of identity*. The request of recognition of identity entails the contention that, if recognition is not granted, something most harmful or even existentially endangering may happen to the identitary group: it is suggested that, in the absence of recognition the very 'identity' of the group is put to risk.[4] This, in turn, favours the claimants' self-styling in the mode of a *victim*, the argument being that what is promoted as a general principle is in some way denied to them.

Obviously, the construction of 'human rights' offers a privileged support to this type of claims. To be able to exploit the human rights background, the claimant group has to argue that what they claim to be a lesion in their identitary essence constitutes a violation of their human right. To establish this connection, identitary strategists have to profile themselves, within the construction of human rights, as the 'other' as the instance which represents the *limit* to everyone's exercise of their own human rights and liberties.[5] Identitary claimants subsume their cause under the *universal* principle of human rights by what may be called the 'hypochondriac turn': this turn consists in inscribing oneself into the field defined by the universal principle, as the 'wronged other'. Or, in other words, the turn consists in locating oneself in the *specific exterior* defined by the universal principle as the zone of violation. Contrary to the popular belief that identitary ideologies are presumed to be incapable of 'the relation to the other', I would rather suggest that they, from their very inception, *appropriate* the 'position of the other' specifically, the position of the *wronged*, *offended*, or *victimised* other. Identitary strategies are exercised from this 'position of the wronged other', *which is already established within, and by*, the *dispositif* of the human rights.[6] We should therefore abandon another popular prejudice about the identitary strategies according to which they presumably contradict the idea of human rights. Quite the contrary, identitary politics practice this doctrine.

Formalisation of Identity-formation

The mechanisms of identity-formation can be formalised,[7] and are presented here with the help of examples chosen for their simplicity. The same formalisation will show that the culturalised pseudo-political discourse transforms the social support of a state (which, in the modernity, used to be the 'nation') into an identitary community.

I. Albanians are fighting against the mono-ethnic Macedonian state which excludes their participation in its structures.

(Arbë Xhaferi, Chairman of the Democratic Party of Albanians, at the time Vice-Prime Minister of the Macedonian government, as quoted in *Delo*, Ljubljana, 20. 3. 2001).

The interesting feature in [I] is the tension between the generalist description of the Macedonian state (introduced by the use of the learned expression 'mono-ethnic'), and the particular case for the Albanians; it is this particular case which is the explicit point of the utterance.

To conduct our analysis, we will adapt the conceptual apparatus proposed by Oswald Ducrot.[8] We will present the relevant elements of Ducrot's theory and adapt them for our purpose while analysing the utterance [I].

The *topos* initially evoked in [I] may be reconstructed as:

T [P: 'the more a state is mono-ethnic' → Q: 'the less it allows allo-ethnic participation'].

The evocation of the *topos* T is evident, and it is explicitly stated that P of T applies to the Macedonian state. The argumentation consequently seems to be:

1. *evocation* of the *topos* T which links together two properties, P and Q, in such a way that the possession of the property Q is presented as the consequence of the possession of the property P: T [P: 'the more a state is mono-ethnic' → Q: 'the less it allows allo-ethnic participation'];[9]

2. *application* of the *topos* T to the case at hand, to the case of the Macedonian state: 'Macedonia is a mono-ethnic state'; or: 'T & P of T applies to the Macedonian state'; this is the *argument* proper which leads to:

3. the *conclusion*: consequently, Q of T applies to the Macedonian state; or: therefore: Macedonian state does not allow allo-ethnic participation in its structures.

Schematically:

$$T [P → Q]$$

Argument: T & Macedonian state is P

|

V

Conclusion: Therefore: Macedonian state is Q

The argument seems to point towards a *general* conclusion about a particular state, the Macedonian state. Contrary to this easy passage, the speaker not only specifies the first term within the predicative paradigm 'mono-ethnic/allo-ethnic' (by pointing out that it is specifically the Macedonian state that is mono-ethnic); he *also* specifies the second term: the mono-ethnic Macedonian state does not allow *the Albanians* to participate in its structures. But this *specific* conclusion *does not follow* from the argumentation presented earlier. We must accordingly assume an implicit introduction of a supplementary *topos*, which introduces the additional specification of the second predicate of the paradigm and in this way accounts for the specified character of the conclusion.

Such a supplementary *topos* can be construed as a topical inversion of T:

T' [P': 'the more a community is allo-ethnic in a mono-ethnic state' → Q': 'the less it is allowed by the mono-ethnic state to participate in the state-structures'].

The implicit supplementary argumentation, which leads to the explicitly stated conclusion, would then be:

1. the *background* topos: T' [P': 'the more a community is allo-ethnic in a mono-ethnic state' → Q': 'the less it is allowed by the mono-ethnic state to participate in the state-structures'];

2. the *argument*: 'the Albanians are P' = an allo-ethnic community in the mono-ethnic Macedonian state';

3. the *conclusion*: 'therefore, the Albanians are Q' = not allowed to participate in the state-structures of Macedonia'.

Schematically:

$$T' [P' \rightarrow Q']$$

Argument: T' & the Albanians are P'

|

V

Conclusion: Therefore: Albanians are Q'

The 'Albanians' should be read as 'We, the Albanians'. The application of T' (the 'inverted' initial *topos* T) to the specific case is therefore an 'identitary' application. It articulates the identitary inscription of a 'we' into the general field opened by the general *topos* T.

However, in order to construe this articulation between a general *topos* and an identitary 'we', it is necessary to insert a mediating *topos* T': this 'inverted' *topos* presents, in general terms, what it means to be the victimised party within the field opened, in general terms, by the initial *topos* T. The inversion by the means of which T' is generated from T, is what we have called *the hypochondriac turn*.

Therefore utterance [I] is an example of identitary strategy: it subsumes an identitary 'we' under a general *topos* T' which explains what it is like to be *the wronged other* within the horizon of an initial general *topos* T of which T' is an inversion. Besides relying upon the typical rhetorical para-logics, utterance [I] exerts important 'moral' pressure upon its audience: both the identitary nature of the application of the *topos* (i.e., of the argument proper) and the moral prestige of the two *topoi* themselves (the doctrine of human rights and minority rights) present the argumentation as a request for identitary recognition. In our analysis, though, the recognition takes no metaphysical paths: what is to be recognised is simply the appropriateness of the subsumption of a 'we' under a general common-place on the theme of the wronged other.[10]

Let us schematically present this analysis of utterance [I]:

T [P → Q] T' [P' → Q']

Argument: T & Mac.st. is P

  | M.st.is Q

  | T' & *we* are P'

V

Conclusion: Therefore: *we* are Q'

The sequence of the argumentation which we have put into the quadrangle is not explicitly stated in the actual utterance. Yet, without this 'not stated' section, the argumentation cannot reach its explicit conclusion: the general conclusion about the particular Macedonian state is necessary for the particular Albanian case to be inserted under the general *topos* about victimisation. The argumentation then seems plausible, especially since the focal opposition 'mono-ethnic/allo-ethnic' appears to be, or rather, is presented as being, 'lexical', and the argument therefore seems 'analytical', i.e., trivial, self-evident. Still, considering that in strict 'lexical' terms the opposition to 'mono-ethnic' is 'poly-ethnic', something more is needed for the argument to run smoothly. This additional element is the same as the one which provides for the dramatic relevance of the attribution of the adjective 'mono-ethnic' to the noun 'state': it is the conception of the state as 'ethnically blind', as the warrant of human rights, etc. A 'mono-ethnic' state is then a monstrosity which, in clear violation of its own concept, treats its Albanian citizens as 'allo-ethnic' and victimises them. By appealing to the universalist notions of contemporary politics, utterance [I] requests the recognition of the Albanians as the victimised party and pleads for the condemnation of the 'mono-ethnic' Macedonian state as the perpetrator. The argument sets all the *dramatis personae* upon the scene and establishes appropriate relations among them. And, it will work if its audience: (*a*) shares its universalist juridical–political background; (*b*) acknowledges to the speaker's group the status of the victim in terms of the universalist normative background.

Condition (*a*) is secured by the present global ideological hegemony; the fulfilment of condition (*b*) seems to depend upon a judgement about 'facts'. What matters, though, is that the judgement about 'facts' under (*b*) is to be passed by the same instance which is supposed to 'share' the universalist ideological background under (*a*). The 'addressee', supposed to 'share' the universalist background, is also supposed to have the competence of its 'application to the facts'.[11] This means that (*a*) invests its 'addressee' with privileged access to the ideological background of its own operations: it installs the 'addressee' upon the structural position of the 'subject-supposed-to-know'.[12] Submission to the hegemony of a universalist ideology is an immanent feature of identitary revendication: what is more, identitary revendication defines its 'addressee' as the 'hegemon' of this hegemony, it promotes its 'addressee' to the position from where a legitimate 'recognition' can be conceded. Since the 'hypochondriac turn' is only completed if recognised as justified, and since the recognition can only come from the 'subject-supposed-to-know' of the universalist ideology, submission to the hegemony and to its concrete, 'material' *Träger* is an essential component of the identitary operation.

From Hypochondria to 'Risk Society'[13] and to Apocalyptic Revelation[14]

Identitary hypochondria is one of several possible strategies under the hegemony of universalism—the one which negotiates an affirmation of culturalist nativism with the submission to hegemonic universalism. Strategies that do not take the nativist detour but directly take the universalist position while keeping the hypochondriac turn, assume the voice of a 'cosmopolitan' hypochondriac community, i.e., of an 'imagined global community' of possible victims. At this level, it is almost impossible to avoid a certain 'reflexivisation' of the mechanism: for, if we are all united in our status of possible victims, any harm that may befall us can, regardless of the contingency of its empirical origin, be imputed to our lack of vigilance. The alienating blackmail is perfect: we are permanently under threat, and if occasionally the threat materialises, we are guilty of negligence. Guilt and anxiety, what better cement of domination could one imagine? You either live in anxiety or you die in guilt. Or, others die and you survive in guilt. So, we must anticipate our guilt to escape anxiety; but anticipated guilt is present anxiety.

This is really a 'reflexive' modernity: in classical situations the individual was faced with an impossible dilemma which, retroactively, generated her or him as a subject; now, the existence of the subject is nothing but this oscillation between two impossibilities. At the dawn of modernity, Corneille's Chimène was torn between genealogical loyalty and the loyalty to her emerging bourgeois Ego: an impossible dilemma which could only be resolved by having recourse to the alibi of the monarchic authority. But if Chimène needed complex ideological backgrounds to construe *cette généreuse alternative*[15] with which she addressed the king, nothing so redundant is needed any more: the 'ideological background' is now the alternative itself. We have finally reached the founding moment of the social contract where the effect precedes the cause.[16]

The case of 'reflexive modernity' is indeed argued for in classical terms, but negatively: 'modern societies, having dissolved all givens and transformed them into decisions'.[17] Since the 18th century, 'nature' has been colonised by humanity, humanity is only facing itself as a decision-making instance. The 'reflexivity' hypothesis seems to be spelled out in classical terms not so much to appeal to sociological rationalism or to profit from some popular Heideggerianism, than to covertly impose an implicit hypothesis of a different kindone regarding a certain 'interior' absence and not the absence of 'exterior'. This simultaneously vague[18] and seemingly precise talk about 'decisions', further specified as 'the socialisation of shared risks or shared risk definitions', actually suggests that there is no antagonistic contradiction within contemporary society or societies. All the possible risks then come as a sort of 'collateral damage' to the global development. This, in turn, opens the possibility to envisage the rational construction of a world community around the *possibility of involuntary self-inflicted harm*.

What follows is a blueprint for argumentation within this horizon:

II. The promotion of human rights is not just a kind of international social work. It is indispensable for our safety and wellbeing because governments which do not respect the rights of their own citizens will in all likelihood not respect the rights of others either. Such regimes are also more likely to trigger unrest by persecuting minorities, offering a safe haven for terrorists, smuggling drugs or clandestinely manufacturing weapons of mass destruction.

(Madeleine Albright, at the time, Secretary of State)[19]

This is a scheme that can be filled in as needed: 'Governments who violate human rights of their citizens are a threat to others as well. And X is such a government. Consequently, X is a threat to others as well. Whoever encounters such a government is threatened by it. And, we are facing such a government. Consequently, we are in danger'.

This seems satisfactory and offers a plausible argument for preventive war. However, socialisation of risk has been achieved through 'de-antagonisation' of society, and this has seriously reduced chances for a rational explanation of the danger. This void can metonymically be filled in by enumeration of 'shared risk definitions' (the familiar list: terrorism, weapons of mass destruction, etc); or it can metaphorically be acknowledged and fuel the development of an apocalyptic vision:

III. God is not neutral.

(George W. Bush, jr., 20 September 2001)

The analysis must explain why the spontaneous interpreter understands [III] as meaning: 'God is with us'. Restitution of the argumentative chain shows why: 'The harder the evil presses, the more God protects the victims of the evil. And the evil is now pressing hard. Consequently, God is protecting its victims. The more one is a victim of the evil, the more God protects one. And *we* are now victims of the evil. So: God is protecting us'. The rest is lexical: 'If one is protecting somebody, then one is not neutral; and God is protecting us. Therefore, God is not neutral'.

This digression was necessary to show that identitary strategy enters into a wider context of strategies possible within a universalist ideology. We can now return to our more immediate concerns.

Victimisation and Identification

Victimisation in terms of the hegemonic universalist ideology then functions as the *einziger Zug* of Freudian identification, as the 'single trait'[20] around which 'identity' will be constructed. Construction of identity is a cultural operation, a fabrication of a patch-work of elements fished out of the Sargasso Sea of freely floating autonomised cultural *débris*:[21] it needs anchorage, though, and this point of attachment comes from the 'outside', from the hegemonic ideology, as the recognition of victimisation. Once this solid core has been provided in universalist terms, the remaining work of identity construction will be carried out by the idiosyncratic powers of the native consciousness. This perfect fit between the particular (native) and universal (hegemonic) is mediated by the status of the victim—claimed from a particularist position, but already in universalist terms, and recognised from the universalist hegemonic position.[22]

This mechanism situates a 'native' identitary group into a universalist hegemonic context without hurting its cultural idiosyncrasies. However, it paradoxically also retroactively produces the native group itself—at least in its specific identitary constitution. Social construction of identity which makes various identitary features crystallise around the 'single trait' of victimisation, stabilised in the hegemonic ideology, *integrates* the identitary community. The mechanism of such integration is analogous to the Freudian mechanism of the constitution of the Ego. According to Freudian analysis, the psychological identity of the Ego is produced when past Ego-identifications crystallise around a privileged 'single trait' borrowed from the person who is the object of the individual's identification. It is this single trait that brings together various Ego-identifications and integrates them into a solid Ego. Sociological construction of the identitary group that integrates itself on the basis of the 'single trait' of victimisation is analogous to the individual psychic processes described by Freud, and is thus quite an exceptional historical case: it is a situation where *mechanisms of social cohesion are the same as the mechanisms of individual psychic integration.*[23]

But we should give full import to the fact that construction of identity is only made possible by a heterogeneous universalist element which comes from an ideology whose privileged mode of existence is *juridical*.[24] This feature provides for another conversion which completes the one we have noted in the dimension of the relations between the psychic and the social, and which gives its full meaning to the transformation of the psychic process, individual by definition, into a form of socialisation, that is, into a mechanism of social cohesion. The juridical apparatus, especially in its modern form (with the abstract, free and equal individual), essentially keeps individuals apart.[25] In an identitary community, though, elements of juridical ideology, such as human rights, provide support for the mechanisms of recognition and secure foundations for the identity construction. In such a community, *what separates individuals as individuals, binds them together as a group*.

The *form* of individual freedom (limitation of its performance by the freedom of the other) becomes the core element of the *contents* of collective belonging. Correlatively, the *contents* of socialisation (individual psychic processes of Ego-integration) become the *form* of the mechanisms of social integration. What used to be the support of the 'autonomous political sphere' and the medium of a certain political articulation of social tensions and conflicts (freedom and equality of abstract individuals), now becomes the axis of 'culturalisation'[26] of those tensions and conflicts. 'Culturalisation' is the imposition of a relatively arbitrary set of 'native' ideological ('representational') elements, disconnected from the practices they have initially mediated,[27] as the social link, constitutive of the identitary group. This 'set' can only hold together if it is amalgamated around the core of identitary construction the heterogeneous universalist element; the articulation to the universalist core element is also the absolute condition for identity-construction *to be imposed as the (ideological) mechanism of social cohesion*.

Identity as a Mode of Ideological Interpellation

We can now see that 'identity' is what Simmel's stranger has: more precisely, 'identity' is what the stranger has *for the native*for Simmel takes care to give a relational, or topical, description, and not to substantiate a social relation.[28] The native's relation to the stranger:

1. is a more abstract relation than the relation with the members of the native's own group, and is based on the commonality of more general qualities;

2. stresses, against the background of the general shared features of humanity, 'that which is not common'.

3. is not individualised and takes the stranger as representative of her or his group of origin.

With the stranger, then, what is individual and particular operates as an element of distance; and what is collective and general is an element of closeness. Conceived in this way, identity is not a property, it is a relation; the relation between the individual who has identity, and the individual who perceives this individual as having an identity. If the two individuals are distinct, then the identity is an *ascribed* one. If it is the same individual who figures on both sides of the relation, then the identity is an *assumed* one. If both modalities coincide, then it is a *recognised* identity.

The ascribed identity of Simmel's stranger is also composed on the background of the 'generally human.[30] Furthermore, his construction of the stranger's identity uses the 'native element as well: it uses the 'native' element on both sides. On the side of those who produce the construction as well as on the side of the stranger. To the stranger, the 'native' features are being ascribed. However, since these features in the stranger are those which are 'non-common', their perception presupposes a 'native point of view, the perspective which distinguishes between the 'familiar' and the 'stranger', the 'common' and the 'non-common'. The *ascriptive* perspective[31] then presupposes a happy cohabitation of the particular and the general view, of the 'native' standpoint and of the view that perceives the 'humanly common'. It presupposes an instance from where it is possibly naively to arbitrate about both both dimensions. Contrary to this, the *assumed* identity presupposes a separation of the two perspectives, the 'native' one and the 'generally human' one. While it is constructed or declared by the 'native' instance, it appeals to the 'generally human' instance: construction of the assumed identity cannot be completed until it is sanctioned by the 'general' instance. This sanction is the 'recognition'- by the way of which the 'general' instance grants to the subject of the assumed identity the access to the 'generally human'.

In less descriptive terms, in conceptual terms of the theory of ideological interpellation; in identitary construction, the native subject-supposed-to believe is separated from the instance of the subject-supposed –to-know, and appeals for its recognition. A direct identification with the subject-supposed-to-know is not possible and needs the sanction of its representative to be consummated. On the other hand, this means that even the identification with the subject-supposed-to-believe will not be possible until it acquires the recognition. Already on the native level, the core element of identity construction is the one borrowed from the 'general', more specifically, from the universal domain, controlled by the subject-supposed-to-know. On the other side, however, the instance of recognition is not just 'general', it is 'universal'. Two consequences follow from this , one permissive and the other restrictive. The first consequence is that, the instance of recognition being universal, any collage of identitary features can, in principle, pretend to be recognized by it (since, being universal, it is by definition bound to embrace all the identities[32]). The second consequence is restrictive: an identitary collage can only be recognized under the condition that it is centred round some universal element. Such a universal element can be, and usually is, the claim that some universal 'right' of the identitary community and its members has been violated. However, such a claim actually actually acknowledges that the identitary collage cannot affirm itself without external assistance. An identitary collage is therefore recognised only under the condition that it is *not* self-sufficient. The actual recognition, then, does not depend upon any consideration of the content of the identity construction and its relation to the universal background. The recognition entirely depends upon conditions external to the frame within which the problem has been articulated: it depends upon the relations of power, the perceptions of the 'interests' of the involved parties, etc.[33]

Identity then is a type of ideological interpellation which, to succeed, needs neither to support its identification with the subject-supposed-to-know by the unconscious desire[34] nor to squeeze the interpellated individual into a *vel*-situation.[35] To succeed, identitary interpellation does not need to strike upon an unconscious fantasy in the interpellated individual; but neither does it need to present itself as the solution to the unsolvable dilemmas of a pluralistic socio-ideological context. The belief background to which its subject supposed to believe is referring has the structure of an Ego-integration. Structuration of this background, though, can only be completed by the incorporation of a universalist element as the axis of its articulation. While incorporation of the universalist element completes the identitary construction, it also makes its validity depend upon the sanction which can only come from the univer-salist field. In this sense, the identitary individual yields to the ideological interpellation even *before* s/he has been granted the right to identify with the subject-supposed-to-know (of the universalist background) which supports the interpellation. Identitary interpellation is, *sit venia verbo*, a *vel*-alternative 'in action': identitary construction is incomplete until it incorporates the universalist element; this means that the identitary individual cannot identify with her or his (native, local) subject-supposed-to-believe until the belief background to which this subject is ascribed is *recognised* by the subject-supposed-to-know of the universalist background. Once the recognition is granted, identity is saturated. But it *still* remains within the register of 'belief', i.e., of the possible, the conditional. As a consequence, identitary interpellation traps the interpellated individual into an incessant oscillation between the possible and the necessary, between the conditional and the unconditional. Until s/he completes her or his identity with a universalist element, it is only 'possible, conditional'; after the inclusion of this element, the identity makes itself depend upon an external sanction; if it succeeds in obtaining the sanction ('recognition'), it is recognised precisely as a 'native' identity, i.e., as something 'possible and conditional', appended to a subject-supposed-to-believe which, again, needs the sanction of the 'necessary and unconditional'. Recognition cannot be given once and for all; it has to be reiterated, gained, 'deserved' again and again.[36] Identity, then, is the state of being constantly blackmailed. It is the perfect ideology for the 'comprador' political classes, as it can equally well mediate both their disciplinary local activities and their servility upon the global scene.

What follows is a schematic presentation of the Althusserian 'ideological interpellation'[37] as the inversion of Lacan's scheme of the analytical process:[38]

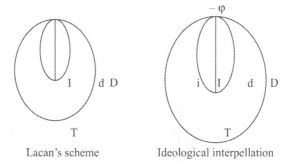

Lacan's scheme   Ideological interpellation

D   demand (of sense)
I   identification
T   point of transference (subject-supposed-to-believe/know)
$-\varphi$ position of the subject (the unconscious fantasy or a *vel*-alternative)
i   ideological interpellation

The interpretation starts from the addressee's '*demand* of sense' (D), which is confronted with a 'sense/nonsense' alternative; the interpreter solves this alternative by *identifying* her/himself (I) with the *subject-supposed-to-believe* (T) 'all that is necessary to believe' for a particular string to 'make sense'; from this quasi-neutral pivotal point of communication (to which both the addresser and the addressee implicitly appeal), the 'sense' comes back to the addressee. This back-lash of the interpreter's demand of sense is, in general, the 'sense' of the utterance; in certain cases, though, the 'return' of the sense to the addressee takes the form of *ideological interpellation* (i).

The conditions of a 'happy' interpellation are suggested by the very scheme that we have borrowed from Lacan: if, at the point of the 'sense/nonsense' alternative, the individual is located *as subject* ($-\varphi$), i.e., if the individual is, at that point, squeezed into what Lacan calls a '*vel*-alternative' (of the type: 'give your money or I take your life!'), then the process does not proceed directly to the point of identification (to the 'subject-supposed-to-*believe*'), but *takes an unconscious loop and is mediated by the individual's (unconscious) desire* (d). (The same happens if the utterance activates an unconscious fantasy in the interpreter.) In this case, the identification is no longer 'conditional' it becomes unconditional, the background beliefs are assumed as necessary, the identification is consequently with the 'subject-supposed-to-*know*', and the interpellation succeeds.

Our general theory sets the condition: 'no interpellation without (unconditional) identification', or 'no interpellation without identification to the subject-supposed-to-know'. In the general formula, then, it is the transformation of identification from 'conditional' to 'unconditional' that provides an unproblematic transformation of the subject-supposed-to-believe into the subject-supposed-to-know. Identitary interpellation specifies the general formula by *maintaining* the distinction between the two 'subjects-supposed-to'...The identitary formula would then be: 'no identification to the subject-supposed-to-believe without identification to the subject-supposed-to-know; but with the identification to the subject-supposed-to-know, you only get identification to the subject-supposed-to-believe; but then: no identification to the subject-supposed-to-believe without identification to the subject-supposed-to-know' etc.

What strikes us as a very specific feature of the identity interpellation is that what in interpellation in general and, indeed, in the various specific forms of interpellation we have hitherto investigated,[39] are ideological mechanisms which operate on the level of the individual, are here displaced into the extra-individual, into the social dimension. The social counterpart of the individual *vel*-alternative is the aporetic *regressio ad infinitum* we have noted earlier and which operates on the level of the identitary community, not 'within' its particular members; the social counterpart of the individual fantasy in the hypochondriac turn which, again, is articulated in a *we*-mode, and not individually.

This inversion in the location of interpellative mechanisms, their displacement from 'the individual as subject' to 'the group as identitary community' can best account for the inversion of the whole problematics of interpellation that we have already noted: while in other types of interpellation different ideological discourses and apparatuses struggle to 'catch' the individual, in identitary interpellation the individual has always-already yielded to interpellation, but without any certainty that the trans-individual, 'social' conditions for the identitary interpellation are secured at all. While in other types of interpellation the theoretical problem, accordingly, is to define the conditions of a 'happy' interpellation, in identitary interpellation, given that it seems to be always-already successful at the individual level, the theoretical problem seems to be to define the larger social conditions where identitary interpellative mechanisms can be deployed at all. This, of course, is an over-simplification, but it will help us to advance in grasping the specificity of identitary interpellation.

The general 'interest' an individual has to yield to ideological interpellation is the satisfaction of her or his 'demand of sense': s/he cannot understand others, nor her- or himself, without the fixation provided by interpellation. The general philosophical principle of 'charity of interpretation' cannot, in itself, secure this tasknot because some utterances, discourses of inter-subjective relations would be too 'exotic' for the principle to be stretched to cover them, but because too many utterances, discourses and relations may be too 'un-exotic', too 'common', too *binding* not to exact decisions impossible without the 'fixation' which interpellation provides. Identity statements, usually embedded in some more general ideology (totemistic, genealogical, familial, communal, corporate, political, etc.), perform precisely this kind of 'fixation' of social relations. Georges Devereux, who starts from a rather 'technical' notion of identity,[40] underlines that 'it must be possible for ethnic identity to be enunciated, and it has to be enunciated, by an auto-ethnographer'.[41] This condition of reflexivity holds for our type of identity as well; it logically originates from a statement like, A says: 'I am a P'. Such a statement provides the speaker with an important social 'anchorage', for it affirms the identity of *sujet d'énonciation*, the subject of enunciation, the speaker as a concrete individual being, and of *sujet d'énoncé*, the 'social individual', the individual as member of a group. This 'fixation' provides the speaker both with the control over her or his utterances, and the access to her or his 'social being'. It is her or his tie to social ties. If the identity statement is embedded in some other ideology, it is only the effect of the ideological inter-pellation having been successfully performed upon the speaker as a particular individual. As a consequence, it submits the interpellated individual to the obligations of group membership, and to the fear of the group eventually withdrawing its autho-risation for further identity statements. If the background ideology is an identitary one, though, its interpellation confronts the interpellated individual directly with the anxiety as to the very existence of the identitary group. Since the tie to her or his social ties, and, it should hardly be added, to her- or himself, comes to the individual through her or his belonging to the identitary group, the eventuality that the group will not be able to constitute itself presents an immediate danger to the individual.[42] 'If *we* do not have the right (~s pertaining to an identitary group), *I* cannot be my (identitary) Self'.

The social tie which binds together identitary communities comes from the threat of losing, or not being able to achieve, their specific form of sociality. It is a tie which founds itself on the possibility of its own absence.[43]

Identitary Ideology in Social Struggles

As already noted, identitary ideology, by constructing social aggregates under the threat of the loss of elementary mechanisms of inter-subjectivity, is a powerful *mechanism of domination*. As such, it has amply been used by political classes to destroy the Yugoslav Federation, to wage wars, and to fabricate social consensus as the basis for new political constructions[44] whose primary effects were the installation of new forms of exploitation,[45] inequality,[46] discipline and control. Identitary ideology is now an important component in these newly imposed political constructions. It fits well into the status of 'limited sovereignty' of these new entities, reproduces their dependence at the international level, and mediates their disciplinary action over their own populations.

Contemporary debates mostly focus upon the tension between the 'citizenship principle' and the 'identitary principle' which identitary ideological constitution presumably introduces into the body politic. The remedy proposed is to *separate* the two domains and, at the same time, to *reformulate* the identity-complex. Accordingly, 'citizenship' as the *political* domain is separated from the *cultural* domain, which, in turn, is re-constituted upon the principle of 'cultural diversity'. As cultural diversity is deduced from cultural rights, and as 'cultural rights' are supposed to be part of (individual) human rights, reformulation of the cultural sphere submits it to constitutive principles of the modern juridical–political sphere, and the presumed 'separation' is rather an *annexation* of culture by the political sphere. This does not mean that identitary construction has been superseded by some universalist political construction: it only means that the identitary construction has been more or less rigorously articulated to a universalist juridical–political frame. In other words, and in the light of the theory we have tried to present here, it is at this point that *the identitary construction has actually been completed*. Not only does the standard solution to the identitary problem complete the logic of identitary construction, it also deeply contaminates the supposedly 'autonomous' political sphere with this logic. But here, in the *political* dimension, the standard solution does bring a solution: not the solution to the problem it is supposed to confront, but a solution to a problem it does not pose. Contamination of the traditional political sphere by the logic of identitary construction brings a solution to the crisis of the liberal democratic *political* model—it replaces political processes by juridical and para-juridical procedures, transforms political confrontations into cultural struggles, dissolves the relics of the 'political sphere' into a 'civil society' composed of various identitary groups, and submerges the relics of the public sphere under a flood of authenticist and solipsist identitary discourses. What seemed to be an annexation of the identitary culture to the political sphere proves to be 'culturalisation' of politics, and its replacement by apparatuses and procedures of Foucauldian[47] governmentality.[48]

Notes

1. The logic of this reasoning reminds one of a joke related by Freud in *Jokes and their Relations to the Unconscious*: 'In the temple at Cracow the Great Rabbi N. was sitting. Suddenly he .exclaimed: 'At this very moment the Great Rabbi L. has died in Lemberg.' .At last it was established .that the Rabbi L. had not died .he was still alive. A stranger took the opportunity of jeering at one of the Cracow Rabbi's disciples...: ''Your Rabbi made a great fool of himself that time, when he saw the Rabbi L. die in Lemberg. The man's alive to this day'. 'That makes no difference', replied the disciple. 'Whatever you may say, the *Kück* from Cracow to Lemberg was a magnificent one' (1921: 63). The stranger believes that a vision needs to be true if it is to be a vision—as we may believe that elections should be democratic if they are to be elections; the disciple, to the contrary, knows that a vision only has to happen to be fascinating—as

Mr. Bush knows that elections, to generate legitimacy, only have to take place.

2. *Matryoshka* is a wooden folk-art doll from Russia. On opening it one finds inside it a smaller, likewise doll which, in turn, contains yet another smaller doll, and so on.

3. 'Identity' may even be promoted to the status of a legal category. This is a particularly strong tendency within those legislations which otherwise enforce the neo-liberal submission of cultural sphere to the mechanisms of 'free market', i.e., in the post-socialist legislation. The following is an example from Slovenia. According to the implicit philosophy of the Council of Europe suggestions (which were later built into the Slovene 'Law on the Enforcement of Public Interest in Culture'/*Uradni list* RS, no. 96-4807/2002, November 14, 2002; also in *Predpisi s področja kulture*/Regulations in the area of culture/, Ljubljana: *Uradni list*, 2003), the 'natural life' of culture is provided by the invisible hand of the 'free market'. However, the law explicitly considers the eventuality that the self-regulated cultural market may fail to provide goods and services of sufficient quality, or in sufficient quantity, or may not provide for their sufficient accessibility, on certain points of public interest. It is upon these points of 'public interest' that the state and the local communities should intervene. The horizon of the public interest is generally defined as 'the cultural development of Slovenia and the Slovene nation', and is further specified as 'securing the conditions for: cultural creativity; accessibility of cultural goods; cultural diversity; Slovene *cultural identity*; common Slovene cultural space.' In a programme document (*National Program for Culture 2004–2007*), special state responsibility for vulnerable groups (specified as disabled, children, immigrants) is formulated as the 'enforcement of cultural rights as a dimension of human rights', and materialises in 'securing the conditions for authentic expression of cultural needs of various minority ethnic communities, vulnerable groups .and the basic conditions for conservation and development of their cultural *identities*' (italics mine).

4. Hence 'the politics of recognition'. See Taylor (1992).

5. 'La liberté consiste à pouvoir faire tout ce qui ne nuit pas à autrui: ainsi, l'exercice des droits naturels de chaque homme n'a de bornes que celles qui assurent aux autres membres de la société la jouissance de ces mêmes droits'. (Art. 4 of the *Déclaration* of 1789).

6. This position of the 'wronged other' is inscribed in the field of human rights by the 'structuring' opposition *'tout homme / nul homme'*: *everybody* should be included, *is* (by nature) included within the horizon of human rights; correlatively, *nobody* should be excluded, can be excluded from this horizon. It is inscribed also as a 'structured' effect, punctually, by the figure of *'autru'*, *'autres membres de la sociét'*.

7. To conduct our analysis, we will adapt the conceptual apparatus proposed by Ducrot (1996). We will develop Ducrot's theory, a theory of argumentation *in language*, so as to embrace problems of argumentation *in discourse*. Ducrot epistemologically supports his theory of argumentation with reference to the work of Mikhail Bakhtin. Since Bakhtin's is a theory of discourse, not of language, we will obviously elaborate our extension of Ducrot's theory within the epistemological direction taken by Ducrot himself, while taking into account also other contributions of the same school: Medvedev (1928); Vološinov (1929); Bakhtin (1963). The general concept under which these problems were elaborated by the 'Bakhtin's school' is the concept of 'orientation towards another discourse', *ustanovka na čužoe slovo*.

8. Ducrot (1996).

9. The *topos* evoked remains on the level of the 'background'; schematically, we will mark this by writing T *above* the horizontal line *under* which we will present the [argument → conclusion] chain.

10. Yet, this simple rhetorical turn accomplishes a major political shift: from the concern for the minority rights *(in general)* in a 'mono-ethnic' state, it transfers the emphasis upon the confrontation between two *(particular)* 'ethnic' formations. This displacement by which conflict and negotiation between the major ethnic groups marginalises smaller ones was denounced by Jean-Arnault Déens: 'La logique qui a prevalu au Kosovo s'est repeté en Macedoine, où la mosaique ethnique, confessionnelle et linguistique est particulierement complexe. ... le dialogue politique favorisé par la communauté internationale s'est reduit à un face-à face entre représentants macedoniens et albanais, 'oubliant' les Turcs, les Roms, les Serbes, les Vlachs ou les Macedoniens musulmans, appelé Torbeš. Dans le conflit, des méhanismes de reduction de la complexité sociale à un affrontement entre deux 'grands' nationalismes se mirent en oeuvre, de mène qu'une assimilation des petits groupes à ces 'grands' nationalismes' (2003: 16; trans. *http://mondediplo.com/2003/08/04derens*).

11. This 'application to the facts' of the universalist ideology, or the assessment of the 'facts' in terms of the background universalism, is a delicate if not impossible task: it has to measure an absence, and to invent the measure of an absence ('which allo-ethnic individual, excluded from the state structure, makes the state mono-ethnic?'). (If the utterance [I] approaches a well-known sorites on the side of its interpretation, it nears pragmatic paradox on the side of its production: its enunciation, at least to some extent, falsifies it.) The decision about the 'facts' cannot be 'fully motivated' and will always suffer from insufficient support: it is consequently an act of power and has to compensate its relative arbitrariness by a position of authority. This

is precisely our point here: revendication of the recognition of identity invests the instance to which it is addressed with *the authority of arbitration* about the proper 'use' of the universalist juridico–political apparatuses.

12. In this sense, the plea for a recognition of identity is the inversion of ideological interpellation in the Althusserian sense. The Althusserian interpellation endeavours to elicit, from its 'addressee', the interpellated individual, an unconditional identification to the 'subject-supposed-to-believe' of its belief-background, i.e., to promote its 'subject-supposed-to-believe' into a 'subject-supposed-to-*know*'. Contrary to this, the identitary claim poses the interpellation as always-already achieved on the part of its speaker, and situates its 'addressee' upon the structural *locus* from where the identitary speaker has always-already been interpellated (upon the *locus* of the 'subject-supposed-to-know'). Identitary speech is the contemporary counterpart to the voluntary servitude, *la servitude volontaire*.

13. Beck (1992) and (1999).

14. Lapham (2003).

15. 'She asked the king to give him (= Rodrigo de Bivar, 'el Cid') to her for husband, for she was much taken by his qualities, or to punish him according to the laws for the death he had afflicted to her father': Corneille opens his 'Avertissement' (1648) to *Le Cid* by quoting the passage in Spanish.

16. 'Pour qu'un peuple naissant pût gouter les saines maximes de la politique et suivre les règles fondamentales de la raison d'Etat, il faudrait que l'effet pût devenir la cause, que l'esprit social qui doit etre l'ouvrage de l'institution presidât à l'institution même, et que les hommes fussent avant les lois ce qu'ils doivent devenir par elles' (Rousseau 1762: 262; English trans. 1993: 215).

17. Beck (2000: 95).

18. To be fair, the players on this field are identified few lines above: 'state, business and a society of citizens' Beck (2000: 94).

19. Albright (1998: 25); quoted from Beck (2000: 82).

20. Freud (1921: 107); Freud also uses the terms 'point of coincidence' (1921: 107) and 'common quality' (1921: 108).

21. The constitution of the modern 'autonomous cultural sphere' can theoretically be presented in various ways. An explicit classical attempt is the one proposed by Georg Simmel (cf. his texts: 'Das Geheimnis'; 'Die Grossstädte'; . *Philosophie des Geldes*; For English translation, see Wolff (1964). In a kind of historical dialectical process, Simmel binds together the expansion of 'money economy', the emergence of the modern public sphere ('publicity' which encompasses 'politics, administration and jurisdiction'), and the polari-

sation between the 'objective culture' and the individual culture. For Simmel, 'cultural differenciation', 'culture which outgrows all personal life', are inseparably linked with the constitution of the modern state as a sphere of, as he puts it, 'publicity', with the correlative imposition of the money economy as the dominating form of exchange, but also with the growth of *modern individualism*. Simmel emphasises the *integrative* character of the 'cultural ideal' and, most importantly, links its integrative force to a *suspension of* 'the inherent value' of the elements which form the cultural 'ideal'. The cultural sphere constitutes itself by a process in which particular 'achievements' 'evaporate' out of the regions of their origin, and coalesce to form a separate and autonomous domain. These 'achievements' are liberated from their particularist boundedness and transformed into the 'glue' of *human* relations by a certain suspension of, or abstraction from, their original, authentic and particularist 'inherent value'. Thus, the 'ontological mode' of culture as an autonomous social sphere is constitutively *distanciation* from 'origins', is *suspension* of 'authenticity'. Simmel's insight suggests the image of a Sargasso Sea of uprooted 'achievements', both integrated into a *humanising* 'cultural ideal' *and* crashing down upon the individual as 'an overwhelming fullness of crystallised and impersonalised spirit'. An alternative way to present the constitution of the modern 'culture' would be to explain it as a consequence of the expansion of commodity exchange: the history of modernity can be described as progressive annexation of one social sphere after the other into the generalised commodity economy. Commodity exchange, as the dominant form of exchange, over-determines all other forms of exchange simply by imposing the necessity upon individuals to apprehend all kinds of exchange as *economic* exchange. This is the result of the historical constitution of economy into an 'autonomous' social sphere, the dominant social sphere. The counterpart of this historical constitution is the autonomisation of other 'social spheres', and of the cultural sphere among them. The modern sphere of culture would then be the dumping ground of ideological elements made superfluous by their substitution with the *commodity fetishism* as the dominant symbolic mediator of social practices. Culture, as it has historically emerged with modernity, is like a *cabinet de curiosités*, stuffed with 'native representations', abstracted from practices and processes of their origin.

22. This 'fit' is the ideological counterpart to the chain of dependency as classically analysed by Gunder Frank (1969).
23. It is only from this point on that the term 'identity' can be considered to possess theoretical conceptual value. Thus admitted into the field of theory, the concept immediately calls for further elaboration. The

situation is *not* one of the invasions of the social field by psychological mechanisms~~which~~ would require, as the epistemological counterpart, the abandonment of sociological conceptuality to the profit of some psychological or psychoanalytical conceptual apparatus. What we have just described is rather what Georg Simmel calls 'the autonomisation of contents'. In the chapter 'Die Geselligkeit (Beispiel der Reinen oder Formalen Soziologie)', in: *Grundfragen der Soziologie* (1970), Simmel first establishes the distinction between 'the *content*, .the *material* .of sociation' (defined as: 'Everything present in the individuals .in the form of drive, interest, purpose, inclination, psychic state, movement.').and the *form* which is sociation (*Vergesellschaftung*) itself ('Sociation thus is the form .in which individuals grow together into units that satisfy their interests.'). Simmel then proceeds to describe a phenomenon which he calls 'the autonomisation of contents'. Although he considers this process to be essential, he only describes it as already given, without asking what may be the reasons for its emergence: 'But it happens that these materials .become autonomous in the sense that they are no longer inseparable from the objects which they formed and thereby made available to our purposes. They come to play freely in themselves and for their own sake; they produce or make use of materials that exclusively serve their own operation or realisation' (quoted from Wolff 1950: 40 **ss)**. What Simmel does not explicitly state, but what is implicit already in the quoted passage and what even more obviously follows from the examples he is giving, is that the 'contents', by 'autonomising' themselves, *convert themselves into 'forms' of sociation*. This region of Simmel's theoretical elaboration may well be an ingenuous anticipation-in-action of what much later Merab Mamardašvili developed under the concept of ' *converted forms*'. (At one point, Simmel actually uses the expression translated as 'this complete turnover', but then banalises the idea into the transition from a situation where 'the material determines the form' to a situation where 'the form determines the material'.) Identity-formation, then, is a type of sociation where processes of identification and Ego-integration, otherwise the '*material*' of various forms of sociation, become themselves the 'form' of social integration of individuals.

24. The central component of the presently hegemonic ideology is actually the 'proto-juridical' condition of contemporary juridical apparatuses: the ideology of human rights. It is the complex of human rights which nowadays occupies the position of what Althusser called '*le petit supplément d'idéologie morale*' without which the Law (*le Droit*) could not exist. This shows the capacity of the modern juridical ideology to structure its 'supplement' according to its own logic; this logic is one of *abstraction, homogenisation*, which permits

the presently hegemonic ideology to avoid being caught in any particular moral ideology, and, consequently, to hegemonise them all; it is therefore *via* its supplement that the juridical ideology now performs its 'dominant' role in the domain of 'practical ideologies' (cf. Althusser 1995: 99, 203).

25. 'Die *Konstitution des politischen Staats* und die Auflöung der bügerlichen Gesellschaft in die unabhägingen *Individuen*deren Verhätnis das *Recht* ist []vollzieht sich in *einem und demselben Akte*' (Marx 1958: 369).

26. Boris Buden (2002: *Kaptolski kolodvor*, Beograd: Centar za savremenu umetnost) writes of 'culturification' of political conflicts, while Kuzmanić (2002) speaks of 'disappearance' of politics from political apparatuses.

27. This accounts for the paradoxical 'traditionalism' of identitary ideologies.

28. 'For, to be a stranger is naturally a very positive relation; it is a specific form of interaction' (Wolff 1964: 402).

29. '[the stranger], who is close by, is far, and .he, who also is far, is actually near .is near and far *at the same time*.(. *ibid*.: 402, 407).

30. The relation to the stranger is 'founded only on generally human commonness' (*ibid*.: 407).

31. The one which, against the background of the general shared features of humanity, 'stresses that which is not common' (*ibid*.).

32. Theoreticians of the 'cultural translation' may pretend that such an additional integration of an excluded element can only be achieved through a struggle that shakes the existing notion of the universal and results in a revolutionary re-articulation of the universal. I think this is an exaggeration: the universal is articulated in juridical terms, it is abstract and formal. The content from which it is abstracted is not this or that identity—it is the relations of production and exploitation. See Althusser (1995).

33. Denunciations that the actors involved in these transactions do not act 'consistently' do not make much sense since the field itself is structured so as to exclude any possibility of 'consistency'. This is most probably one of the important sources of violence, so frequent in 'identitary' situations.

34. See the concluding remarks to my text 'Ideology and Fantasy' in Kaplan and Sprinker (1993).

35. See my piece 'Should the theory of ideology be conceived as a theory of institutions?' in Cindrič (1998).

36. What has widely been interpreted as 'neo-nationalism' seems rather to be identitary politics. For example, 'nationalist' post-communist political classes have engaged in a long-term 'politics of recognition': their struggle for the recognition of their new states, accession to

EU, entering NATO, etc., have been styled as 'struggles for recognition'; the same endeavour has been evoked as the motive for joining the coalition invading Iraq, for the Vilnius declaration, for participation to the occupation of Iraq ...

37. As first proposed in Althusser (1970, rpt. 1976; Eng. trans. 1971).

38. In: 'From Historical Marxisms to Historical Materialism: Toward the Theory of Ideology' (Rosenthal and Lal 1991).

39. The 'extremist' interpellation *via* individual fantasy; the 'national' interpellation *via* 'the nation as a zero-institution'. See my texts quoted earlier.

40. 'Quite simply,/ethnic identity/is a tool of triage and labeling.' ('L'identitéethnique: fondations logiques et dysfunctions' (1970) in Devereux (1985)).

41. *Ibid.*

42. In the words of Ubu-Roi: 'Il n'y a pas de Polonais sans Pologne'.

43. In this sense, identitary community is distinct from the Freudian *Masse*. We can now sketch the relation between the two. Freud distinguishes three modalities of identification: 'First, identification is the original form of emotional tie with an object; secondly, in a regressive way it becomes a substitute for a libidinal object-tie, as it were by means of introjection of the object into the ego; and thirdly, it may arise with any new perception of a common quality shared with some other person who is not an object of the sexual instinct. The more important this common quality is, the more successful may this partial identification become, and it may thus represent the 'beginning of a new tie' (Freud 1921: 107–8). The *Masse*-formation proceeds from a combination of the second and the third modality of identification. It starts from a particular inflexion of modality no. 2 in which the regressive 'introjection' puts the object not in the place of the ego, but in the place of the *ego ideal* (which, actually, is defined as 'a differentiating grade in the ego'). It is completed by modality no. 3 when individuals who share this common quality identify with each other on its account. 'A primary group of this kind is a number of individuals who have put one and the same object in the place of their ego ideal and have consequently identified themselves with one another in their ego' (*idem*: 116). The Freudian *Masse* is constructed through two processes on the level of individual psyche. Contrary to this, our construction of the identitary group is trans-individual from the very beginning since the instances of the 'subject-supposed-to-'.with which individuals identify ('in their ego') are *inter-subjective* instances.

44. Cf. Rosenthal (2002).

45. This is a clear case where ideology, in its 'material existence', importantly, if not decisively, participates to the *installation* of a new

type of 'relations of production'. It has been reproached to Althusser, among others by Hall (1996: 12), that he led the theory of ideology back into the classical dead-end by 'normatively' (*ibid*.) defining its 'function' (sic!) as 'to reproduce the social relations of production'. Althusser's formulation is different: reproduction of relations of production is, to a very large degree, secured (*assurée*) 'by the exercise of the state-power in the state-apparatuses, the repressive apparatus on one side, and the ideological state-apparatuses on the other'; Althusser (1970: 286, rpt. 1971). Schematically, installation of new relations has been achieved: (*a*) through *replacement* of former relations by new ones (privatisation, denationalisation, redefinition of the general function of the state from protector of labour to the agent of capital), enacted primarily by the *repressive* state-apparatuses; (*b*) by *re-articulation* of the existing apparatuses, performed mostly by *ideological* apparatuses. Identitary ideology, in its 'material existence' (apparatuses, discourses, images), has an *over-determining role* in these processes: 1. It '*represents*' the violent *replacement* of one type of social relations (of production) by another type as the advent of a historical *telos* (the national state) which, at the same time, is a '*return*' to a presumed state of 'normality' and 'authenticity' (liberal capitalism). The new political construction is presented as a 'true expression' of identitary authenticity to which the identitary community is presumed to have a fundamental 'right'. Here, identitary ideology, playing on two of its components, the 'native' 'subject-supposed-to-believe' and the collective 'right', 'represents', in Althusser's words, 'the imaginary relation of individuals to their real conditions of existence'. 2. It attempts to *unify* the *re-articulation* of existing ideological elements under its domination. Here, it 'interpellates' individuals. In this dimension again, a 'replacement' is at stakeidentitary ideology attempts to 'replace' the national ideological construction. In this, however, it can only fail: the instance that could take over the 'program managing' operations formerly performed by the 'nation as a zero-institution', the native, 'subject-supposed-to-believe', is not autonomous and depends upon an external recognition; but even if this recognition is granted, the 'native' instance can only engage in composing a 'native culture' whose collage is limited in its principle. The result is paradoxical: identitary ideology can only work if supported by statist (or, in the case of non-recognised identities, by para-statist, 'civil society') constraint, and the more successful it is, the more it weakens its statist or para-statist political construction by submitting it to the conjuncturally determined representative of the universalist sanction.

46. In all 'post-communist' countries where identitary ideology has been of primary importance during the past decade, social inequalities have begun rising after the change of system. Cf. Močnik (2002).

47. 'Maybe what is really important for our modernity that is, for our present is not so much the *étatisation* of society as the governmentalisation' of the state' (Foucault 1991: 103).

48. This structural transformation is already the object of a positive policy-notion: 'the increasing tendency to conscript communities as agencies of cultural governance' (Bennett 2001: 18). Bennett specifies the process in terms of governmentality and offers a 'political' classification for it: 'A noted recent tendency has consisted in the increased emphasis that is placed on communities of various sorts (ethnic, indigenous, regional, neighbourhoods, lifestyle communities) to assume responsibility for organising and managing themselves and their members. This renewed stress on the role of communities as an intermediary between the state and its citizens has been strongly associated with the political agendas of the third way' and, in more general terms, needs to be seen as a response to the concern to roll the state back out of the lives of its citizens that has been such a marked characteristic of neo-liberalism' (Bennett 2001: 49).

10

Constitutionalism in Pakistan: The Lingering Crisis of Dyarchy

Mohammad Waseem

This chapter deals with the nature and direction of constitutional thinking and practice in Pakistan. It is argued that the country reflects the general malaise of post-colonial societies characterised by a tension between the locus of power in the politico-administrative machinery and the source of legitimacy in the constitution. In the classical formulation, a constitution represents the way a nation wants to live its collective life in terms of various laws and institutions as well as powers and duties of public office holders. In other words, the institutional–constitutional edifice of the state functions as the 'vehicle of a nation's life'.[1] One finds comparable theories in the tradition of structural Marxism, for example in Poulantzas, which consider the state as a condensate of the power structure of the society.[2] It is argued that there is a conceptual tension in the formulation of such theories. In the context of post-colonial societies, transplantation of institutions and constitutions from a different era and a different continent, played a formative, almost deterministic, role in the way the state's authority was conceived and operationalised. For more than a 100 years, British India remained a laboratory for implementation of political, economic, legal and administrative values and norms. On the one hand, this shaped the way people came to look at their relations with the state in terms of new implements of power such as non-arbitrary sources of authority, codified law, rational–legal bureaucracy and rule of public representatives. On the other hand, it created the mass public itself which, in due time, rose to stake a claim for societal input into the business of the state.[3] In other words, our discussion needs to go beyond the ahistorical approach to constitutionalism in Pakistan and elsewhere, as embedded in such concepts as the reflection of either the nation's will or the social power structure in a microcosm. The relative autonomy of state apparatuses of military, bureaucracy and judiciary, as well as constitutional provisions ranging from writ jurisdiction, equality before law and equality of protection from law to neatly defined roles of police and magistracy and fundamental rights in general predate independence.

In the post-independence period, the state increasingly absorbed pressures from the newly enfranchised public, which sought to reshape politics along nationalist goals. The institutional–constitutional framework of the post-colonial state was ill-equipped to accommodate much less to sponsor and pursue these goals in earnest. This led to a general outcry of institutional decay, leading to a crisis of democracy.[4] Research on post-independence India and Pakistan gradually moved into a consideration of the bifocal nature of public authority. At one end, the bureaucratic core of the state, supported by the armed forces (overtly as in Pakistan and covertly as in India), represented the bedrock of conservatism in terms of continuity of policy, locus of power and ideological framework. In the common parlance, this came to be known as 'establishment'. At the other end, the political leadership purportedly claimed to represent the public, project its grievances and seek re-allocation of state's resources to meet the demands of their constituents. In this process, they vacillated between the two poles of upholding the establishment's commitment to what was often billed as 'national interest' in terms of internal and external security, and representing the society's demand structure couched in the idiom of 'public interest' to be articulated through the channels of decision-making on top. The 'centralising' tendencies of the former often overwhelmed the disaggregated nature of the latter in the context of the pluralist framework of vote politics in regional, religious, ethnic, caste and tribal terms. Rajni Kothari's formulation of 'state against democracy' in the context of Indian politics, though considered cynical by some, is even more applicable to Pakistan.[5]

The logic underlying this line of argument often led to placement of India and Pakistan along a continuum moving from democracy to authoritarianism. Hamza Alavi analyses the post-colonial state in South Asia and elsewhere as an institutional framework that is relatively autonomous of the dominant classes while at the same time mediating between their rival interests.[6] In this context, he sees differences between countries in a comparative framework such as between India and Pakistan, though formidable, as less than deterministic. In the same way, differences between the democratic and military phases of rule within Pakistan in a longitudinal framework are less than substantive. In Ayesha Jalal's view, the two countries displayed covert and overt authoritarianism respectively. She gives credit for civilian supremacy over military in India to the 'pre-existing unitary central apparatus' and similar propitious circumstances, rather than to politicians ruling the country.[7] This perspective sought to challenge the scholarly orthodoxy which looked at the two countries in the context of a dichotomy between democratic and military rule. The argument is that given the shared British legacy and the similar starting point of independent statehood, the difference between the two countries was more of degree than kind. Both systems displayed an obsessive concern with centralisation of power at the cost of provincial autonomy, securitisation of the national vision, use of ideology to subvert the process of articulation of regional or class interests, and discouragement of politics of issues in favour of politics of identity.

For the purposes of the present study of constitutionalism in Pakistan, we propose to look at the structural transformation of politics in the country inasmuch as the ruling elite sought to change the juridical framework of the exercise of state's authority. This process took place in a direction which was fundamentally different from the one pursued in its neighbouring country. As opposed to the classical approach to the constitution as being a reflection of the nation's will and the power structure of a society, it has been argued that the constitutional tradition inherited by Pakistan did not necessarily correspond to the reality of the distribution of power on the ground.[8] The inherent institutional imbalance between bureaucracy and politicians in Pakistan made a mockery of such constitutional provisions as parliamentary sovereignty, procedural and substantive aspects of the legislative process at the federal and provincial levels and the principle of the government's accountability to public representatives. The Government of India Act 1935 as amended by the Independence of India Act 1947 remained operative for more than a decade after partition. On the way, the state elite faced a tremendous pressure from the 'political class' that was marginalised under the prevalent ruling set-up. As the crisis deepened between the parliamentary and extra-parliamentary forces on the issue of constitutionality of certain policy and administrative measures taken by the government, to be discussed later, judiciary was brought in as a referee and the ultimate source of legitimacy. The 1954 Tamizuddin Case started a process whereby the higher courts continually interpreted the constitution throughout the following half-century. The tenacity of the struggle between the two sides has been amply reflected through a lingering crisis of constitutional understanding between the two. On the one hand, various attempts at constitutional engineering were taken up by extra-parliamentary forces, led by civil bureaucracy during the first quarter and military during the second quarter of a century after independence. On the other hand, parliamentarians struggled to keep the constitutional framework inherited from British India intact and thwart attempts from outside the parliament to change its character.

The most contentious issue, which has been at the core of the constitutional crisis of Pakistan, is parliamentary sovereignty. The founding fathers heralded the independent statehood of Pakistan from a starting point, which was fundamentally different from India contrary to general understanding. It was considered almost mandatory by the ruling elite to discount with the parliament even as power was formally transferred to the Constituent Assembly. Apparently, cross-migration of Muslims from India and Hindus and Sikhs in the reverse direction after partition was a shared experience of the two countries. In reality, the phenomenon of migration had an entirely different impact on their political development. In (West) Pakistan, refugees accounted for 20 per cent of the population as opposed to only 1 per cent of the population in India. Refugees in India came from peripheral areas of British India in the northwest and northeast. Refugees in Pakistan came from what had long been the imperial centre of India, along with presidencies of Bombay and Calcutta, to the periphery of the erstwhile empires. These people had led the movement for Pakistan, which was established in what became their land of migration. The migratory elite provided the new state with its governor general and prime minister, leadership of the ruling party Muslim League, two-thirds of higher bureaucracy as well as three-fourths of the emergent bourgeoisie. As opposed to structural continuity in India as a successor state of British India, it was structural discontinuity that characterised Pakistan as a seceding state par excellence. From the beginning, the migrant-led executive of the new state grappled with the issue of dealing with the Constituent Assembly, which had been elected by the legislative assemblies of Muslim majority provinces now constituting Pakistan and which was, therefore, dominated by 'locals'. Migrants from the Muslim minority provinces who had been converted to the Pakistan cause at the time of the 1936–37 elections enjoyed a sense of state legitimacy higher than the late converts from the Muslim majority provinces. Pakistan became a migrant state par excellence.

The new state was characterised by a disdain for legislature. The executive, along with bureaucracy, assumed the sub-legislatory activity in various important fields. Recourse to mass mandate— which would have meant exit from power for the migrant-cum-bureaucratic elitewas considered dysfunctional for the system. Elections were postponed *ad nauseum*. Constitutional formulas that promised to restore parliament to its rightful place at the centre of the state as the custodian of state legitimacy were brushed aside. One such attempt led to the first coup in Pakistan's history executed by the civil bureaucracy in 1954. Governor-General Ghulam Mohammad dissolved the parliament and dismissed Prime Minister Nazimuddin who enjoyed the support of majority in the Constituent Assembly. The Federal Court upheld the decision on a technical ground that the relevant provisions under Article 223-A to issue writs of *mandamus* and *quo-warranto* to annul the dissolution and restore the government had not been given assent by the Governor-General. The fact that the governor general could give or withhold assent as per the Court's verdict indirectly made him a constituent part of the legislature.[9] Subsequently, in response to the Governor-General's reference to the Federal Court in the midst of the prevalent constitutional crisis where the supreme law-making body had been dissolved and no other law-making institution was in existence, the Court validated the dissolution of the Constituent Assembly following the doctrine of state necessity. By now, extra-parliamentary forces had become fully entrenched in the state system. The doctrine of state necessity became an essential part of the judicial lexicon of Pakistan, whereby maintaining public order was defined as the paramount function of any ruling set-up even if it involved an extra-constitutional step. An orthodoxy was born whereby judiciary developed a 'statist' perspective on constitutional issues in line with the ruling elite on top of what was fast becoming an administrative state.

On the other hand, the Federal Court also refused to empower the governor general to validate laws in the absence of the Constituent Assembly. As opposed to the Governor-General's efforts to organise a Constituent Convention on 10 May 1954 to make a constitution, the Court ordered the summoning of a new Constituent Assembly for that purpose. It duly recognised the continuation in force of the Independence of India Act as the supreme law of the land according to which an elected Constituent Assembly alone could make a constitution. The Court clearly displayed a 'constitutional' outlook. In its view, the executive must refer to a superordinate body of laws for submitting itself to the principle of legality of its actions. However, in this respect there were two opposite consequences of these court cases. Constitutionalism became the final point of reference for the courts sitting on judgement on the legitimacy of all presidential measures to bring about a change of government through extraordinary means, such as dissolution of the Constituent/National Assembly, e.g. in 1954, 1988, 1990, 1993 and 1996. More significantly, the courts took recourse to constitutionalism even when army directly took over power through extra-constitutional means. The 1958 and 1969 military coups abrogated the 1956 and 1962 Constitutions respectively, while the 1977 and 1999 coups suspended the 1973 Constitution. Each time, the courts sat on the judgement of the act of dissolution of parliament by army notwithstanding the fact of abrogation or suspension of the relevant constitutions. They conducted elaborate hearings about the constitutional vires of the act of dissolution and gave their verdict on the basis of contemporary or classical approaches to constitutional law in UK and the Commonwealth in general. The critics of judiciary's role in Pakistan have accused it of following the word rather than the meaning, and the letter rather than the spirit of the constitution, thus turning a blind eye to the actual issue of uses and abuses of constitutional provisions by the supra-parliamentary office of the Governor-General (and later the president). Constitutionalism remained a consistent, latent, all-pervasive and morally superior source of legitimacy under both civil and, paradoxically, military dispensations. General Iskandar Mirza declared, soon after launching a military coup on 7 October 1958, that Pakistan would be governed under the new set-up in accordance with the last constitution as much as possible.[10] Subsequent to each successful military takeover, the coup-maker promised constitutional continuity sans those articles, which provided for the elective principle and rule of public representatives.

The obvious casualty in the process of successive acts of dismissal of elected assemblies was parliamentary sovereignty. Even apart from the issue of dissolution of the Constituent Assembly, the latter's legislative potential was seriously circumscribed during the first decade after partition. In 1950, the Sindh Chief Court had observed that there was no limit on legislative powers of the Constituent Assembly.[11] However, the reality was different. The first Constituent Assembly sessions were few as well as brief. For seven years, it met for only 51 days per annum on an average. Government bills consumed the whole session time, leaving little space for private member's bills. Successive governments resorted to steamrolling the bills through various stages without eliciting public opinion or allowing full debate on the floor or sometimes even informing members about the oncoming legislation. Very few bills were referred to select committees. The National Assembly under the first Constitution (1956–58) passed 72 bills, which included 50 presidential ordinances already entered on the statute book.[12]

Within a decade after independence, there had emerged two power centres in the country. One comprised the political executive, civil bureaucracy, business community and intelligentsia, all dominated by the Urdu-speaking migrants (later called 'mohajirs') from U.P., Bombay and to a lesser extent Hyderabad Deccan. In close proximity followed the migrants from East Punjab. These groups were socially embedded in the middle class, which gradually expanded from its mohajir core to include Punjabis and, to some extent, Pathans. It was essentially the mohajir-Punjabi middle class that laid the institutional foundations of the state, defined its ideological profile and shaped its cultural, economic, diplomatic and financial policies. With no electoral constituency of its own, it distrusted the process of elections since these were destined to bring the tribal and landed elites into power. The middle class in Pakistan has been socially progressive but politically conservative. It looked at electoral democracy in an illiterate society such as Pakistan as disruptive of social order and destabilising in its political impact. In Hamza Alavi's formulation, this was the *salariat* that heralded the movement for Pakistan essentially to get out of its potentially under-privileged position vis-àvis its better-educated Hindu counterpart. [13] In Pakistan after partition, the middle class thinking was reflected through the bureaucratic abhorrence for mass politics, commitment to unitary forms of government and hostility against the political class in general that was condemned for nepotism, corruption, factionalism, and parochialism. The way out was establishment of control over politicians from outside the elected assemblies. Not surprisingly, it was exactly at a moment in history when the Constituent Assembly was considering a move to transfer some of the overarching powers of Governor-General away from him when the latter dissolved it in 1954.

The second power centre was the parliament itself. It represented politicians from all the provinces, East Bengal, Punjab, Sindh, NWFP and Baluchistan. Having been elected before partition, the parliament did not correspond to the new realities of power and privilege as well as ethnicity and demography. Under the prevalent constitutional framework, especially after the 1954 Tamizuddin Case followed by the 1955 Governor-General's reference to the Supreme Court, a dyarchy set in whereby the legislators were required to adjust to the idea of a non-sovereign parliament. The 1956 Constitution formalised the strong role of president vis-àvis a weak prime minister. This model was patterned after the Montague-Chelmsford Reforms 1919 which provided for dyarchy at the provincial level. Under dyarchy, the provincial administration was divided between 'reserved subjects' administered by the official councilors belonging to the civil bureaucracy who were essentially accountable to the executive, and 'transferred subjects' handled by political councilors responsible to the legislative council. The India Act 1935 provided responsible government at the provincial level but reserved veto power for the Governor. It also provided for the principle of dyarchy for the ruling dispensation at the centre—principle that was operationalised rather late in the form of 'interim government' (1946–47). In the immediate post-independence years, the extra-parliamentary office of Governor-General Jinnah made it a matter of routine to initiate information, guide policy as well as take political and administrative decisions largely bypassing the parliament. This pattern of authority has been described as the 'vice-regal system'.[14] The moral authority of Jinnah was manipulated by a coterie of bureaucrats around him led by Secretary-General Chaudhary Mohammad Ali. They held initiatives in their own hands in matters ranging from administrative reorganisation, revenue and police administration, allocation of resources, posting and transfer of civil bureaucracy, and appointment of service chiefs, judges of higher courts and diplomats abroad. In fact, an informal 'parallel cabinet' of bureaucrats ran the administration.[15] Meanwhile, the Constituent Assembly constantly debated legal formulas and constitutional frameworks to bring about a consensus on the floor between parties, communities and provinces, often at the bidding of the increasingly powerful president operating from outsidein this case, President Iskandar Mirza. He openly took credit for putting in place coalition after coalition to form the government in the centre for several years.[16] Two ex-bureaucratsGovernor-General Ghulam Mohammad and President Iskandar Mirza were responsible for dismissing six prime ministers from 1953 to 1958.

The parliament remained a patch-work of political stalwarts belonging to various provinces, who were elected before independence. Karachi exercised a firm control over provinces through the central bureaucracy. The Independence of India Act empowered the governor general to declare emergency in any part of the country vide Article 93. He could also dismantle the administration of a province and put it under governor's rule vide a new Section 92-A. This amounted to constitutional terrorism. The Centre dismissed nine provincial governments in 11 years after independence. The migrant-dominated Centre was inspired with an all-Pakistan institutional and constitutional outlook. Faced with security threats from India and laced with disdain for outlandish morals and manners of the periphery of yesterday's empires which formed today's Pakistan, it showed complete antipathy to sub-national identities. The shifting coalitional arrangements on the floor of the parliament, leading to a persistent crisis of government formation, reflected a pattern of manipulation of factional groupings inside the house by the president. Whenever provinces asserted their demands, for example, East Bengal after the 1954 elections which brought in new firebrand politicians into the second Constituent Assembly in 1955 demanding maximum provincial autonomy, the Centre sought to play parliamentary parties and party factions against each other. Various ideas started to take shape in the official circles: that provinces were the hot-bed of controversy; that a unitarian rather than a federal system was the guarantee against political instability; that the parliamentary system turned the chief executive into a hostage in the hands of public representatives since he needed to keep the support of majority in the house to save the government from falling; and that the presidential system provided the requisite level of stability because a president would be elected for a fixed term and would be shielded from the obligation of being accountable to the parliament. This was considered a solution of the perceived failures of several dyarchic arrangements for distribution of power. Although, the president led a constellation of powers operating from outside the parliament, which firmly controlled political and administrative initiatives, he was nevertheless inherently constrained to seek legitimacy from the parliament as enjoined by the Federal Court in the two constitutional cases of 1954 and 1955. In the establishment's view, the parliamentary system was a curse on the country's destiny, which held back its development and security. Therefore, it had to go. But the 1954 civilian coup had failed to deliver in this regard because the ultimate source of legitimacy remained with the India Act 1935 and Independence of India Act 1947, which together provided for parliamentary rule with prime minister as chief executive. Bureaucracy could not rule in its own name.

This paved the way for military takeover within a few years. Army units had been involved in the refugee evacuation effort during partition, in the war of 1947–49 in Kashmir and in the aid of civilian authority for keeping law and order on several occasions. The first Pakistani Commander-in-Chief General Ayub had already emerged as one of the principal players on the chessboard of politics in the Centre. In the following decades, the army emerged as an ally, and gradually, as the leader of extra-parliamentary groups and institutions. It became the shaper and maker of governments and constitutions. It became the bedrock of political conservatism represented by the dominant groups, communities and institutions in the society. Approaches to the phenomenon of praetorianism in Pakistan generally highlight a dichotomy between constitutional politics and military politics.[17] However, one may argue that a military government in Pakistan looks at its own role in transitional terms, as a facilitator to bring about change in the constitutional edifice according to its own preferences and priorities. The 1958 coup in Pakistan took place at a time when the prospects of general elections under the 1956 elections loomed large on the horizons, threatening to take the initiative away from where it had been for a decade. Elections would have shifted the source of legitimacy from the constitution (as interpreted by judiciary and implemented by the executive) back to the parliament, which would then become the repository of the national will and state sovereignty. That would have been the undoing of the military–bureaucratic establishment's cherished goals defined in terms of establishing a presidential form of governmenta– unitarian model of rule, a strong executive opposite a weak legislature and a strong Centre against weak provinces.

The 1958 military coup clearly identified the new locus of power in Pakistan. Punjab as the major catchment area for the army pro- vided a much needed power base for the migratory elite. This eventually led to the *punjabisation* of the state in Pakistan over the following decades leading to alienation of other ethnic communi- ties.[18] The military high command's exposure to the US admini- stration after Pakistan entered military alliances of CENTO and SEATO in the mid-1950s brought new awareness about the unity of command and tenurial security enjoyed by an American president. Military input in terms of political and constitutional engineering served the function of transition from parliamentary to presidential system through promulgation of the 1962 Con- stitution. Meanwhile, the famous 1958 Dosso Case, which deliber- ated over, and finally, validated the military coup provided a new perspective on the phenomenon of military politics in Pakistan. The 1955 Governor-General's Reference had dwelled on the doctrine of state necessity. The Dosso Case instead deliberated on the effect of a successful revolution as a law-creating fact. This interpretation heavily relied on Kelsen's theory couched in the principles of legal positivism. Joseph Conrad compared the two extra-constitutional acts of 1954 and 1958 as examples of com- missarial and constituent dictatorship respectively.[19] The sub- sequent history of dissolution of parliaments in Pakistan moved along these two poles of jurisprudence. The 'necessity cases' such as the 1955 Reference, the 1972 Asma Jillani Case and the 1977 Begum Nusrat Bhutto Case where the higher courts focused on the argument of safeguarding the prevalent social and political order from total collapse through extra-constitutional action relied on the implied mandate of the state. The Kelsen Cases, for which the Dosso Case remains the prime example, by default brings in the question of acknowledgement of the *fait accompli*. Together, the two types of judicial cases provided 'legal' ways of resolving constitutional crises emerging out of dissolution of elected assemblies.

All along, the judiciary's role as referee in the struggle between parliamentary and extra-parliamentary forces transformed it into a symbol of ultimate legitimacy. Higher judiciary found space between the two power centres, and thereby arrogated to itself the function of judicial review. By upholding the principle of constitutionalism over and above the principle of parliamentary sovereignty, the courts generally supported the executive. Also, by consistently referring to the doctrine of necessity for legitimising extra-constitutional actions, it followed a 'statist' approach to matters of governance. All along, judiciary safeguarded and vigorously defended its own right to overview official actions of controversial nature. Institutionalism, constitutionalism and statism became the leading characteristics of the judiciary's perspective in the context of a persistent constitutional crisis. The instinctive response of judiciary to the executive's overbearing attitude, which often amounted to emasculation of lawful opposition in the country, was to keep the latter's authority bound by the word of law and thus to maintain its own role as interpreter of law. Subsequently, the two military takeovers of 1977 and 1999 and dissolution of elected assemblies in 1988, 1990, 1993, and 1996 within an ongoing constitutional set-up even further consolidated the role of judiciary in making and breaking of governments.

The 1962 Constitution is the epitome of the presidential system in Pakistan. It has been remembered as such by its protagonists like the army, bureaucracy, the business community and conservative elements of intelligentsia for more than three decades now. They hark back to the halcyon days of Ayub when there was political stability and politicians were kept under control. Unfortunately, there was no way of entering the Ayub system available to the politicians belonging to major political parties, especially from East Pakistan and smaller provinces of West Pakistan. The popular uprising against Ayub in 1968–69 followed by the 1970 elections (held on a parliamentary basis) represented a setback for the presidential system in thought and practice. The 1973 Constitution revived the parliamentary form of government. It provided for a prime minister as chief executive, a bicameral parliament to assuage the fears of smaller provinces vis-àvis Punjab and a titular president. Parliament was *de facto* and *de jure* sovereign from 1972 to 1977. Zia's martial law government (1977–85), while making a departure from the previous practice of abrogating the constitutions, had only suspended the 1973 Constitution. There was a tacit understanding in the official circles that the presidential system had led to accumulation of anger and frustration among Bengalis and that even in West Pakistan Sindh, NWFP and Baluchistan had strong reservations against it.

The 1985 elections were again held under the parliamentary system. The military-led state elite faced the challenge of keeping the political initiative in its own hands while formally transferring power to elected representatives. Military's withdrawal from politics in 1985 was carefully managed to keep its covert role intact, as opposed to the previous withdrawal in 1971 after the defeat in East Pakistan. The two models correspond to the Brazilian and Argentinian models: in the former case (1980–84), military withdrawal represented a phased process in order to ensure continuation of policy and personnel after what was, at best, a partial transfer of power. In the latter case, the military regime collapsed after the defeat in the Falklands War in 1982. This led to emergence of a strong civilian government which was able to take innovative measures in terms of policy, institution-building and accountability of generals.[20] The Bhutto government (1971–77) approximated the Argentinian model as he introduced various economic, political and administrative reforms. The Zia-Junejo government (1985–88) represented the Brazilian model. If the Ayub era was the symbol of presidentialism, the Bhutto era is a reified model of populist politics cushioned by parliamentary sovereignty and mass mandate. The military junta under Zia was inimical to the idea of allowing back anything remotely similar to what was alleged to be dictatorial powers of prime minister. The argument was that if the constitution had a provision for dissolution of the

National Assembly at the hands of the president, then the conflict between the Pakistan People's Party (PPP) government and the Pakistan National Alliance (PNA) movement in 1977 would have been resolved within the constitutional framework by dissolving the parliament, and martial law would not have been imposed.

The civilianisation process in 1985 led to a new political and constitutional orthodoxy. It is characterised by a two-pronged constitutional approach: carving out a new legal and institutional edifice in order to accommodate the populist sentiments in favour of a parliamentary form of government; and at the same time keeping the control over policy and personnel in both operational and structural terms in the hands of the president. The new political idiom revolved around the theme of a balance of power between the president and the prime minister. This was a euphemism for lack of parliamentary sovereignty whereby the president could dissolve the National Assembly and dismiss the government of prime minister and his/her cabinet under the 8th Constitutional Amendment. From 1985 to 1997, the new arrangement for division of powers between the president and the prime minister as enshrined in the 8th Amendment remained a hotbed of controversy. It promises to remain so in the latest incarnation of 'dyarchy' after the 2002 elections. The April 1997 13th Amendment annulled the relevant clauses of the 8th Amendment, thereby taking the presidential power of dissolution of the National Assembly away from him. During the tussle between President Leghari and Prime Minister Nawaz Sharif in December 1997, Chief Justice Sajjad Ali Shah suspended the amendment, thereby restoring the presidential powers to dissolve the National Assembly, ostensibly to pave the way for the president to do exactly that. However, within minutes of the Court's verdict, the other and larger faction of the divided Supreme Court restored the 13th Amendment. Later, in 2003, the controversial Article 58(2) (b) was reinstated in the 17th Amendment, again enabling the president to dissolve the National Assembly.

The 1985 8th Amendment formalised a situation that had existed *de facto* during the 1950s. Under this, 'dyarchy' provided the substantive principle of constitutional rule, thereby effecting the replacement of a prime ministerial-dominant form of government with a presidential-dominant system.[21] The 8th Amendment was a culmination of various political and constitutional developments under Zia's rule. Fearing the PPP's potential to return to power in an event of elections, the military ruler along with the anti-Bhutto political grouping PNA representing various major and minor political parties sought to checkmate the prospect of a PPP victory by tilting the balance of power in favour of the president. First and foremost, President Zia sought to perpetuate his own role over and above a future parliament in order to keep in place the policy structure and a plethora of laws, regulations amendments and ordinances issued by him during his eight-year long military rule. He held a referendum for his own election as president outside the framework of the constitution in November 1984, prior to holding the general elections in February 1985. The referendum remained at best a fraud, for, barely 10–12 per cent voters turned up. However, it demonstrated the fact that the regime was committed to getting legitimacy through a formal exercise in mass mandate. The political forces belonging to the mainstream, ethnic and Islamic parties, the emergent civil society in general and the lawyers community in particular continued to struggle for restoration of parliamentary rule, which climaxed in 1983. The regime was convinced that elections needed to be held to avoid another Bangladeshin this case Sindh which was the epicenter of the movement, and not the least because Z. A. Bhutto belonged to that province. However, elections were to be held on a non-party basis. This triggered the boycott of elections by the alliance of political parties MRD (Movement for Restoration of Democracy). After the elections were held, but before the new parliament met, Zia promulgated the Restoration of Constitution Order. This Order empowered the president to dissolve the National Assembly when, in his view, an appeal to the electorate was necessary. Later, this provision became part of the 8th Amendment with some minor changes. As a classic case of deliberate insertion of contradictions within a constitution, the new amendment formally declared parliamentary sovereignty. In a similar case, the president was mentioned as the chief executive even as the prime minister was responsible for the operational side of the government as leader of the house.

Even as the National Assembly was elected on a non-party basis, parties were restored soon after the lifting of martial law on 30 December 1985. The majority in the house joined Prime Minister Junejo in forming the Pakistan Muslim League (PML). The old phenomenon of King's party under Ayub, as a loyalist group of legislators operating along the supra-parliamentary will of the president, re-emerged as a necessary part of the dyarchic arrangement for sharing power between the president and the prime minister. This helped keep the procedural aspects of the legislative process in line and maintain a profile of parliamentarism in operation. Junejo presided over the process of transition from the one-party dominant model of the 1970s to the two-party model in the late 1980s, as he rebuilt the PML as a classic king's party. After dissolving the National Assembly and dismissing Junejo in May 1988, Zia once again called for non-party elections. But, he seemed to have lost touch with reality as the political community had already got engaged in a thriving political struggle between PML and PPP on the right and left of the centre respectively. The more Zia sought to lace himself with legal safeguards against the much-dreaded prospects of Benazir Bhutto's comeback to power through elections, which he was obliged to hold in 90 days after dissolution of the National Assembly, the more he lost ground in moral and political terms.

This was the time when judiciary staged a comeback. Zia had emasculated higher courts under martial law. He had forced judges twice to take a new oath, first in 1977 and again in 1981, and thus pledge allegiance to his 'constitutional' set-up. He amended Article 199 of the Constitution in 1980 to bar the courts from reviewing cases against official orders or challenging military courts' verdicts. However, the Baluchistan High Court declared the amended Article 199 and 212(A) ultra vires of the Constitution and thus invalidated restrictions placed on the judicial review. Indeed, civil courts had continued to provide relief to various politicians whom Zia's military government tried to convict of crimes against martial law. The Provisional Constitutional Order (PCO) 1981 again sought to restrict the jurisdiction of civil courts and therefore alienated the bar and the bench still further. After dismissal of the Junejo Government, Zia sought to contain the party-based political dynamics of the country. He required all parties to be registered with the Election Commission and submit their accounts annually. When Benazir Bhutto challenged the amendment in Section 3 of the Political Parties Act 1962 to this effect, the Supreme Court declared them null and void. Later, the Lahore High Court declared the dissolution of elected assemblies by Zia 'unconstitutional'. However, it stopped short of restoring the dissolved assemblies as the election process was already under way. Subsequently, the Supreme Court gave its verdict in favour of party-based elections as opposed to the announcement of Zia, who had meanwhile died in an air crash. Through what is often called judicial activism, courts demonstrated a new sensitivity to popular and unfettered mandate being the ultimate source of legitimacy for government formation. However, two years later, the Supreme Court upheld the dismissal of Benazir Bhutto's government via the dissolution of the National Assembly, in 1990. But next time, it set aside the dismissal of Nawaz Sharif government in 1993. The Court observed that the prime minister was answerable for his actions to the National Assembly, not to the president, and the latter was bound by the advice of the former and it was not the other way round. The judiciary demonstrated its commitment to 'populism', i.e. to the institutional expression of the rule of public representatives. However, it remained allegedly selective in its approach. For example, it found the dismissal of the two governments of Junejo and Nawaz Sharif in 1988 and 1993 respectively unconstitutional but declared the dismissal of Benazir Bhutto's governments in 1990 and 1996 as constitutionally valid. The former headed the king's party in the parliament and thus represented a constitutional tradition from within the establishment's trajectory of policies and profiles. The latter fell outside the circle drawn by the establishment, even as it some times played ball with it with the lure of office, if only to keep politics from getting out of hand.

The second phase of parliamentary sovereignty under Nawaz Sharif after the passage of the 13th Amendment in 1997 did not last long. The army was simply not ready to countenance loss of control over what it perceived as selfish, wayward, corrupt and immature politicians operating from the floor of the parliament. The Supreme Court validated the 1999 coup but gave relief by providing for transfer of power back to elected representatives in three years, i.e. by 11 October 2002. Drawing on the precedent of the 1979 Begum Nusrat Bhutto Case, the Court also gave the new chief executive General Musharraf the right to amend the constitution, short of altering its basic character defined by federalism, parliamentarism and judicial independence. Three years later, when President Musharraf enacted constitutional amendments by issuing an LFO (Legal Framework Order) prior to elections, he restored dyarchy in letter and spirit. LFO revived the presidential powers to dissolve the National Assembly, appoint services chiefs and judges of higher courts, and establish the National Security Council. Later, an amended version of LFO was passed by the parliament with the help of the new king's party PML (*Quaid-I-Azam*) and the Islamic alliance MMA (*Muttahida Majlis Amal*). Despite an uproar of criticism from the political community, lawyers and intelligentsia in general, the new law has stayed the course during the last two years. Meanwhile, President Musharraf got himself elected through a controversial referendum prior to parliamentary elections in the footsteps of President Zia, followed by a vote of confidence from the parliament and provincial assemblies in December 2003. The current dyarchic arrangement for sharing power between the parliament and extra-parliamentary forces is heavily tilted in favour of the latter. While Prime Minister Jamali (2003–4) was at least the nominee of the king's party PML-Q, Prime Minister Shaukat Aziz (2004–present) is the nominee of the president, even as he was not a member of the National Assembly at the time of his nomination.

The dyarchy remains fully operational in Pakistan in the year 2007. This is the constitutional expression of dichotomy between the state elite and political elite. It reflects the institutional imbalance between the state apparatuses of army and bureaucracy along with judiciary as a maverick partner on the one hand and parliament and political parties on the other. The initial attempt of army's project of constitutional engineering in the form of a presidential system (1962–69) collapsed in the face of a nation-wide movement, which led to the revival of parliamentarism enshrined in the 1973 Constitution. The two subsequent military governments took recourse to establishment of dyarchy as a semi-presidential system without parliamentary sovereignty. It has been argued that Pakistan suffered from incomplete constitution-making which led to constitutional interpretation by institutions such as the bureaucracy, military and judiciary, thereby reconstituting the State.[22] However, even more significantly, it is the structural discontinuity in Pakistan that precluded the possibility of a smooth constitutional development from the beginning. The migrant-turned-military state sought to grapple with the model of one-province-dominates-all as a product of, first, partition of India in the case of East Bengal and, then, the break-up of Pakistan in the case of Punjab. The commitment of the wider political community to a parliamentary form of government points to the efficacy of the neo-institutional approach to analyse the prevalent constitutional norms in the country. We can argue that constitutionalism in Pakistan has moved along priorities of the state apparatuses in a substantive sense, to the great dissatisfaction of the political community. This is an inherently tense situation, which continues to engage the bar and the bench, often on opposite sides of the political spectrum representing the political community and the state elite respectively.

Notes

1. Woodrow Wilson's words quoted in Raza (1985: 11).
2. See for discussion, Poulantzas (1982: 48–50).
3. See for a detailed discussion Waseem (1989: 66–84, 116–36).
4. See Kohli (1990).
5. Kothari (1988).
6. Alavi (1979: 54–57).
7. Jalal (1995: 43).
8. Alavi (n.d.: 66).
9. Khan (2001: 137).
10. *The Pakistan Times*, 11 October 1958.
11. Khan (2001: 137).
12. Ahmed (1970: 91–98, 120).
13. Alavi (1990: 32).
14. Sayed (1968: 253–71).
15. Alavi (1990: 42).
16. *The Pakistan Times*, 8 October 1958.
17. See Rizvi (2000: xiv–xix).
18. See Samad (1995: 124–35).
19. Dieter Conrad in 'In Defence of the Continuity of Law: Pakistan's Courts in Crises of State' (Zingel and Zingel Ave-Lallemant 1985: 125).
20. See Viola and Mainwaring (1985: 2, 38, 193–97).
21. Kennedy (1995).
22. Newberg (1995: 47).

Bibliography

Abramovich, Victor and Courtis Christian. 2002. *Los derechos sociales como derechos exigibles*. Madrid: Trotta.

Academie des Sciences Coloniales. 1933. Paris: Societe d'Editions.

Agamben, Giorgio. 2005. *State of Exception*, trans. Kevin Attell. Chicago: The University of Chicago Press.

Agnes, Flavia. 2004. *A Study of Family Courts in West Bengal*. Calcutta: Women's Commission.

Ahmed, Mushtaq. 1970. *Government and Politics in Pakistan*. Karachi: Space Publishers.

Alavi, Hamza. n.d. 'Constitutional Changes and the Dynamics of Political Development in Pakistan', in *Collection of Seminar Papers on Constitutional Changes in the Commonwealth Countries*. London: University of London, Institute of Commonwealth Studies.

———. 1979. 'The State in Postcolonial Societies: Pakistan and Bangladesh', in Harry Goulbourne (ed.), *Politics and the State in the Third World*. London: Macmillan.

———. 1990. 'Authoritarianism and Legitimation of State Power in Pakistan', in Subrata Mitra (ed.), *The Postcolonial State in South Asia*. London: Harvester-Wheatsheaf.

Albright, Madeleine. 1998. 'Menschenrechte und Außenpolitik', *Amerika-Dienst*.

Alexy, Robert. 1997. 'Grundrechte im demokratischen Verfassungsstaat', in Aulis Aarnio, Robert Alexy and Gunnar Bergholtz (eds), *Justice, Morality and Society: A Tribute to Aleksander Peczenik*. Lund: Juristförlaget.

Althusser, Louis. 1970 (rpt. 1971). 'Ideologie et appareils ideologiques d'Etat', *La Pensee*, vol. 151; rpt. in *idem, Lenin and Philosophy and Other Essays*. London: New Left Books.

Ansari, Iqbal. 1999. 'The Politics of Constitution-Making in India', in D.L. Sheth and Gurpreet Mahajan (eds), *Minority Identities and the Nation-State*. Delhi: Oxford University Press.

Anweiler, Oscar. (1958) 1972. *Les Soviets en Russie*. Paris: Gallimard.

Arendt, H. 1958. *The Human Condition*. Chicago: The University of Chicago Press.

———. 1965. *On Revolution*. Harmondsworth: Penguin Books.

———. 2002. *Les Origines du totalitarianisme*. Paris: Editions Gallimard.

Azan, P. 1925. *L'armee indigene nord-africaine*. Paris: Ch-Lavauzelle & Cie.

Bakhtin, Mikhail. 1963. *Problemy poétiki Dostoevskogo*. Moscow: Sovetskij Pisatel.

Balagopal, K. 2000. 'Law Commissions' View of Terrorism', *Economic and Political Weekly*, 35 (25): 2114–22. 17–23 June.

Balibar, Étienne. 2001. *Nous citoyens d'Europe? Le frontières, l'État, le people*. Paris: La Découverte.

———. 2003. *L'Europe, l'Amérique, la guerre*. Paris: La Découverte.

Bandopadhyay, Upendranath. (1921) 1999. *Nirbashiter Atmakatha*. Calcutta: National Publishers.

Bandopadhyay, Sandip. 1993. *Agnijuger Banglaye Biplabimanas*. Calcutta: Progressive Publishers.

Banerjee, Paula. 1998. 'Refugee Repatriation: A Politics of Gender', *Refugee Watch*, vol. 1.

———. 2002. 'Aliens in the Colonial World', in Ranabir Samaddar (ed.), *Refugees and the State*. New Delhi: Sage Publications.

Banerjee, Sumanta. 1991. 'Colonial Laws: Continuity and Innovations', in A. R. Desai (ed.), *Expanding Governmental Lawlessness and Organized Struggles*. Bombay: Popular Prakashan.

Barthélemy, J. and P. Duez. 1933 (1985). *Traite de Droit Constitutionnel*. Paris: Economica.

Baxi, Upendra. 1982. *Crisis of the Indian Legal System*. Delhi: Vikas.

Bayley, D. H. 1962. *Preventive Detention in India*. Calcutta: Firma K. L. Mukhopadhyay.

Beaumont, G. De. 1843. *Rapport fait au nom de la seconde sous-commission, 20 June 1842*. Paris: Imprimerie royale.

Beck, Ulrich. 1992. *Risk Society*. London: Sage Publications.

———. 1999. *World Risk Society*. Cambridge: Polity Press.

———. 2000. 'The Cosmopolitan Perspective: Sociology in the Second Age of Modernity', *British Journal of Sociology*, 51 (1): 79–105.

Beck, Ulrich and E. Grande. 2004. *Das kosmopolitische Europa*. Frankfurt/M: Suhrkamp.

Bennett, Tony. 2001. *Differing Diversities: Transversal Study on the Theme of Cultural Policy and Cultural Diversity*. Strasbourg: Council of Europe Publishing.

Bhaumik, Madan Mohan. 1985 rpt. *Andamaney Dosh Batsar*. Calcutta: Lekhak Samabaye Samiti.

Bickel, Alexander M. 1975. *The Morality of Consent*. Yale: Yale University Press.

Billiard, A. 1901. 'Etude sur la condition politique et juridique a assigner aux indigenes des colonies', *Congres international de sociologie coloniale*.

Borrelli, G. (ed.). 2004. *Governance*. Naples: Libreria Dante & Descartes.

Bonet-Maury, G. 1900. 'La France et le movement anti-esclavagiste au xix siecle', *Revue des Deux Mondes*, vol. 160. July.

Bourdieu, Pierre. 1991. *Language and Symbolic Power*, trans. Gino Raymond and Matthew Adamson. Cambridge, MA: Harvard University Press.

Buden, Boris. 2002. *Kaptolski kolodvor*. Beograd: Centar za savremenu umetnost.

Butalia, Urvashi. 1998. *The Other Side of Silence: Voices from the Partition of India*. Delhi: Viking Press

Butler, Judith and Joan W. Scott (eds). 1992. *Feminists Theorize the Political*. London: Routledge.

Chakrabarty, D. 2004. *Provincializing Europe: Postcolonial Thought and Historical Difference*. Princeton: Princeton University Press.

Chakraborty, Trailokya Nath. 1981. *Jeley Tirish Bochor o Pak–Bharater Sangram*. Calcutta: Anushilan Bhavan Trust Board.

Chakravorty Spivak, Gayatri. 1999. *A Critique of Postcolonial Reason: Toward a History of the Vanishing Present*. Cambridge, MA: Harvard University Press.

Charvériat, Ch. 1889. *À travers la Kabylie et les questions kabyles*. Paris: Plon.

Chatterjee, P. 2004. *The Politics of the Governed: Reflections on Popular Politics in Most of the World*. New York: Columbia University Press.

Chattopadhyay, Jogesh Chandra. 1977. *Swadhinatar Sandhaney*. Calcutta: Kishore Trust.

Chopra, P.N. 2003. *A Comprehensive History of India*, vol. 1. New Delhi: Sterling Publishers.

Cindrič, Alojz. 1998. *Čarnijev zbornik – A Festschrift for Ludvik Čarni*. Ljubljana: Oddelek za sociologijo Filozofske fakultete v Ljubljani.

Constituent Assembly Debates. 1939. Vol. 7. New Delhi: Government of India.

Constituent Assembly Debates. 1948. Vol. 7, 9 April. New Delhi: Government of India.

Constituent Assembly Debates. 1948. Vol. 7, 22 November. New Delhi: Government of India.

Cuvillier-Fleury, R. 1907. *La main-d'oeuvre dans les colonies françaises de l'Afrique occidentale et du Congo.* Paris: Larose.

Dareste, P. 1931. *Traité de Droit colonial.* Paris: Publisher Unknown.

Das, Pulin Bihari. 1987. *Amar Jiban Kahini* (ed.) Amalendu De. Calcutta: Anushilan Samity.

Datta, Bhupendra Nath. 1390 B.S. rpt. *Aprakashito Rajnitik Itihas.* Calcutta: Nababharat Publishers.

———. 1983 rpt. *Bharater Dwitiya Swadhinata Sangram.* Calcutta: Nababharat Publishers.

———. 1973. *Biplaber Padachinha.* Calcutta: Orient Longman.

'Dawn of a New Life after Years of Struggle'. 2001. *The Hindu.* 2 October.

Debats parlementaire, Chambre des deputes. 1888. Session ordinaire, 9 February.

Derrida, Jacques. 1984. 'Déclarations d'indépendance', in *Otobiographies.* Paris: Galilée.

———. 1987. 'Envoi', in *idem, Psyché : Inventions de l'Autre*, pp. 109–42. Paris: Editions Galilée. Eng. trans. *Psyche: Inventions of the Other* (eds) Peggy Kamuf and Elizabeth G. Rottenberg. Stanford: Stanford University Press.

Dérens, Jean-Arnault. 2003. 'Les "Petits Peuples" oubliés des Balkans', *Le Monde Diplomatique* (English Edition), 50(593). August. *http://mondediplo.com/2003/08/04 Derens*.

Devereux, Georges. 1985. *Ethnopsychanalyse comple´mentariste.* Paris: Flammarion.

Dislère, P. (1886) 1914. *Traité de législation coloniale.* Paris: P. Dupont.

Doucet, Robert. 1926. *Commentaires sur la colonisation.* Paris: Larose.

Ducrot, Oswald. 1996. Slovenian lectures/Conférences slov'enes. Course given at the Institute of the Humanities (ed.), Igor Z. Zagar. Ljubljana: ISH.

Dumas, Ch. 1914. *Liberez les indigenes ou renoncez aux colonies.* Paris: Figuere & Cie.

Dupont, O. 1990. 'Apercu sur l'administration des indigenes musulmans en Algerie', *Congres international de sociologie coloniale.*

Eboué, Félix. 1941. *Politique indige'ne de l'Afrique équatoriale française*. Brazzaville: Imprimerie officielle de l'A.E.F.

Eerde, J. C. Van. 1927. *Ethnologie coloniale (l'Européan et l'Indigéne)*. Paris: Éditions du monde nouveau.

Farringdon, Karen. 1996. *History of Punishment and Torture*. London: Chancellor Press.

Ferreira, Camila Duran *et al*. 2004. *O Judiciário e as Políticas Públicas de Saúde no Brasil: o caso AIDS*. São Paulo: Faculty of Law of the University of São Paulo.

Foucault, Michel. 1991. 'Governmentality', in Graham Burchell *et al*. (eds), *The Foucault Effect: Studies in Governmentality*. London: Harvester-Wheatsheaf.

Frank, Andre Gunder. 1969. *Underdevelopment and Capitalism in Latin America*. New York: Monthly Review Press.

Freud, Sigmund. 1921. 'Group Psychology and the Analysis of the Egó, in *The Standard Edition of the Complete Psychological Works of Sigmund Freud*, vol. 18: 69–143.

Furet, François and Denis Richet. 1973. *La révolution française*. Paris: Fayard.

Gaddis, John Lewis. 1987. *The Long Peace: Inquiries into the History of the Cold War*. New York: Oxford University Press.

Girault, A.1903. 'Des rapports politiques entre metropole et colonies'. Preliminary report at the London session, 26 May 1903. Brussels: L'Institut Colonial International.

———.1906. 'Condition of the Indigenous Populations from the Point of View of Civil and Criminal Law and Distribution of Justice', *Congres international de sociologie coloniale, debut du xx siecle, Cinq ans de progress, 1900–1905*. Marseille: Barlatier.

Girault, A. 1921. 'Condition of the Indigenous Populations from the Point of View of Civil and Criminal Law and Distribution of Justice', in *Congres international de sociologie coloniale*, Paris.

Government of Bengal. 1926. *Terrorist Conspiracy in Bengal*. Calcutta: BG Press.

Grandmaison, Olivier Le Cour. 2005. *Coloniser, Exterminer: Sur la guerre et l'Etat colonial*. Paris: Fayard.

Guha, Ranajit. 1997. *Dominance without Hegemony: History and Power in Colonial India*. Cambridge, MA: Harvard University Press.

Gutman, Amy (ed.). 1994. *Multiculturalism*. Princeton: Princeton University Press.

Habermas, Jürgen. 1992. *Faktizität und Geltung: Beiträge zur Diskurstheorie des Rechts und des demokratischen Rechtsstaats.* Frankfurt/M: Suhrkamp.

——. 1994. 'Human Rights and Popular Sovereignty: The Liberal and the Republican Versions', *Ratio Juris*, 7 (1): 1–13.

Hall, Stuart. 1996. 'Who Needs Identity?', in Stuart Hall and Paul du Gay (eds), *Questions of Cultural Identity*, pp. 1–18. London: Sage Publications.

Hampate' Bâ, A. 1994. 'Amkoullel, L'enfant peul', *Le Mejan*, Arles: Actes Sud.

——. 1992. 'Amkoullel, l'enfant peul', *Le Mejan*, Arles: Actes Sud.

Harmand, J. 1910. *Domination et colonization.* Paris: Flammarion.

Hasan, Zoya. 2001. 'Gender Politics, Legal Reform, and the Muslim Community in India', in Patricia Jeffery and Amrita Basu (eds), *Resisting the Sacred and the Secular: Women's Activism and Politicised Religion in South Asia.* New Delhi: Kali for Women.

Hazarike, Sujata Dutta. 2005. 'Feminism as a Resource for Autonomy'. Paper presented at the conference, 'What is Autonomy?'. Mimeograph. Calcutta, 29 July.

Hegel, G.W.F. 1956. *The Philosophy of History*, trans. J. Sibree. New York: Dover Publications.

Hillyard, Paddy. 1993. *Suspect Community: People's Experience of Terrorism Acts in Britain.* London: Pluto Press.

Hofer, Cristina B., Mauro Schechter and Lee H. Harrison. 2004. 'Effectiveness of Antiretroviral Therapy among Patients who Attend Public HIV Clinics in Rio de Janeiro, Brazil', *Journal of Acquired Immune Deficiency Syndromes*, 36: 967–71.

Holmes, Stephen and Cass R. Sunstein. 1999. *The Cost of Rights: Why Liberty Depends on Taxes.* New York: W.W. Norton.

Honig, B. 1991. 'Declarations of Independence: Arendt and Derrida on the Problem of Founding the Republic', *American Political Science Review*, 85 (1): 97–113.

Iampolskii, Mikhail. 2004. *Vozvrashchenie Leviafana.* Moscow: Novoe literaturnoe obozrenie.

Jalal, Ayesha. 1995. *Democracy and Authoritarianism in South Asia.* Cambridge: Cambridge University Press.

Jayal, Niraja Gopal. 1999. *Democracy and the State: Welfare, Secularism and Development in Contemporary India.* Delhi: Oxford University Press.

Kanamura, Alberto. 2003. 'O dilema do gestor da saúde', *Folha de São Paulo*, 10 July.

Kanungo, Hem Chandra. 1928 (rpt. 1984). *Banglaye Biplob Prachesta*. Calcutta: Chirayata Prakashan.

Kaplan, Ann and Michael Sprinker. 1993. *The Althusserian Legacy*. London: Verso.

Kapur, Ratna and Brenda Cossman. 1996. *Subversive Sites: Feminist Engagements with Law in India*. New Delhi: Sage Publications.

Kennedy, Charles H. 1995. 'Presidential–Prime Ministerial Relations: The Role of the Superior Courts', in Charles Kennedy and Rasul Baksh Rais (eds), *Pakistan 1995*. Boulder: Westview Press.

Ker, J. C. 1917 (rpt. 1973). *Political Trouble in India*. Delhi: Oriental Publishers.

Khan, Hamid. 2001. *Constitutional and Political History of Pakistan*. Karachi: Oxford University Press.

Khasbulatov, Ruslan. 1993. 'Slovo o Sovetakh', *Pravda*, March 4.

Kishwar, Madhu. 1999. *Off the Beaten Track*. Delhi: Oxford University Press.

Kohli, Atul. 1990. *Democracy and Discontent: India's Growing Crisis of Governability*. Cambridge: Cambridge University Press.

Korzhikhina, T. P. 1995. *Sovetskoe gosudarstvo i ego uchrezhdenia: Noiabr' 1917–dekabr'*. Moscow: RGGU.

Kothari, Rajni. 1988. *State against Democracy*. Delhi: Ajanta Books.

Kuzmanic, Tonči. 2002. *Politika, mediji: UZI in WTC*. Ljubljana: Mirovni inštitut.

Lapham, Lewis H. 2003. 'Une grande lumière est apparue au président', *Le Monde diplomatique*, 50 (592).

Larcher, E. Trois. 1902. *Annees d'etudes algeriennes, legislatives, socials, penitentaires et penales*. Paris: A. Rousseau.

Larcher E. and G. Rectenwald. 1923. *Traite elementaire de legislation algerienne*. Paris: A. Rousseau.

Law Commission of India. 2000. *173rd Report on Prevention of Terrorism Bill*.

Lawless Roads: A Report on TADA 1985–1993. 1993. Delhi: People's Union for Democratic Rights.

Les lois organiques des colonies. 1906. 'Documents official procedes de notices historiques', t.2–3. Brussels: L' Institut Colonial International.

Lefort, Claude. 1988. *Democracy and Political Theory*, trans. D. Macey. Cambridge: Polity Press & Basil Blackwell.

Legislative Assembly Debates. 1939. 12 April. New Delhi: Government of India.

Lok Sabha Debates. 1984. 9 August. New Delhi: Government of India.

Lok Sabha Debates. 1985. 'Progress of Indian Women in Social, Educational, Political and Economic Fields in the International Women's Decade', 24 April. New Delhi: Government of India.

Lok Sabha Debates. 1985. 19 November. New Delhi: Government of India.

Lok Sabha Debates (Eighth Lok Sabha). 1986. Vol. J (17). New Delhi: Government of India.

Lopes, José Reinaldo de Lima. 1994. 'Direito subjetivo e direitos sociais', in José Eduardo Faria (ed.), *Direitos humanos, direitos sociais e justice*. São Paulo: Malheiros.

Magun, Artemy. 2003a. 'Poniatie i opyt revoliutsii', *Novoe literaturnoe obozrenie*, 64: 54–79.

———. 2003b. 'The Concept and the Experience of Revolution'. Ph.D. dissertation. Ann Arbor: The University of Michigan.

———. 2006. 'La révolution négative', *Les Temps Modernes*, 640: 163–89.

Mahanta, Aparna. 1994. 'The Indian State and Patriarchy', in T. V. Sathyamurthy (ed.), *State and Nation in the Context of Social Change*, vol. 1. Delhi: Oxford University Press.

Maine, H.S. 1875. *The Effects of Observation of India on Modern European Thought*. London: John Murray.

Marx, Karl. 1958. 'Zur Judenfrage' (1843), in *Marx – Engels Werke*, vol. 1. Berlin: Dietz. Trans. 'The Jewish Question', in *Collected Works of Marx and Engels*, vol. 1.

Masson, P. 1906. 'Introduction', in *idem, Les colonies francaises au debut du xx siecle: Cinq ans de progress (1900–1905)*. Marseille: Barlatier.

Mau, Vladimir and Irina Starodubrovskaya. 2001. *The Challenge of Revolution: Contemporary Russia in Historical Perspective*. Oxford: Oxford University Press.

Maunier, R. 1938. *Repetitions ecrites de legislation coloniale*, (troisiemme annee d'etudes). Paris: Les Cours du Droit.

Mayer, F. and I. Pernice. 2003. 'La Costituzione integrata dell'Europa', in G. Zagrebelsky (ed.), *Diritti e Costituzione nell'Unione europea*. Roma – Bari: Laterza.

Medvedev, Pavel N. 1928. *Formalnyj métod v literaturovedenii*. Leningrad: Priboj.

Melia, J. 1936. *La triste Sort des indigenes musulmans d'Algerie*. Paris: Mercure de France.

Menon, Ritu and Kamala Bhasin. 1998. *Borders and Boundaries: Women in India's Partition*. New Delhi: Kali for Women.

———. 1993. 'Abducted Women, the State and Questions of Honour', in *Gender Relations Project Paper 1*. Canberra: Australian National University.

Merle, I. 2002. 'Retour sur le regime de l'indigenat', *French Politics, Culture & Society*, 20 (2).

Metha, U.S. 1999. *Liberalism and Empire: A Study in Nineteenth-Century British Liberal Thought*. Chicago: The University of Chicago Press.

Mezzadra, S. 2002. 'Immagini della cittadinanza nella crisi dell'antropologia politica moderna. Gli studi postcoloniali', in R. Gherardi (ed.), *Politica, consenso, legittimazione. Trasformazioni e prospettive*. Roma: Carocci.

———. 2004a. 'Confini, cittadinanza, migrazioni', *Scienza & Politica*, 30.

———. 2004b. 'Le vesti del cittadino. Trasformazioni di un concetto politico sulla scena della modernità', in S. Mezzadra (ed.), *Cittadinanza. Soggetti, ordine, diritto*. Bologna: Clueb.

———. (ed.). 2004c. *I confini della libertà. Per un'analisi politica delle migrazioni contemporanee*. Roma: Derive Approdi.

——— and F. Rahola. 2006. 'The Postcolonial Condition: A Few Notes on the Quality of Historical Time in the Global Present', *Postcolonial Text*, 2 (1), http://www.pkp.ubc.ca/pocol/index.php.

Michelman, F. I. 2003. 'The Constitution, Social Rights, and Liberal Political Justification', *International Journal of Constitutional Law*, 1: 13–34.

Močnik, Rastko. 1993. 'Ideology and Fantasy', in Ann Kaplan and Michael Sprinker (eds), *The Althusserian Legacy*. London: Verso.

———. 1998. 'Should the theory of ideology be conceived as a theory of institutions?', in Alojz Cindrič (ed.), *Čarnijev zbornik: A Festschrift for Ludvik Čarni*. Ljubljana: Oddelek za sociologijo Filozofske fakultete v Ljubljani.

———. 2002. 'Social change in the Balkans', *Balcanis*, 2 (3).

Montesquieu. 1748 (rpt. 1951). *De l'esprit des lois*, vol. 11. Paris: Gallimard Bibliothéque de la Pléiade.

Moulier Boutang Y. 2003. 'E pluribus multiplico, e pluribus, multitude: remarques sur le désordre dans la future constitution', *Vacarme*, 23.

Nancy, Jean-Luc. 2002. *La création du monde ou la mondialisation*. Paris: Galilee.

Negri, Antonio. (1992) 1999. *Insurgencies: Constituent Power and the Modern State*, trans. Maurizia Boscagli. Minneapolis: University of Minnesota Press.

Newberg, Paula. 1995. *Judging the State: Courts and Constitutional Politics in Pakistan*. Cambridge: Cambridge University Press.

Nielly, A. 1898. *Codes coloniaux de l'Inde anglaise*. Alger: Zamith & Cie.

Nilsson, Martin. 1964. *History of Greek Religion*. New York: W.W. Norton.

Oliveira-Cruz, V. J. Kowalski, and B. McPake. 2004. 'Viewpoint. The Brazilian HIV/AIDS "Success Story": Can Others Do It?', *Tropical Medicine & International Health*, 9: 292–97.

'On Godhra, Gujarat Rejects POTA Review Panel Report'. 2005. *The Indian Express*. 10 June.

Parliamentary Debates. 2002. 26 March.

Penant, D. 1905. *Congres colonial francais de 1905*. Paris: Secretariat general des congres coloniaux francais.

Pettman, Jan Jindy. 1996. 'Boundary Politics: Women, Nationalism and Danger', in Mary Maynard and June Purvis (eds), *New Frontiers in Women's Studies: Knowledge, Identity and Nationalism*. London: Zed Books.

Plamenatz, J. P. 1960. *On Alien Rule and Self-government*. London: Longmans.

Podlech, Adalbert. 1984. 'Repräsentation', in Otto Brunner and Reinhart Koselleck (eds), *Geschichtliche Grundbegriffe*, vol. 5: 509–50. Stuttgart: Klett-Cotta.

Poulantzas, Nicos. 1982. *Political Power and Social Classes*. London: Verso.

Prevention of Terrorism Ordinance 2001: Government Decides to Play Judge and Jury. New Delhi: South Asia Human Rights Documentation Centre.

Rachum, Ilan. 1999. *'Revolution': The Entrance of a New Word into Western Political Discourse*. Lanham, NY: University Press.

Rameshwari Nehru Papers. Speeches and Writings, Sub. File no. 25. New Delhi: Nehru Memorial Museum and Library.

Raza, R. 1985. 'The Continuous Process of Re-writing the Constitution', in W.P. Zingel and S. Zingel-Ave Lallémant (eds), *Pakistan in the 1980s: Law and Constitution*. Lahore: Vanguard.

Regismanset. Ch. 1912. *Questions colonials*. Paris: Chez Larose.

Regismanset, Ch., G. Francois and F. Rouget. 1924. *Ce que tout Francais devrait savoir sur nos colonies*. Paris: Chez Larose.

Report of the Government of Eastern Bengal and Assam on Deportation. 1909. Political Branch, File no 706, *TIB* (Terrorism in Bengal), vol. 4: 1281–331.

Report of the Simon Commission. 1929. vol. 1, para. 138, 139.

Report of the Committee on Reforms of the Criminal Justice System (Malimath Committee Report). 2003. Government of India: Ministry of Home Affairs, March.

Rigo, Enrica. 2005. 'Citizenship at Europe's Borders: Some Reflections on the Post-colonial Condition of Europe in the Context of EU Enlargement', *Citizenship Studies*, 9 (1): 3–22.

Rizvi, Hasan Askari. 2000. *Military, State and Society in Pakistan.* London: Macmillan.

Romano, S. 1918. *Corso di diritto coloniale.* Roma: Athenaeum.

Rosenthal, John. 2002. 'Le fantôme de l'autodétermination', *Les temps modernes.*

Rosenthal, John and Radhika Lal. 1991. 'Marxism and Contemporary Philosophy', *Graduate Faculty Philosophy Journal*, 14 (1): 7–21.

Rousseau, Jean Jacques. 1762 (rpt. 1970). *Du contrat social ou Principes du droit politique.* Paris: Garnier.

———. 1988. *The Social Contract*, trans. G. Cole. New York: Prometheus Books.

Salam Us, Ziya. 1999. 'Caught in the Cross five', *The Statesman.* 25 June.

Samad, Yunas. 1995. *A Nation in Turmoil.* New Delhi: Sage Publications.

Samaddar, Ranabir. 2002. 'Colonial Constitutionalism', *Identity, Culture and Politics*, 3 (1). *www.codesria.org/Links/Publications/icp/july_2002.htm.*

Sanyal, Sachaindra Nath. 2001 rpt. *Bandi Jeevan*, (ed.) Ajijul Haq. Calcutta: Nandanik.

Sarrault, A. 1923. *Discours a l'ouverture des Cours de l'Ecole coloniale.* Paris: Edition du journal' La presse coloniale.

Sastri, K.A. Nilakantha. 1987. *A Comprehensive History of India*, vol. 2. New Delhi: People's Publishing House.

Sautayra, E. 1883. *Legislation de l'Algerie.* Paris: Maisonneuve & Cie.

Sayed, K. B. 1968. *Political System of Pakistan.* Boston: Houghton Mifflin.

Sedition Committee Report. 1918. Government of India.

Sen, Satadru. 2000. *Disciplining Punishment: Colonialism and Convict Society in the Andaman Islands*. New York: Oxford University Press.

Shablinskiy, Igor. 1997. *Predely vlasti. Bor'ba za rossiskuiu konstituzionnuiu reformu (1989–1995)*. Moscow: MONF.

Shapiro, Michael. 2005. 'Every Move You Make: Bodies, Surveillance, and Media', *Social Text*, 233.

Shourie, Arun. 2001. *Courts and their Judgements: Premises, Prerequisites, Consequences*. New Delhi: Rupa and Co.

Sieyès, E. (1789) 1970. *Qu'est-ce que le Tiers-État*. Geneva: Librairie Droz.

Simmel Georg. 1900. *Philosophie des Geldes*. Leipzig: Duncker and Humbolt.

———. 1903. 'Die Grossstädte und das Geistesleben', in K. Bücher, F. Ratzel, G.V. Mayr, H. Waentig, G. Simmel, Th. Petermann and D. Schäfer, *1903: Die Grossstadt*. Dresden: Zahn und Jaensch.

———. 1908a. 'Das Geheimnis und die geheime Gesellschaft', in *Soziologic, Untersuchungen über die Formen der Vergesellschaftung*. Leipzig: Duncker und Humbolt.

———. 1908b. 'Exteurs über den Fremden', in *Soziologic, Untersuchungen über die Formen der Vergesellschaftung*. Leipzig: Duncker und Humbolt.

———. 1964a. 'The Metropolis and Mental Life', in Kurt H. Wolff (ed., trans., intro.), *The Sociology of Georg Simmel*. New York: The Free Press.

———. 1964b. 'The Secret and the Secret Society', in Kurt H. Wolff (ed., trans., intro.), *The Sociology of Georg Simmel*. New York: The Free Press.

———. 1964. 'The Stranger', in Kurt H. Wolff (ed., trans., intro.), *The Sociology of Georg Simmel*. New York: The Free Press.

———. 1970. *Grundfragen der Soziologie: Individuum und Gesellschaft*. Berlin: De Gruyter.

Singh, Ujjwal Kumar. 2004a. 'State and the Emerging Interlocking Legal Systems in India: Permanence of the Temporary', *Economic and Political Weekly*, 39 (2): 149–54. 10–16 January.

———. 2004b. 'POTA and Federalism', *Economic and Political Weekly*, 39 (18): 1793–97. 1–7 May.

Skirda, Alexander. 2003. *Vol'naia Rus': ot veche do sovetov*. Paris: Gromada.

Sogrin, Vladimir. 1999. 'Zakonomernosti russkoy dramy', *Pro et contra*, 4 (3): 155–69.

Sol, B and D. Haranger. 1930. *Recueil general et methodique de la legislation et de la reglementation des colonies francaise.* Paris: Societes d'editions geographiques.

Solus, H. 1927. *Traite de la condition des indigenes en droit prive.* Preface to A. Girault. *Principles de legislation coloniale.* Paris: Recueil Sirey.

Stokes, Eric. 1982. *The English Utilitarians and India.* Delhi: Oxford University Press.

Strouvens L. and P. Piron. 1945. *Codes and Laws of Belgian Congo.* Leopoldville: Editions des codes et loi du Congo.

Sunstein, Cass R. 2001. *Designing Democracy: What Constitutions Do.* New York: Oxford University Press.

Supiot, A. 1991. *Homo juridicus: Essai sur la function anthropologique du Droit.* Paris: Seuil.

Supreme Court Cases (Criminal). 2002. Part 7, July.

Sylvain, B. 1901. *Du sort des indigenes dans les colonies d'exploitation.* Paris: L. Boyer.

Tabb, William K. 2003. 'After Neoliberalism?', *Monthly Review*, 55 (2): 25–33.

Talukdar, Mrinal. 1999. 'TADA lives on in Assam Jails', *The Indian Express*, 20 October.

Taylor, Charles. 1992 (1994). 'The Politics of Recognition', in Amy Gutmann (ed.), *Multiculturalism.* Princeton: Princeton University Press.

Terray, Emmanuel. 2003. 'Law Versus Politics', *New Left Review*, Second Series (22): 71–91.

Terror by Proxy. 2003. Delhi: People's Union for Democratic Rights.

Terrorism in India. 1937 (rpt. 1974). Compiled and prepared by the Intelligence Bureau, Government of India. Delhi: Deep Publications.

Terrorism in Bengal: A Collection of Documents on Terrorist Activities from 1905 to 1939. 1995. Calcutta: Government of West Bengal.

Tharu, Susie and K. Lalita (eds). 1991. *Women Writing in India: 600 B.C. to the Present*, vol. 1. Delhi: Oxford University Press.

Thomas, N. 1995. *Colonialism's Culture: Anthropology, Travel and Government.* Princeton, NJ: Princeton University Press.

Tilly, Charles. 1990. *Coercion, Capital, and European States, AD 990– 1990.* Oxford: Basil Blackwell.

Tocqueville, A. de. 1991. 'Travail sur l'Algerie'. *Oeuvres.* Paris: Gallimard.

Traite de Droit Constitutionnel. 1933 (rpt. 1985). Paris: Economica.

Trial of Errors: Critique of the POTA Court Judgement on the 13 December Case. 2003. Delhi: People's Union for Democratic Rights.

Vattel, E. de. 1758. *Le droit de gens, ou principes de la loi naturelle appliqués à la conduite et aux affaires des Nations et de Souverains.* Washington, D.C.: Carnegie Institution.

Vernier J. de Byans. 1912. *Rapport au Ministre des colonies.* Paris: Imprimerie nationale.

Viola, Eduardo and Scott Mainwaring. 1985. 'Transition to Democracy: Brazil and Argentina in the 1980s', *Journal of International Affairs*, 38 (2): 193–219.

Vološinov, Valentin N. 1929. *Marksizm i filosofija jazyka.* Leningrad: Priboj.

Wallerstein, Immanuel. 2003. 'Citizens All? Citizens Some! The Making of the Citizen', *Comparative Studies of Society and History*, 45 (4): 650–79.

Walters, W. 2002. 'Mapping Schengenland: Denaturalizing the Border', *Environment and Planning Society and Space*, 20 (5): 561–80.

———. 2004. 'Secure Borders, Safe Haven, Domopolitics', *Citizenship Studies*, 8 (3): 237–60.

Waseem, Mohammad. 1989. *State and Society in Pakistan.* Lahore: Progressive Publishers.

Wolff, Kurt H (ed., trans. and intro.). 1950 (rpt. 1964). *The Sociology of Georg Simmel.* New York: The Free Press.

Wortman, Richard. 2000. *Scenarios of Power: Myth and Ceremony in Russian Monarchy.* Princeton: Princeton University Press.

Young, R. J. C. 2001. *Postcolonialism: An Historical Introduction.* Oxford: Blackwell Publishers.

Yuval-Davis, Nira, Floya Anthias and Jo Campling (eds). 1989. *Woman–Nation–State.* New York: St. Martin's Press.

Zingel, Wolfgang Peter and Stephanie Zingel-Ave Lallemant (eds). 1985. *Pakistan in the 1980s: Law and Constitution.* Lahore: Vanguard.

Zizek, Slavoj. 2005. 'The Constitution is Dead: Long Live Proper Politics', *The Guardian*, 4 June.

Notes on Contributors

Paula Banerjee is currently teaching at the Department of South and Southeast Asian Studies, University of Calcutta and is a member of Calcutta Research Group. She was Visiting Professor at the Maison Des Sciences de l' Homme, Paris. Specialising in issues of conflict and peace in South Asia, she has also worked on women's issues in general. She has published extensively on issues of forced displacement, histories of borders and women in conflict situations. Besides working on diplomatic history, particularly on American foreign policy in South Asia, she has also been a recipient of the prestigious Taft Fellowship at the University of Cincinnati. She has received a number of international and national awards and grants, including the WISCOMP Fellow of Peace Award in 2001-2002 for her work on women's dialogue across borders in South Asia.

Virgilio Afonso da Silva is Professor of Law at the University of São Paulo, where he coordinates a research group on 'Courts and Social Rights in Brazil'. He has several publications to his credit in Brazil and other countries, including *Grundrechte und gesetzgeberische Spielräume* (2003) and *A constitucionalização do direito* (2005).

Olivier Le Cour Grandmaison teaches political science and political philosophy. He directed and led several seminars at the *Collège International de Philosophie* in Paris (France). He has published, most notably, *Les citoyennetés en Révolution 1789-1794* (1992). *Les étrangers dans la Cité. Expériences européennes*, with C. Wihtol de Wenden, preface by M. Rebérioux, (1993). *Le 17 octobre 1961 : un crime d'État à Paris* (2001). *Passions et sciences* humaines, with C. Gautier, (2002). His most recent books are: *Haine(s). Philosophie et Politique*, preface by Etienne Balibar, (PUF, 2002) and Coloniser. Exterminer. *Sur la guerre et l'Etat colonial*, (2005). *Le retour des camps ? Sangatte, Lampedusa, Guantanamo*, with G. Lhuilier et J. Valluy. (2007). *In* *preparation La République impériale : 'sciences coloniales' et racisme d' Etat* (2009).

Artemy Magun is Political Philosopher at European University at Saint-Petersburg and Smolny Institute of Liberal Arts and Sciences, Russia. He has published articles in *Modern Language Notes, Les Temps Modernes, Les Lignes, Scienza & Politica, Novoe Literaturnoe Obozrenie, Polis.*

Sandro Mezzadra teaches History of Political Theories at the University of Bologna, Faculty of Political Science. His research work focuses on German constitutional history and on the history of political sciences in Germany between the 19th and the 20th century (particularly in the Weimar age), on the history of the concept of citizenship in the 20th century, and on the main issues of political theory in the age of globalization (particularly the relationship between citizenship and migration). Among his publications: *Diritto di fuga. Migrazioni, cittadinanza, globalizzazione,* Verona, ombre corte, 2006. *I confini della libertà. Per un'analisi politica delle migrazioni contemporanee,* Roma, DeriveApprodi, 2004 (editor) *La costituzione del sociale. Il pensiero politico e giuridico di Hugo Preuss,* Bologna, Il Mulino, 1999.

Rastko Močnik teaches theory of discourse, theoretical sociology and epistemology of the humanities and social sciences at the University of Ljubljana, Slovenia. He is co-chairperson of the International Board of Directors of the Institute for Critical Social Studies, Sofia and Plovdiv, and is also member of the international advisory board of the journal *Eszmélet*, Budapest. His recent publications include *Altercations* (1998); *How much Fascism?* (1998); *Theory for Our Times: Lévi-Strauss, Mauss, Durkheim* (1999); *Encounters: Histories, Transitions, Beliefs* (2001); *Theory for Politics* (2003); *3 Theories: Ideology, Nation, Institution* (2004); *World Economy and Emancipatory Politics* (2006); *Julia Primic in Slovene Literary Studies* (2006).

Dietmar Rothermund is Emeritus Professor at the University of Heidelberg. Prior to this, he was Professor in South-Asian History at the University of Heidelberg. His publications include *Die politische Willensbildung in Indien* (1965), *Landlord, Government and Peasant in India* (1978), *India in the Great Depression* (1992), *The Global Impact of the Great Depression* (1996), *A History of India* (2004).

Ranabir Samaddar is Director, Mahanirban Calcutta Research Group, and has been vitally involved in initiating peace studies programmes in South Asia. He has worked extensively on issues of justice and rights in the context of conflicts in South Asia. The *Politics of Dialogue* is the culmination of his work on justice, rights, and peace. His specific research focuses on migration and refugee studies, the theory and practices of dialogue, nationalism and post-colonial statehood in South Asia, and technological restructuring and new labour regimes. He has completed a three volume study of Indian nationalism; the third one titled as, *A Biography of the Indian Nation, 1947–1997*.

Ujjwal Kumar Singh is Reader in the Department of Political Science, University of Delhi, Delhi. Earlier, he was a Fellow at the Centre for Contemporary Studies, Nehru Memorial Museum and Library, Teen Murti Bhavan, New Delhi. His articles have appeared in *Economic and Political Weekly*, *Diogenes*, *Scienza & Politica*, *Ethnic Studies Report*, *Contemporary India* and *Indian Journal of Human Rights*. His publications include *Political Prisoners in India* (1998) and *The State, Democracy and Anti-Terror Laws in India* (2007). He has written and published extensively on laws and institutions, electoral governance and issues concerning democratic rights.

Mohammad Waseem is Professor of Political Science in the Department of Social Sciences, Lahore University of Management Sciences (LUMS).. He has written on ethnic, Islamic, constitutional, electoral and sectarian politics of Pakistan. Professor Waseem was Pakistan Chair at St Antony's College Oxford from 1995 to 1999. He has been a visiting professor in Sciences Po Paris; visiting scholar in International Programme for Advanced Studies MSH, Paris; Fulbright Fellow in New Century Scholars Programme at The Brookings Institution, Washington DC; fellow of the Ford Foundation at Oxford; DAAD fellow at the University of Heidelberg; Fulbright Fellow at Columbia University New York; fellow of the Indian Historical Research Council New Delhi; fellow of the British Council in London; and fellow of the American Political Science Association in Washington DC. His books include: *Politics and the State in Pakistan* (1989), *The 1993 Elections in Pakistan* (1994), *Strengthening Democracy in Pakistan* [jointly with S. J. Burki] (2002) and *Democratization in Pakistan* (2006).

Index

1955 Reference, 220
1972 Asma Jillani Case, 221
1977 Begum Nusrat Bhutto Case, 221
Abducted Persons (Recovery and Restoration) Bill, 152
Abducted Persons Act, 154
abduction, women's vulnerability to, 154
absolutism, 2
activism,
    judicial, 226
    legal, 164
    unprepared judicial, 177
administration, wisdom of the colonial, 61
adultery, Aggravated, 146
Afro-Guyanese community, 25
Age of Consent Act, 146
Age of Consent Bill, 145–46
agenda-setting, 18
    and Arena Setting, 15
    British style of, 16
    French type of, 17
    of the political, 18
Alipur Conspiracy Case, 64
All India Muslim Personal Law Board, 160
All-Russia Congress of Soviets, 140
American Revolution, 129
arena-setting, 19
Armed Forces Special Powers Act (AFSPA), 56, 94

Armed Forces,
    civilian control of the, 24–26
    control of the colonial, 24
    politically neutral professional, 25
Arms Act, 1959, 67, 108
army, internal command structure of an, 26
Article 109 of the Constitution of the Second Republic, 33
association, safeguard against implication through, 109
Autonomy,
    discourses on women's, 145
    provincial, 19, 21
    women's, 154
    women's, in India 144–64

Babri Mosque demolition, 100
backlash against demands of the women's movement, 161
Backward Tracts Act of 1919, 56
Bahadur Shah II, exile of, 55
Balasore Conspiracy Case, 57
Balkanisation of Africa, 20
Bengal Act VI of 1930, 59
Bengal Criminal Law Amendment Act of 1925, 59, 65
Bengal Ordinance, 65
Bengal Partition, 73
Bengal Provincial Congress Committee, 61
Bengal Suppression of Terrorist Outrage Act of 1932, 67

Bhutto government, 222
Bolshevik Party, 133
Bolsheviks, 133–34
Bombay blasts, 100
British Commonwealth of
    Nations, 20
British governing and military
    establishments, 55

capitation, forced labour and, 38
Central Recovery Project, 152
centralism, amalgamation of,
    and federalism in
    independent India, 22
Chittagong Armoury Raid, 59, 61
Citizen,
    and the Subject, 80
    distinction between, and
        subject, 83
Citizenship Act of 1955, 156
citizenship, 199
    concept and discourse of, 81
    European, 89
    heterogeneity of European,
        89–90
    principle, 198
    relationship between, and
        property, 82
civil rebellion in North Cachar,
    55
Code of Gentoo Laws and
    Ordinations of the Pundits
    (1775), 69
colonialism, educational
    character of modern
    European, 83
Colonisation, 44
colonists, supremacy of, 37
communication, interception of,
    113
Communist Party, 132
confessions made to a police
    officer, 108
conflict, ethnic, 19

conflict, problem of, and law as a
    function of legality, 6
Congo, history of, 25
Congress of People's Deputies,
    134
Congresses of Soviets, 133
conquest, colonial wars of,
    annexation and suppression,
    54
conservatism, political, 219
Constitution (42nd Amendment)
    Act, 1976, 103
Constitutional Treaty, 80
Constitutionalism, 3, 6, 8, 10, 12,
    57–58, 214
    and decolonisation, 10
    and law-making, 10
    colonial, 50, 74
    in Pakistan, 210
    law and, 10
    liberal, 121
cosmopolitan hypochondriac
    community, 188
creativity, economic, 139
creativity, political, 138–39
Criminal Procedure
    (Amendment) Act, 104
cultural diversity, 199
Culturalisation, 192

Dayabhaga, 149
Declaration of the Rights of Man
    and the Citizen, 27, 35
decolonisation, 14, 22
    history of, 85
    the British, 23
Defence of India (Consolidation)
    Rules of 1915, 67
Defence of India Act, 1915, 65
Defence of India Act, 1962, 103
Defence of India Ordinance,
    1962, 103
Defence of India Rules, 58, 73
    intelligence advice, 61

Defence of the Realm Act, 72
democracy,
    benefits of, 30
    electoral, 216
    establishment of, 182
    historical concept of
        representative, 141
    national security and, 94
    Parliamentary, 16
    Representative, 129–30
    Russian revolutionary, 132
    Western model of, 136
desovietization, 136
detention,
    preventive, by the
        government, 103
    Preventive Detention System
        (PDS), 106
de-territorialisation,
    concept of, 89
    of the border, 89
Dhaka Conspiracy Case, 59
Disruptive Activities
    (Prevention) Act, 1985
    (TADA), 94
Discrimination, Discussing, on
    the basis of sex, 151
domo-politics, 91
Donoughmore Constitution of
    1931, 17
Dosso Case, 220
Dowry Prohibition Act, 1961, 157
Dutch East Indies, 38
duties, distinction between
    negative and positive, 169

East African mutinies of 1964, 25
elections, Benazir Bhutto's
    comeback to power through,
    225
emergency legislation, 76
Equal Remuneration Act, 1976,
    157
equality of sexes, 146

ethno-racial division of work in
    Europe, 90
Evidence Act, 107
Excluded and Partially Excluded
    Areas Act of 1935, 56
Explosives Act, 1984, 108
Explosives Substances Act, 67,
    108

Factory and Mines Act of 1953,
    amended, 157
Fall,
    of Delhi, 55
    of Tipu Sultan and
        Seringapatnam, 55
Family Courts Act, 161, 162
federalism,
    imposed by the colonial
        rulers, 21
    uses and abuses of, 17
    uses and abuses of, 19–24
French Colonial Law, 27–44, 27
French Revolution of 1789–99,
    43, 129–31, 137
fundamentalism, Muslim, 98
Fundamentals of Colonial Law,
    28–40

Gandhi–Irwin Pact of 1931, 61
globalisation, 88
Government of India Act of 1935,
    21
government, existence of
    representative, 83
governmentality, 11

Hindu Code Bill, 148
Hindu Code, debate on, 152
Hindu Law Code, 155
Hindu Marriage Act, 1955, 155
Hindu Succession Act, 155
Hindu Widows Remarriage Act,
    146

Hindu Women's Right to
  Divorce Bill, 146
Hindu Women's Right to
  Property Act of 1937, 147
Hinduism, orthodox, 150
human rights, 199

Identification, Victimisation and,
  191–92
identitary principle, 198
Identity,
  and the 'Politics of
    Recognition, 183–84
  as a Mode of Ideological
    Interpellation, 192
Identity-formation,
  Formalisation of, 184
Ideology, Identitary, in Social
  Struggles, 198–99
ill-treatment, 147
imperial orientation in France, 31
Implementation of Social and
  Economic Rights, Cost of,
  173–75
Independence of India Act 1947,
  212, 215, 218
  and its impact on the Indian
    constitution, 14
independence,
  declaration of, proclaimed by
    Sukarno, 20
  judicial, 226
India under Prime Minister
  Jawaharlal Nehru, 25
Indian Criminal Law
  Amendment Act XIV of 1908,
  65
Indian Divorce Act, 146
Indian Marriages Act, 145
Indian National Congress, 21, 62
Indian National Educational
  Board, 62
Indian State's attitude to women,
  152

Indian Succession Act of 1865, 146
Indo–China War of 1962, 103
Inflammable Substances Act,
  1952, 108
intelligence gathering, 50–51, 58–
  60
internment,
  administrative, 40–43
  juridical conditions of the, 41
  modalities of, 41
  procedures of, 41
interpellation, Identitary, 194–95

Kelsen Cases, 221

Lahore Conspiracy, 65
Law,
  anti-terror, 95
  Anti-Terror, and Shifting
    Contours of Jurisprudence
    in India, 93–126
  Anti-terror, in India, 122
  Extraordinary, 107
  Limits of Constitutional,
    167–79
  making and administration,
    76
  Metropolitan, in the Colonies,
    31–34
  permanence of, 34
  relative stability of, 34
legality, definition of, 6
London County Council, 17

Maharashtra Control of
  Organised Crime Act, 1999
  (MCOCA), 112–13
Maintenance of Internal Security
  Act, 103
Malimath Committee, 111
  report of, 110–12
Maniktola Bomb Conspiracy
  case, investigation of, 59
Maniktola Conspiracy Case, 53, 60

marginalization, women's, in society, 157

Memorandum on the History of Terrorism in Bengal, 65

metropolitan country, authority of, 37

migrants, selective and differential inclusion of, 90–91

migration, re-colonising of, 90

militancy, religious fundamentalist, 99

minority, targeting of, communities, 94

Mitakshara, 149

Moderate government, 6

moderation, 6
    as a function of legality, 6

modernity, reflexive, 189

modification of the Hindu and Muslim personal laws, 145

monogamy, 149

Montague-Chelmsford Reforms 1919, 217

Morley-Minto Proposals, 72

Movement for Restoration of Democracy, 224

Muslim Women's (Protection of Rights on Divorce) Act in May 1986, 158, 160
    controversy over the, 159

Muslim, Migrants from the, minority, 214

mussalmans, indigenous, 37

Mutiny, suppression of, 68

Nairobi Declarations in 1985, 162

narco-terrorism, 114

National Emergency of 1975, 103

National Security Council, 227

national sovereignty, 182

nationalism, militant, 61–62

Nigeria, constitutional development of colonial, 23

Non-Cooperation Movement, 61

observations and recommendations of the Central POTA Review Committee, 118

October Revolution, 135

Organisation of African Unity (OAU), 21

Pakistan Muslim League (PML), 224

Pakistan National Alliance (PNA), 223
    movement in 1977, conflict between the PPP government and the, 223

Pakistan,
    break-up of, 227
    constitutional crisis of, 213
    constitutional thinking and practice in, 210
    punjabisation of the state in, 220
    refugees in, 213

Pakistan People's Party (PPP), prospect of a, victory, 224

Pan-Africanism, 21

Paris Commune of 1871, 137

Parliament,
    attack case, 93, 120
    attack on, on 13 December, 96

parliamentarism, 225

Parsi partial civil code, 146

partition,
    of India, 25
    of the British Indian army, 25
    of the Indian subcontinent in 1947, 152

Personal Law, sanctity of, 158

Politics,
    colonial, and decolonization, 9
    democratic, 130

modern, and terror, 53
of assimilation, 30
of gender during partition, 152
of identity, 212
of issues, 212
realignment of, 160
positivism, 29
Prevention of Terrorism Act, 2002 (POTA)
distinction between, 113
expansion of the scope of, 109
inception of, 93
judgements, 96
provisions, 116
removal of, from the statute books, 115
Repeal Act, provisions of, 117
Repeal Ordinance, 119
Repealing, and Amending UAPA, 115–19
Statement of Objects and Reasons of, 96
trials under, 112
power,
constituent, 86
expression of the constituent, 86
juridical definition of, 6
Prevention of Terrorism (Repeal) Act, 2004, 95, 116
Prevention of Terrorism Bill, 99, 104, 113
Prevention of Terrorism Ordinance (POTO), 94, 101, 104
Preventive Detention Act, 1950, 94, 102–04
property, concept of, 82
Public Safety Acts (PSAs), 94

Ramakrishna Mission, 62
recognition, mechanisms of, 192

Regulation of 1781 (Impey's Civil Code), 69
relations between deputies and their electorates, 134
Responsibility, Collective, 42–44
revolution,
anti-communist, in Russia, 131
concept of, 132
municipal, 139
Russian post-communist, 137
Revolutionary and Anarchist Crimes Act of 1919, 65
rights,
classical basic, 172
community, 156
cost of, 171
cultural, 199
implementation and protection of individual, 170
implementation of social and economic, 175
implementation of social, 170, 174
individual, 169
individualisation of collective, 176
legal provisions on women's, and representations, 145
of maintenance, 147
of Man and the Colonies, 28–31
of the widow, 147
of women in regard to inheritance, 150
promotion of human, 190
social and economic, 172–73
social, 169–70, 177
to discuss changes in the position of women, 148
to equality, 151
to health, 170

women's, 156
women's, to inherit
    agricultural land, 155
women's, to maintenance, 149
Rowlatt Act, 67
Rowlatt Committee's Report, 73
Royal Proclamation of Amnesty
    in 1919, 65
rule of law, 11
Russia, post-communist
    transformation in, 131
Russian revolution, second, 133
Russian Supreme Soviet, 142
Sati Act, Abolition of, 145
Sati, abolition of, 145
Scheduled District Act of 1874, 56
Schengen agreement, 89
sex, discrimination on the basis
    of, 151
Shah Bano case, 157–59
Shankar Math, 62
Shariat Laws of 1939, 155
SIMI,
    constitution of, 97
    motive of, 97
Social and Economic Rights and
    Positive Duties, 170–71
society, political, 91
sovereignty, parliamentary, 212,
    222
Sovety narodnykh deputatov, 134
Soviets,
    History of, in Russia 132-36
    of People's Deputies, 134
    of the working people
        (*Sovetytrudiashchikhsia*), 134
    the Congresses of the, 134
    the revived system of, 135
Special Marriage Act, 1956, 155
Stalinist' constitution of 1936, 134
Students Islamic Movement of
    India (SIMI), 97
Subjects, Indigenous, and French
    Citizens, 34–40

subject-supposed-to-know, 193
Swarajya party, the, 62

TADA, 101
    judgements, 96, 112
Telegraph Act, interceptions
    under the, 108
telephone interceptions, 107
terror,
    and violence, 83
    relation between, and law, 50
terrorism,
    and mutiny, 69
    and organised crime, 112–15
    concept of, 114
    consensual' effort against
        global, 96
    constitutional, 218
    definition of, in POTA and
        UAPA, 120
    discourse on, in India, 96
    global Islamic, 99
    insurgency-related, 100
    international consensus
        against global Islamic, 94
    international cooperation
        against 'global, 121
    Islamic, 98
    legal definition of, 73
    menace of, 99
    Pakistani Link with
        International, 96
    permanent legal measures
        against, 96
    threat from transnational
        Islamic, 98
terrorist activity, 121
Terrorist and Disruptive
    Activities (Prevention) Act,
    104
Terrorist and Disruptive
    Activities (Prevention) Act,
    1987, 105
terrorist, 68

attrition between the, and the colonial state, 66
organizations, banning of, 116
Towards Equality Report of 1975, 157–58, 162
transformation of estates, 140

UAPA 1967, replacement of, by UAPA 2004, 115
UAPA Amendment Act, 2004, 95
Uniform Civil Code, 150, 156–57, 163
Universal suffrage, 17
universalism and uniform centralisation, 29
universality, 4
    concrete, 5–6
    concrete, of law, 10
    of law, 5
Unlawful Activities (Prevention) Act, 103
Unlawful Activities (Prevention) Act, 1967, 97, 108, 110, 115
Unlawful Activities Prevention Act (UAPA), amendment of the, 94
Unlawful Activities Prevention Act, 2004, 119–21

Unlawful Activities Prevention Ordinance (UAPO), promulgation of the, 119

violence, the spread of, and terror, 53

West Indies Federation, 22
women, Muslim, divorced, 158
women,
    abducted, 152, 154
    condition of, in India, 144
    debate on status of, 151
    Demands for the reservation of seats for, 160
    Dowry deaths among landless, 163
    marginalisation of, in polity, 145
    marriageable age for, 146
    Muslim, in India, 152
    non-Muslim, in Pakistan, 152
World Trade Centre, attacks on, 98

Zia's martial law government (1977–85), 222
Zia-Junejo government, 222